THIS BOOK IS VOLUME VI

IN

The Pioneer Heritage Series

THE PIONEER HERITAGE SERIES

BOSS COWMAN

BOSS COWMAN

THE RECOLLECTIONS

OF ED LEMMON

1857–1946

Edited by

NELLIE SNYDER YOST

UNIVERSITY OF NEBRASKA PRESS · LINCOLN · 1969

Publishers on the Plains

UNP

FOREWORD

Ed Lemmon had no notches on his gun, no medals for broncbusting or prizes for roping or trick riding. But according to the National Livestock Association, he held the world's record for saddle handling more cattle (over one million head) in his lifetime than any other man. He also held the record for the largest number of cattle (nine hundred) cut out, roped, and brought to the branding fire in a single working day.

In his years on the range he was a cowhand, trail rider, wagon boss, range manager, and ranch owner. He covered virtually every foot of the range in western South Dakota and parts of Wyoming, Montana, and Nebraska on horseback, and once knew every important brand in the West. He was noted for having at one time (1902) managed the largest fenced pasture in the world—865,000 acres on the Standing Rock Indian reservation (a tract larger than the state of Rhode Island)—and for bossing the biggest single roundup in history.

He knew the West as it was in its earliest cattleman period, knew the big cattlemen in their halcyon days, and was a part of those days himself. He saw the homesteaders block off the range with barbed wire and turn under the fine grasses, saw them fold up and leave, too, and finally saw the slow return of the grass and the cattlemen.

In the 1880's, when he first became associated with the Sheidley Cattle Company on a permanent basis and moved into the L7 head-quarters, there were no fences to hem in the vast herds. It was during those years and the nineties and the first few years of the new century that he built the company herds to a peak of fifty-three thousand head.

Toward the end of 1906 the Chicago, Milwaukee and St. Paul Railroad crossed the Missouri River at Mobridge, South Dakota, and stretched its tracks on westward, reaching the location of what became the town of Lemmon late in 1907. Almost overnight a busy city of tents sprang up at the site. Mr. Lemmon owned the land where the new town took root, and the Milwaukee Townsite Company at once bought 163 acres from him for $3,260. The town was christened Lemmon and its lots auctioned for a total of nearly $100,000. Lemmon himself, who had reserved the right of first choice of lots at the sale, chose a corner lot and paid the top price of $2,650 for it—almost as much as he had received for the entire original acreage. In the county seat fight that followed, the town of Lemmon lost to Bison, a little town down in the center of the county. Bison won by the slim margin of fourteen votes in the election of January 26, 1909, but Lemmon continued to outgrow its rival, soon becoming the largest town in the county. Today its population is 2,412, as compared to Bison's 457.

During its early years Lemmon was a boisterous place. Real estate offices were crowded, saloons and gambling houses almost never closed. The first Fourth of July celebration was put together by G. E. Lemmon and the other businessmen, who contributed most of the $2,250 cost of entertaining the five thousand people who crowded into the town for the three-day jamboree held in 1908. That same year Mr. Lemmon sold out his cattle interests and moved into the town named in his honor. Although he ran more sheep than cattle after 1908, he continued his active life in the saddle for another fifteen years, making fifty-three years as a cowman altogether.

A charter member of the South Dakota Stock Growers Association, a faithful worker in the organization and regular in attendance at its meetings, he several times turned down the honor of filling the president's chair because he didn't like to make speeches. Because of the death of his son George, who drowned in Lake Isabel just before the annual convention of 1936, he missed the meeting. But three years later (the same year that South Dakota celebrated a half-century of statehood), when the biggest convention of them all was held in Lemmon, Ed was there—one of the three old charter members still able to attend. In fact, it was said of him that until well up in his eighties he was still enthusiastically going to every rodeo and stock growers' convention that came along.

By then, though, the once lively town had become a far less colorful but progressive and modern city, with fine schools, parks, brick buildings, and paved streets. But it was still the headquarters and favorite shipping center of stockmen from as far as 150 miles away. And Ed, though likewise tamed by the more than eighty years that had passed over his head, was still stoutly maintaining that cattle ranching would survive the desperate 1930's and be a good business again.

Not long before his death in August, 1946, he was quoted as saying, "I believe the cattle business is on its way back. There will always be enough farmers to hinder stocking cattle in big numbers, and the range will have to be handled with that in mind. But the West-river country is *cow country*, and that's the way it always should've been."

Mr. Lemmon was well into his eighties before he finished his reminiscences. As he looked back over the years he seemed to regret that as a youth he didn't get to kill an Indian, though he later came to know many of them well and to count them as his friends. The name given him by the Sioux was Tazpaze, or Yellow Apple, which was as close as they could come to "lemon."

It is evident that he was a somewhat boastful kid, skilled in the ways of the rough frontier and given to twitting older men who couldn't perform as well as he. Plain, too, is his hero worship for his father and his elder brother Hervey. He ranges them alongside Kit Carson and Davy Crockett, with Hervey even ahead of his father in some respects, for he writes, "Father, with all his physical skill, was no match for brother Hervey with a gun, or in handling cattle or trailing man or beast on foot."

[ix]

This book makes it apparent, too, why, when the National Cowboy Hall of Fame was established in Oklahoma City in 1958, G. E. Lemmon and his friend Scotty Philip were the first South Dakota cowmen to be named to that great shrine for old cowboys.

NELLIE SNYDER YOST

North Platte, Nebraska

CONTENTS

[xi]

Contents

Maps of the Republican and Platte River valleys, of the Dakota area that Ed Lemmon knew best, and of the major cattle ranges follow pages 20, 116, and 216 respectively.

BOSS COWMAN

I

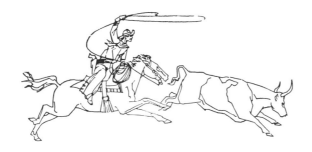

MY FATHER AND THE REST
OF THE FAMILY

M Y FATHER, James H. Lemmon, was born in Fremont, Ohio,
in 1820. In July, 1847, he went to Oregon by land (the first
of seven land crossings and one trip around the Horn) and there
took part in the Oregon Indian War of 1848–1849. Quite a large
body of men volunteered to fight in that war, and at its beginning
most of them furnished their own mounts. Father and a volunteer
named Olney [1] were among these, and before it was over they had
several horses shot out from under them.

On one occasion a big party of volunteers was heading down one
side of a long ridge toward a place known as the Cross Timbers,
where they intended to make a night camp. Where this ridge
connected with the Cross Timbers it drew down to a low, narrow

1. Nathan Olney (probably James N. Olney) fought in the Yakima Indian
War and was an Indian agent in eastern Oregon for several years. In 1852 he
married Annette Hallicola, a member of the Wasco tribe. (Letter of Mrs. Barbara
Elkins, Oregon Historical Society, March 27, 1968.) See Roscoe Sheller, *The
Name Was Olney* (Yakima, Wash.: Franklin Press, 1965).

[1]

point. As the volunteers rode along, they noticed a dust cloud rising above the ridge on its far side. They sent scouts to take a look, and saw a big band of Indians also heading for the Cross Timbers.

The Indians had seen the dust cloud raised by the volunteers, and had likewise sent scouts to the top of the ridge, where the two sets met, so to speak, in the middle. Both details then turned and flew to report, and soon a race for the Cross Timbers was on between a majority of both outfits. As they still had several miles to go, the leads on both sides thinned as their horses tired.

Near the Timbers the ridge flattened out. At that point the Indians and the volunteers were in plain sight of each other and drawing closer with every jump. Here the main body of Indians swung out and gave up. The troops also slowed, leaving the finish to eight men mounted on the fastest horses. From there on they raced a like number of Indians, also riding fast horses.

The Indians made it into the timber just ahead of the volunteers. Father, Olney, and the troop surgeon were a part of this group, which soon killed or badly wounded all but one of the Indians. But while they were poking around in the brush, looking for that one, an Indian with a broken back was getting ready to surprise them. The volunteers knew the crippled Indian's gun was empty, for they had seen him discharge it as he went down, so they hadn't bothered to finish him off. But it seemed that this Indian knew that a dead Indian nearby had a loaded gun and was working himself toward it. When he got hold of it he shot and killed the surgeon. Olney then jumped from his horse onto the Indian and reamed his heart out with his knife. The men then found and killed the last Indian, but still considered themselves poorly paid for the life of their doctor.

Neither Olney nor Father had been able to collect anything from the government for the horses they had lost in the war. When the fighting was about over and the volunteers were on the way back to the Rogue River post to be mustered out, they ran onto quite a band of horses that had once been broken but had gotten away and gone wild again. So Olney, Father, and several other men swung out and surrounded the herd.

Among the captured horses was a fine large blue horse that Olney right away laid claim to, stating he wanted it to replace one of his squaw's that had been shot from under him. But it turned out that the blue horse was what is called a bunch quitter. Whenever they tried to catch him he would take to the wilds, but would hover close and rejoin the bunch when it was put on the trail again.

After they got back to the Rogue post, Olney tried several times to corral the blue horse with the rest of the band, but the blue was so fleet of foot that no horse in the outfit could come up with him while carrying a man. There came a day when Olney got so mad and disgusted that he took his rifle and started to crawl up on the horse, which stood on a distant knoll, defying him. Then one of Father's friends said, "Jim, if the government owed me as much money as it does you, I wouldn't let Olney kill that fine horse." Father said he guessed that was right, so he jumped on his horse, dashed in between Olney and the blue, and drove the horse off several miles to a mountain park he and his Ohio friends had already picked for a horse pasture.

There was good grass and water in the park, and there they grazed their gather of horses. They had quite a herd, for their commander had told them they could keep all horses taken when out scouting on their own, and that only those taken in actual battle belonged to the government. After they had held the blue horse in the park with the bunch for several days, he became used to the men. They then drove the whole band into a natural corral, where a Mexican roper in the outfit roped the blue. As soon as the rope tightened on his neck he came right up to the Mexican and began nosing him. He proved to be well broken, and the most rein-controllable horse Father ever rode. He was so swift that he soon became the pride of the whole command. But Olney several times stated that he was going to take him when they were mustered out to go home, for then each man would be on his own, with no commander to interfere.

Finally the day came, and Father saddled the blue horse and tied him to a hitch rack. There had been a good deal of argument as to whether or not Olney would take the horse, and all the men were watching to see what would happen. Now Father was not an expert with a six-shooter, but he was a master with what was called a pepperbox, a double-action .50-caliber gun with four barrels that revolved, instead of a revolving cylinder. It had no sights, but at close range it would tear a hole in a man that you could shove a fist through. Father did not then own such a gun, but he had a friend who had loaned him one for the occasion, and he had it handy in his pocket that day. And beside his skill with the pepperbox, he was also given up to be the best wrestler and boxer in the command, and all the men knew he had the nerve to back his skill.

Well, Olney finally walked up, his thumbs stuck in his belt where he had two .44 Colts (army cap-and-ball six-shooters) and a skinning knife in a scabbard. "Jim," he said, "I have come for my squaw's blue horse." And then he began reciting his reasons for taking the horse.

"There he is, with my saddle on him," Father said. "And it will stay there unless you are a better man than I am, which I doubt." Then Father went on to say, "Olney, I've seen you do some brave deeds, like cutting the heart out of that Indian, and leading your volunteers in hand-to-hand fighting against long odds of Indians, but I don't believe you have the nerve to go against a white man on an equal footing. If you have, just start to pull one of those guns or that knife, and see how far you get."

He followed his speech by pulling the pepperbox and saying, "Here is a gun that goes off without cocking. I'll drop it on the ground in front of me, and you do the same with your six-shooters. At a signal from a man we'll both agree on, we grab for them—and I'll fill your hide so full of holes it won't hold corn shucks. Or, if you want to leave the guns alone, I'll thrash you until your squaw won't know you."

Olney heard him out, then unconcernedly turned and walked away. "Guess I barked up the wrong tree that time," he said.

In 1879, some thirty years after the trouble over the blue horse, I was at home, near Hastings, Nebraska, for the holidays, when an old Oregon Indian War friend of Father's stopped to visit for a couple of weeks. While they were telling Indian stories one evening, the old fellow said, "Jim you sure made Olney pe-hunk [back down] that time, but his stalling wasn't for lack of nerve. It was because he was in the wrong and he saw the fellows were in sympathy with you, not him." Then he went ahead and told the story of the blue horse, and of how Olney led the vigilantes that cleaned up San Francisco in

'56.[2] Since then I've read about that in California history, and about a descendant of Olney's, a mixed-blood Indian girl from Portland, Oregon, who made the biggest contribution in horses of anyone of Indian blood during a Red Cross campaign for funds for use in the First World War.

Shortly after being mustered out of the Oregon war, Father went into some kind of mercantile enterprises near the gold fields. Since there was little good horse feed in that region, and no use there for his string of high-quality saddle horses, he put eight head (one a fine race horse) out on a road ranch where there was good feed. Because there was an Indian village not far away, he hired a boy about eighteen years old to look after the horses, grazing them by day and penning them at night, for Indians never missed a chance to take horses belonging to whites, or to enemy Indian tribes. It was their nature to steal horses, that being an accomplishment taught them from infancy and supposed to be next to scalping in getting to be a chief in the tribe.

Grass was so plentiful at the ranch that the boy didn't need to let the horses graze far, and so he hardly ever let them out of his sight. He was an expert bareback rider, too, and often rode out to turn the bunch back without even saddling his horse. But one day while he was eating his dinner, the horses did graze out of sight. He had kept up one of the best ones for a herd horse that day, so without stopping for hat, coat, or gun, he ran to the tied horse, jumped on bareback, and dashed off to where he had last seen the herd.

A plain trail led off in the direction of the Indian village. Since these Indians were not true hostiles, the boy took right off on the trail. It led up onto a wide plateau, where he caught sight of the fleeing Indians, five of them, riding the same number of stolen

---

2. A James N. Olney appears in the San Francisco directory of 1854, and a James N. Olney, Jr., in the 1856 directory. The California Historical Society catalog has a reference to a James N. Olney who was connected with the committee of vigilance in 1856. (Letter of James de T. Abajian, California Historical Society, March 26, 1968.)

horses and leading the other two. The boy being lighter than any of the thieves, he gained on them so fast that they split up, each taking a different direction.

When the boy came to the place where the trails divided, he picked out the track of the race horse (it was shod with race plates) and took its trail. He wasn't long coming in sight of the horse, for its rider was an unusually big, fat Indian. And the racer, Father's most prized horse, was tiring fast, while the boy, very light of weight, kept gaining. When the Indian saw he was being overhauled and that his horse was panting like a lizard, he got off and sat down in the shade of a tree on the sandy plain. He was sitting there, grinning, when the boy rode up, because he could see he was unarmed.

The boy got off his horse and motioned for the Indian to give up the lariat he had used to guide the race horse. Of course, the Indian, who would make two of the boy and was armed with all kinds of war tools besides, just laughed at him. The boy kept on begging for the horse, for he could speak the jargon that all West Coast Indians talked, but all the time he had his eye on a dry, warted limb that had fallen off the tree. The old, fat Indian was still sitting flat, with his back against the tree, when the boy suddenly grabbed the limb and smashed him over the head with it, stretching him out in a quivering heap. He actually beat the Indian's brains out, then gathered up the riata and headed for home with the racer.

On the way back he met a posse from the ranch, trailing the dust cloud he raised when he took after the Indians. He took them back and showed them the big, brained Indian, lying there with flies feasting on his remains. Of all the Indian warfare that ever came to his notice, Father said, that was about the nerviest he knew of. So he kept the boy in his employ, at good wages, for quite a while.

It seems to me that my father came by his own courage honestly, for he used to tell us children a story of a heroic deed performed by his great-great-grandfather during the Revolutionary War. The men stationed at one of their outposts in the timber kept disappearing at night. After several men had been lost, that post came to be much dreaded by the rest of the men. One night, when it was the turn of a fairly green young soldier to keep the post, he showed such great fear that the great-great-grandfather, an old hand at that kind of warfare, volunteered to go in his place.

When he had been at his post a while, a hog came rooting along, picking up nuts, or so it seemed. But this grandfather three times gave the usual command to halt, and then he fired, killing an Indian wearing a hog's hide and dragging a spear under him. This ended the loss of men on the post. And a few years after Father told us the story, when we were reading United States history in school, we found the feat recorded to the credit of our great-great-great-grandfather.

Another story Father used to tell us about this ancestor was that, on his way home on a furlough, he put up for the night in an empty log house. A ladder went up to the loft, which was floored with a few loose planks, and the ends of some of the planks stuck out of the loft window a few feet.

Pretty soon this grandfather saw about a dozen Indians coming, so he climbed the ladder and pulled it up after him. The Indians, who were spies armed by the British, stacked their guns outside and started to cook their supper over a campfire. The grandfather decided to crawl out a little way on one of the planks, hoping to get a better look at the Indians by the firelight. But he crawled a little too far and the plank tipped up, dropping him down almost on top of the Indians.

As he was going down he yelled, "Come on, boys. We'll catch the whole lot of them." The spies, taken by surprise, bolted, leaving their guns. The grandfather grabbed the guns, leaped into the house, and kept up such a fusillade that the Indians were convinced the loft was full of men. This great-great-great-grandfather, by the way, was a Mohawk Dutchman.[3]

3. A Dutchman who settled in the Mohawk Valley of New York state.

[7]

Now, to get back to Father. In the spring of 1852 he went back to Marengo, Illinois, and married Elizabeth Whittmore. A year later he headed west again, taking Mother, her brother James, her sister Maranda, and enough men to handle the wagon train. They also took with them seventy head of purebred Shorthorn cattle from his Uncle Van Meter's farm at Fremont, Ohio.

In July the train crossed the Missouri River near where Nebraska City is now located. At Fort Kearny they were held up by the military until a hundred fighting men were gotten together and armed and equipped.[4] Before going on they also teamed up with a mule-drawn Missouri train, and Father was elected captain of both trains, as he was the only man in the outfit who had had experience with Indians.

A few days out on the trail from Fort Kearny, the Missouri train decided Father's ox-drawn wagons and the Shorthorn trail herd were too slow for them, so they pulled on ahead. About this same time my oldest brother, Hervey, was born in our covered wagon on Pole Cat Creek.[5] Near Cottonwood Springs,[6] Father's train caught up with the Missouri train, where it was stranded on the trail with not a single mule left. Indians had killed the night herders and driven off the mules, and the government had to transport the emigrants back to their homes at Pottsville.

At Scotts Bluff the train stopped overnight beside a large camp of friendly Sioux Indians. That evening the Indians came over to visit Father's train. They visited, played games, and the men wrestled.

4. The heavy migration along the Oregon and California trails in the late 1840's and early 1850's had alarmed the Indians (mostly Sioux, Cheyennes, and Arapahos in what is now western Nebraska), who made sporadic raids on the emigrant trains and ran off the horses and mules. At the insistence of the emigrants and western congressmen on military protection along the trails, the army established Fort Kearny at the southernmost point of the big bend of the Platte in 1848. See James C. Olson, *History of Nebraska* (Lincoln: University of Nebraska Press, 1955), p. 67.

5. Also known as Skunk Creek, a small stream flowing into the Platte River a few miles east of where the river forks.

6. An important point on the trail a short distance east of the forks of the Platte, Cottonwood Springs was a stopping place for westbound emigrants and a crossing for Indians traveling north or south. It was later the site of a post known first as Camp McKean and then renamed Fort McPherson.

Father and a strapping young warrior had a wrestling match, and Father threw the Indian flat on his back and somehow ripped his blanket. That made him mad and he wanted to fight, but Aunt Maranda stepped up, took his arm, and led him to her tent, where she sewed up the rip. That pleased him and he rode back to his camp in good humor.

After dark, Father, his train crew, and the Indians sat around a big campfire, still visiting. Pretty quick the young brave rode back again, all decked out in his best Sioux riggings. He called Maranda over to him, then scooped her up in his arms, put her in front of him on the horse, and dashed away. Father had his fast horse picketed close by, and in a minute or two he was on their trail. He overtook them in some rough hills and, as he came up beside them, the Indian gave Maranda a bear hug and dropped her to the ground. Father stopped to see if she was all right, and she said, "He is such a handsome brute. I made sheep eyes at him while he held me on his horse." So he decided not to do anything to the Indian about it.

At daylight the next morning a band of Indians came to the camp, driving a herd of twenty ponies. They offered them all to Father to make up for their love-sick warrior's treatment of Aunt Maranda. Father refused the ponies, because he knew that, according to the Indian code, Aunt Maranda had "claimed" the Indian as her man when she led him to her tent.

Father's train was overtaken by winter at Bountiful, Utah, and there they stayed until we moved back to Nebraska in 1859, except for a trip on out to Oregon in 1854. On that trip they met Kit Carson, and Aunt Maranda danced with him on a stump pavilion.[7]

Father did considerable trading with the Mormons and got along fine with them. During this time he was a special friend of Brigham Young, and he named my second brother, Moroni, born in 1855, after one of the twelve Mormon disciples.[8] But after the United

7. The flat stump of a giant redwood tree.
8. According to the *Book of Mormon*, Moroni was an early prophet and historian who, as the Angel Moroni, appeared to Joseph Smith in 1823.

States government ordered General Harney into Utah in 1857 to put down polygamy, Father decided it was time for us gentiles to move out.[9]

9. In June, 1857, General W. S. Harney, commander at Fort Leavenworth, was ordered to head an expedition of 2,500 men to Utah, ostensibly to "establish and maintain law and order," although the real reasons for the Utah Expedition have never been agreed upon. While the Mormons prepared for war and did destroy several army supply trains, both sides were eager to reach a peaceful settlement; and after a period of occupation the army from Utah withdrew without having exchanged shots with the Mormon settlers. See Leonard J. Arrington, *Great Basin Kingdom: An Economic History of the Latter-Day Saints* (Lincoln: University of Nebraska Press, 1966), pp. 170–172, 175–182, 192–193, 196–198.

II

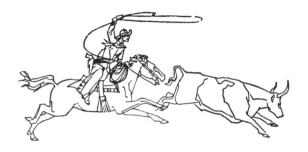

LIBERTY FARM

I WAS BORN at Bountiful, Utah, ten miles from Salt Lake City, on May 23, 1857. Within a few feet of our door ran an irrigation ditch about ten feet wide and very swift, as it was only a short distance to its source in the mountains. Across this ditch was a plank footbridge, onto which we stepped to dip up water for washing. When I was two and a half years old, my brother Hervey, six and a half, flattened out on the plank with a tin tumbler in his hand to dip up a drink of water. The swift current snatched the tumbler out of his hand and he plunged right in after it, hollering "My tumler, my tumler." Someone heard him and pulled him out. Now! How is that for remembering?

That same summer of 1859 my family left by four-horse carriage for the east. There were six of us: Father and Mother, Hervey, Moroni, myself, and my baby sister, Alpharetta, who was named for the beautiful Indian song, "Wild roves the Indian girl, bright Alpharetta." With us, too, was a man named Sam Bell, a close friend who was almost one of the family.

We had along quite a big band of loose horses and ponies for changes, and one of these was Hervey's riding pony, a pinto named

[11]

Lucy. This pony was tough-mouthed and often took the bit in her teeth and ran away. One day, near Green River in what is now Wyoming, we were passing an Indian village. The village was over a mile away, and Sam Bell and Father were speculating as to the Indians being hostiles, when the pinto, scenting others of her kind in large numbers, took the bit in her teeth and stampeded toward the village. Sam, who was mounted, took after them, rather expecting that both he and Hervey would be scalped. It turned out that the Indians were friendlies, though, and they even helped head the pinto and Brother back to our outfit. But a little farther on, when we were some two hundred and fifty miles east of Bountiful, the pinto gave us the slip and disappeared.

At the end of our trip we went onto the Liberty Farm stage station, a division point and supply station on the Ben Holladay stage line, about fourteen miles from the present town of Hastings, Nebraska.[1] Sam Bell went on east for a short visit, then returned by stage to Bountiful, where he found the pinto grazing in the home pasture.

Liberty Creek, for which the ranch was named, emptied into the Little Blue River about a third of a mile below the station, which was on the north bank of the river. For nearly a mile to the west the banks of the Little Blue were steep and muddy, with no good fords. Almost solid timber and brush made fine hiding for roving Indians on the south bank, but the north bank was open and bare. A ten-acre triangle-shaped garden lay in the bend of the river, with the point to the west and the wide end to the east. The road used by the stages, freighters, and emigrants followed the long north side of the garden, then made a sharp turn at the northeast corner and came down to the barn and station, some one hundred and twenty-five yards to the south.

~~~~~~~~~~~~~~~~~~~~~~

1. Benjamin Holladay took over the Central Overland California and Pikes Peak Express Company in 1862, after the original owners, Russell, Majors and Waddell, went bankrupt. He operated it until 1866, when he sold it to Wells Fargo and Company. See Raymond W. and Mary Lund Settle, *War Drums and Wagon Wheels: The Story of Russell, Majors and Waddell* (Lincoln: University of Nebraska Press, 1966), pp. 166–167. The Liberty Farm station was located near present-day Deweese, Nebraska.

Often during the later hostile Indian period, Indians would ride down from their rendezvous in the big timber, only two and a half miles away, and hide in the timber on the south bank, about a third of a mile from the station. Then, as the stage came along, they would dash out and try to cross the Blue to attack it. But they always lost so much time trying to make the steep, muddy crossing that they never managed to get close enough to do any serious damage. Twice they came near it though, once shooting arrows into the body of the stage, and once into a stage horse, but the injury was not fatal. At such times the stage would come around the corner of the garden fence on a dead run with the two off wheels practically off the ground and the passengers, on orders from the driver, all bunched on the off side of the stage to keep it from capsizing.

A roofed passageway between the two main buildings of the house at Liberty Farm made a shelter for some hewn log benches that were fastened to the walls. Passengers coming in on the stages used to put their baggage down on the benches. Once, when I was about five years old, a passenger dropped his California blanket[2] roll on one of the benches, near where I was rolled up in another blanket. When the "all aboard" horn sounded, the passenger, in his rush to get on the stage, gathered the wrong roll under his arm. When it came to life with a howl, he dropped it like a hot potato.

When we first came to Liberty Farm a hunter by the name of Tom Corbit was helping A. C. Beckwith.[3] Corbit supplied game to several stations along the line but, though a good shot, was rather old and slow, so he left the harder work to Beckwith, a much younger man. Spring Ranch, the next station to the west,[4] was run by a fellow named Ute Metcalf. One day an old chap got off the stage at Spring

2. California blankets were made of a finely woven wool cloth with a hard, smooth surface that would shed both soil and water.

3. Ashael C. Beckwith, born in Ohio in 1827, went west as a boy and spent many years as a hunter and trapper. From 1859 to 1866 he furnished meat for various stage stations on the Overland line. He later operated coal mines at Rock Springs, Wyoming, for the Union Pacific; and was the senior member of a mercantile and brokerage firm, Beckwith and Lauder, of Evanston, Wyoming; and in 1893 was appointed to the United States Senate but resigned after a prolonged debate over the legality of the appointment. At his death in 1896 he was one of the wealthiest men in Wyoming.

4. Spring Ranch was about fifteen miles west of Liberty Farm.

Ranch and said he wanted to go on a buffalo hunt. It was haying season and help was scarce, so Ute advised him to go on to Liberty Farm and hire old Tom Corbit, who did quite a lot of such chaperoning.

This he did, and, good buffalo guns being scarce, Corbit gave him his big .50 Yager, a gun that shot a bullet the size of a man's thumb, and then guided him off to the south for a short hunt. Because the banks of the Liberty were so steep and muddy, the buffalo came to water just below its junction with the Blue, where there was a rocky ford. When crossing the ford on foot with his hunter, Corbit showed him some plain buffalo trails, some of which passed right under the limbs of some big cottonwood trees by the stream.

Well, the two men prowled the south breaks for a few hours, but didn't see any buffalo. So the easterner decided he would go back to the ford and wait for some stragglers to come in to water. Back at the ford he climbed onto a big tree limb that overhung the trail and waited. After a while a decrepit old buffalo came wandering down the trail. The hunter cut loose with the old Yager, which shot about as hard backward as forward. A couple of hours later Corbit came back and found his hunter, still unconscious, by the trail. Although he was soon revived with water from the creek, he had had enough of buffalo hunting.

A little later, with Father driving, we all went out one Sunday for an outing in a stagecoach. After a while we drove into a scattering of buffaloes, and all who could muster buffalo guns spread out for a try at bagging game. One old fellow, who couldn't raise anything but a double-barreled shotgun, stayed with the coach.

Pretty soon another decrepit old bull came wending his way down a deep trail that passed near the coach, heading for water. The old fellow grabbed the shotgun and declared he was going to shoot the buffalo's eyes out. Mother tried to talk him out of it, but he went ahead, planted himself directly in the deep path, and pulled off both barrels at once. The buffalo just shook his head and charged, knocking the hunter down lengthwise in the deep trail. After pawing and shoving over him for a while, the bull went on to water. The buffalo had crushed the old fellow enough that he bled some at the lungs and had a mighty sore chest, but otherwise he wasn't hurt much.

About 1864, Ed and Will Stokes, the sons of a wealthy New York saloon family, came to Liberty Farm. Their father had sent them to California by boat to keep them out of the Civil War draft. Now, with the war about over, they were on their way home by stage. They were all primed for a buffalo hunt, and a few days later, when an outrider reported a mammoth herd grazing a few miles away, our whole family drove out in a stagecoach to watch the hunt.

We found the herd grazing peacefully. As we came near it, the living mass parted to make a pathway wide enough for our horses and coach to pass through. From our place on top of the stage we could see Ed Stokes riding among the buffalo, followed by his mounted gun carrier. Ed picked out an old patriarch of the herd and began peppering away with his six-shooter at close range.

The wounded bull jumped, roared, and crowded against the solid wall of the frightened herd, but he was still on his feet when Stokes emptied his gun. His gun carrier handed him another and he shot six more times, but the bull was still up and kicking. The big beast did not go down until the thirty-third shot, and Stokes was so proud of his kill that he had the head shipped east and mounted. For many years it decorated the wall of a famous New York saloon belonging to the Stokes family.

Life at Liberty Farm was always interesting in one way or another. I can remember evenings, after chores were done and night guards set at the stables (because of the Indians who nearly always camped in the timber up Liberty Creek), when we used to gather in front of the fireplace and whittle off dried buffalo meat to eat with the green apples Father freighted in from St. Joe. Of the three four-horse wagon outfits Father used on his trip there for winter supplies, one whole wagon would always be loaded with apples. It was a universal saying that after eating dried buffalo meat and green apples, dreams of Indian fights were sure to follow. No matter how many travelers were staying overnight, all were invited to sit in on our evening feasts, and no doubt dreams followed.

We had to keep quite a few men at the station, some of them just as extra hands to fill the vacancies that were always coming up. At times it was hard for these fellows to find enough to do to while away the time, so all kinds of stunts were pulled off, especially by the stage drivers, who practiced a lot with their four- and six-horse whips. Many of the men got so expert with the whips that they could pick a fly off a leader's ear without touching the ear. Quite often sizable wagers were made as to which man was the best at this sport.

One day two of the men got so wrought up in one of these arguments that they agreed to fight to a finish—with themselves as targets. Each man had made his own whip of selected smoke-tanned elk skin, and now each of them tipped his whip with a short length of fine braided wire. They picked their judges (one was Bill Trotter, king of the stage drivers), and the contest was on. It ended with one of the men having an eye pierced out, and the other with his head and back so cut up he had to be staged to a hospital at St. Joe, where blood poison set in and he died. And the contest didn't prove anything after all, for the wire tips, though very light and thin, threw the whips off balance.

If Father had been at home at the time, he wouldn't have allowed the men to pull off such a foolish fight. And Ben Holladay was so furious about it that he posted notices at every station forbidding all wagers and contests that endangered company property or the lives of the men, especially stage drivers and Pony Express riders, as their experience was too valuable an asset to waste.[5]

This Bill Trotter who helped judge the whip contest was the Pony Express superintendent out of Fort Kearny, and it was under him Buffalo Bill was said to have ridden at the age of fourteen years.[6] Old Bill was known as the most conservative rider and stage driver on

~~~~~~~~~~~~~~~~

5. Although Ben Holladay's name is often erroneously associated with the Pony Express, by the time he bought out the Central Overland California and Pikes Peak Express from Russell, Majors and Waddell (who had operated the Pony Express) in March, 1862, the Pony Express had been out of service for some four months.

6. Born in Pennsylvania in 1836, Bill Trotter went west to Kansas in the late 1850's. He was a stage driver for more than twenty years and was said to have driven 250,000 miles. For a time he was superintendent of the Fort Kearny–Julesburg division.

the whole line. And I believe you could have knocked a bull down with the big silver hunting case watch Holladay gave him as a reward for taking him over his division of the stage line with the *most* speed and *best* judgment combined. Any driver could have whipped his teams over the division faster than Trotter did, but not with such good judgment, which was the important feature.

How I did use to admire Trotter's graceful horsemanship and the way he handled the lines on a four- or six-horse stage team. And I can't recall ever seeing him drive those stage mules with the chain pelter that most drivers used instead of a whip. The pelter was a light chain, two and a half to three and a half feet long, attached to a stock about the same length. In the case of a six-mule team, a blacksnake was used, so the driver, riding the rear wheel mule, could reach the leaders.

When we first came to Liberty Farm they were using mules on the stages, but they proved too slow, and were hard on the drivers besides. So in 1860, shortly before the beginning of the Pony Express, the owners changed from mules to horses. Beginning at the west end of the line, they collected the mules and drove them in a great herd east to St. Joe for use on freight wagons. All of this was in the time of Joe Slade, superintendent of the mountain division of the Holladay stage lines.

It was Slade who cut off the ears of Jules Beni, the man Julesburg was named for, and carried them in his vest pocket as souvenirs. Slade finally went bad and was hung by Montana vigilantes. His remains were staged to Salt Lake City by his devoted wife, Virginia Dale, and laid to rest in the cemetery there.

In 1884, some twenty-five years after the bull-whip fight at Liberty Farm, old Bill Trotter was still driving stages out of Rawlins Spring, Wyoming, on the last star route stage in the United States. He was still as good a stage driver as ever, I was told, though his hair was white as snow.

While that stage line was still active, there was a government investigation known as the great Star route scandal.[7] While it was

7. Star routes were special routes, established before the Rural Free Delivery routes, which were operated at a high rate of pay to the contractors. The Star route scandal occurred in 1883–1884. A group of Washington contractors bid in

going on, the distances between the stations had to be measured, right down to the actual footage. A lieutenant from the troop at Rawlins was detailed to walk to the next station to the north with an odometer locked to his leg.[8] He was to ride back on the stage the next morning. The distance was supposed to be about eighteen miles, but it happened there was a dance going on at the north station that night, so the officer stopped in and danced till morning. The odometer registered every step taken by the wearer, and in the case of the lieutenant a step averaged two feet, eight inches. When the instrument was unlocked from his leg in Rawlins the next day and its mileage computed, it registered 104 miles.

During the time we were at Liberty Farm, Ray Grayson was superintendent of our eastern division. His wife had a little curly white terrier named Sylvia, and at the dances her partners always had to find someone to hold Sylvia while she danced. But it was said it was worth the trouble of finding a holder for the dog, for Mrs. Grayson was considered the best dancer on the whole line, and a good talker besides. Even so, it got to be such a joke about holding Sylvia that the stage men used to twit her dance partners with "Will you please hold Sylvia while I dance?"

As told earlier, the stages sometimes had to outrun Indians on the last dash from the east to Liberty Farm station, and our drivers used to argue as to which of them could bring a stage around that sharp turn with the highest speed and best balance. Now Father, who had done a lot of freighting in the California gold boom days, and had already crossed the plains seven times with four or six horses, was an expert with the reins. So he once wagered one hundred dollars he could bring the stage in on a dead run and hit a stake driven in the road with the inner front wheel. He was to have both wheels off the ground several times, but was to be allowed three

the routes at a low figure, and then subcontracted them to local riders and stage lines at an even lower rate. Later the contractors secured higher rates and pocketed the difference. In the subsequent Senate investigation, which ruined several political careers, it was found that some of the routes existed only on paper.

8. Lemmon apparently means a pedometer. An odometer is an instrument for measuring distance traveled by a wheeled vehicle.

heavy men to ride in the stage and swing to its outer side at these times to keep it from upsetting. Father won the wager, of course, but at the time it was agreed that Bill Trotter was probably the only other man who could have done the same thing.

Besides being an expert driver, Father, in his prime, could make a standing jump as high as his head. He was also known as the best boxer and wrestler on the entire line, and the best fighter for his weight, which was about 175 pounds. This he often proved in rough and tumble fights, for would-be bullies came from far and near to try him out. But Father, although he had trained under the man who trained Heenan for the famous Heenan-Sayers fight of 1860,[9] would never go into the ring on a wager or for money, but would only fight to protect his rights or on behalf of a friend or a principle.

In June, 1886, at Kearney City, I saw him take a roughneck by the ear and boot him through the door of a road ranch barroom. The fellow had just said he'd come from Salt Lake, and then he made an insulting remark about the Mormon people. As Father booted him through the door he told him he wasn't fit to associate with real men. Some of the cheering onlookers then told Father the fellow was apt to waylay him after dark, but Father said the cur was even too yellow to shoot a man in the back. But the ranchkeeper said he and his men would see that there was no ambushing while Father was on his property.

The Pony Express was established the next year after we settled at Liberty Farm. The first runs started from St. Joe, Missouri, and Sacramento, California, on April 3, 1860, with Alex Carlyle riding from St. Joe and Harry Hoff from Sacramento.[10]

Beginning at St. Joe, the stations were: Kennekuk, Granada, Log Chain, Seneca, Ash Point, Guittards, Marysville, Hollenbeck, Rock Creek, Big Sandy, Thompson's, Kiowa, Oak Grove, Little Blue

---

9. Tom Heenan went to England in April, 1860, to meet John Sayers, and the fight was generally considered the first world heavyweight championship bout. It was declared a draw after forty-two rounds. The purse was £200.

10. Other sources name Billy Richardson or Johnny Fry as the first riders out of St. Joseph. The identity of the riders who made the first runs remains a matter of controversy.

station, Liberty Farm, Spring Ranch, Elm Creek, Muddy, Thirty-two-mile Creek, Hungry Hollow, and Fort Kearny. The line went on, past Skunk Creek where Hervey was born, Cottonwood Springs, Bovey [Beauvais] Crossing, across to Ash Hollow, then up the North Platte to Mud Springs, Court House Rock, Chimney Rock, Scotts Bluff, Goshen Hole, Laramie, South Pass, Fort Bridger, and Salt Lake. I knew very little about the Pony Express route from Salt Lake on to Sacramento, but from Salt Lake to St. Joe it was like an open book to me.

The trip covered 1,966 miles and averaged a little more than eight days each way. The dangerous cliff and mountain country runs were made in daylight, the worst Indian region runs in the night. On the plains the riders made lots of detours, since to ride the same route every trip, past places where Indians could wait in ambush, was too dangerous.

The ponies were mostly bought from Brigham Young, who had imported hot-blooded sires in order to raise fast cavalry horses for the Mormons. Brigham had expected U.S. troops would be sent in to put down polygamy, and he wanted his men well mounted. These horses were all racers, weighing about nine hundred pounds and traveling with a long reach when on a lope. They were always kept in the best of trim for long, fast trips. They dashed away from the stations on the run, then slowed to a long, swinging lope that covered about ten miles an hour. In all their time on the route, these Pony Express horses, when under saddle, seldom actually walked a step.

The stations were about twelve miles apart, and each rider rode some thirty-five miles from his home station, then back, making about seventy miles a day for each man. Movies show the rider dashing into a station and leaping from his horse to another one, all saddled and waiting. This is wrong, because no two riders' legs were the same length, and no man could stand such hard riding, day after day, except in his own saddle and with stirrups that exactly fit him.

The light, durable saddles used by the Pony Express were made in the Mormon saddlery at Salt Lake City and weighed about thirty pounds apiece. They had single cinches, so they could be transferred

[20]

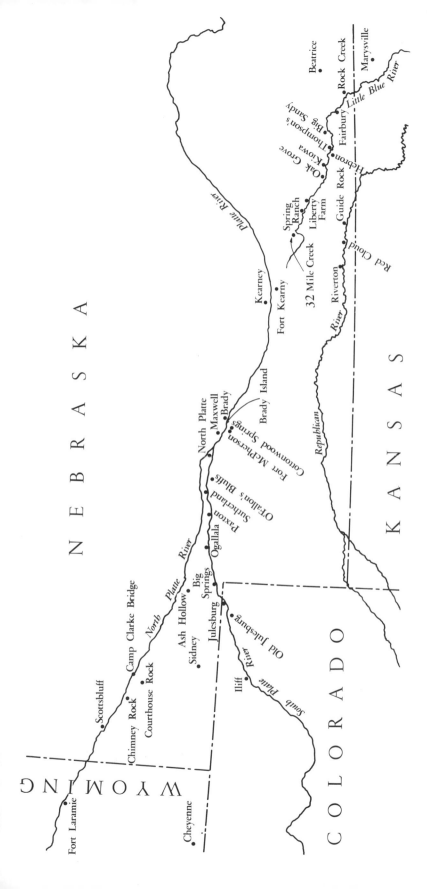

THE PLATTE AND REPUBLICAN RIVER VALLEYS

from one horse to another in seconds. The riders usually wore light brass cavalry spurs and carried a little brass horn that gave out a piercing blast. They blew the horns as they neared the stations, warning the attendants to hurry the fresh horses out. To keep down weight, the riders carried no arms except six-shooters (except on the mountain division) and depended on their fast horses to take them safely through Indian country.

The machiers were leather blankets about as big as the saddles, with slits for the cantle and horn. A pocket on each corner held the forty-pound maximum mail load.[11] As each rider loped into a station, he simply jumped off his horse, unsaddled and threw the saddle, machier and all, onto the fresh horse, buckled the cinch, jumped on, and dashed away again. Only at the end of his run did he jump the machier alone to the saddle of the next rider.

Pony Express riding was much more dangerous and tiring than stage driving and the riders were paid higher wages than drivers. The riders must always go it alone, and only in the dangerous mountain stretches where detours were impossible, could they carry rifles. Even so, I don't recall that any rider was ever killed on our St. Joe to Fort Kearny division.

The champion riders of our section were Jim Moore and Bill Trotter. At times both of them rode out of our Liberty Farm station. The champion ride of all was made by Jim Moore, who rode 280 miles without rest in twenty-two hours.[12] Other noted riders and drivers were Pony Bob Haslam, Keelely [probably Jack Keetley],[13]

11. Leroy R. Hafen, in *The Overland Mail* (Cleveland: Arthur H. Clark Co., 1926), gives the maximum weight of the mail load as twenty pounds. Some writers refer to the leather letter carrier as a *mochila*; others call it a *machier*, as Lemmon does.

12. Moore rode 280 miles without rest in June, 1860, from Midway station to Julesburg and back again. The Julesburg relief rider, who should have made the return trip, had been killed the day before, so Moore jumped into the saddle without even stopping to eat, and headed east. He made the round trip in fourteen hours and forty-six minutes. Jim and his brother Charlie later established a very popular road ranch, the Washington, about forty miles west of old Julesburg. See Frank A. Root and William E. Connelley, *The Overland Stage to California* (Topeka, Kansas, 1901), pp. 28, 386.

13. Keetley, who had the run from St. Joe to Seneca, once rode from Rock Creek to St. Joe, back to Rock Creek, again to Seneca, and back to Rock Creek again, a distance of 340 miles, all without rest or sleep, in thirty-one hours. He rode the last five miles of the run asleep in his saddle. See *ibid.*, p. 125.

[21]

Frank Baker, Bob Emery, John Gilbert, Al Fink, Pete Hammey, and, at times, Jess Owens, a half-brother of Bill Rowland, the fellow who married a Crow squaw and had a big family of mixed-bloods. Pony Bob's longest ride was 380 miles, but he had a break of one nine-hour rest part way.[14]

I have read that the riders were not allowed to use profanity, but I'm sure some of them did not keep this rule. Bill Trotter and Jim Moore, especially, would have made poor Sunday school teachers. The two men were much alike, except that Trotter was not the businessman that Moore was, for Jim later became a big cattleman. He was killed in 1873 by being thrown from a hayrack by a runaway team. His rich widow married R. S. Van Tassell of Wyoming who, at her death, inherited Jim's big JM outfit.

The great mail run lasted only about a year and a half and was discontinued in October, 1861, when the telegraph line across the continent was finished. The Pony Express was started principally to put the Southern Santa Fe, or Butterfield, route out of commission. In this it was a success, but financially it was a complete failure; for Ben Holladay told my father it lost him one million dollars.[15]

During the seven years we kept the Liberty Farm station it was hard for my mother to keep hired girls. This was partly due to the hostile Indians in the country, partly to the girls' getting married pretty quick after they came to the station. Ben Holladay covered his stage line in a buggy about once a month, so on one of his trips Mother had him bring out two girls from St. Joe. One of the girls

14. Robert (Pony Bob) Haslam made the ride, said to be the longest in the history of the Pony Express, in Nevada, because one of the relief riders had been killed and the station burned. See *ibid.*, pp. 130–131.

15. After John Butterfield of the Overland Mail Company, a competitor of Russell, Majors and Waddell, was awarded a six-year contract in 1857 to carry mail over the Southern route, Russell, Majors and Waddell inaugurated the Pony Express to prove the advantages of their shorter Central route and to demonstrate that mail could be carried over it in the winter. Although Benjamin Holladay never owned the Pony Express (see note 5, above), he had advanced money and cashed drafts to help Russell, Majors and Waddell establish and operate it. The Pony Express itself did not bankrupt Russell, Majors and Waddell, who were already deeply in debt, but it did contribute heavily to their ultimate financial disaster. In 1862, Holladay foreclosed his mortgage on the Central Overland California and Pikes Peak Express Company, which owed him $208,000, and bid it in at $100,000. See Settle, *War Drums and Wagon Wheels*, pp. 110–112, 165–167, 249.

was a blonde, the other a brunette. He called the blonde the "Jack of Diamonds," and the brunette the "Queen of Spades."

They were both very chick, of medium height, slender form, and entertaining ways, but not bold. They soon had many admirers, among both the stage hands and the traveling public. Among the last were a Mormon missionary and a western mine promoter. These two seemed to have the inside track and made the stage trip quite often. Of course Mother lost her hired girls—one to the missionary and the other to the promoter—and both went on west to grow up with the country. They used to write to Mother, and from all accounts were living happy and contented lives.

Once when Mother was temporarily out of hired girls, she talked Jess Owens into working for her. One day Jess was baking biscuits. He took them out of the oven and set the pans on one of the wide roof beams to cool, and then went outside for wood or something. This was before the big 1864 Indian raid, and the Sioux of our region were still as welcome at our place as any other neutral tribes. When Jess came back the kitchen was full of Sioux warriors, and some of his pans of biscuits were missing. He went around patting the Indians' robes above their wide belts and soon located his biscuits. Then he reached down, gathered the Sioux' robes, peeled them up and set him down on the hot stove top. That Indian left a lot of his nether skin stuck thereto when he left, and all his friends howled with glee and made no move to help him out. Jess was somewhat of a sport and gambler, and at Spring ranch he one day killed an eastern professional gambler he claimed he caught cheating at cards.

Not too long after we came to the Liberty Farm the Frank Baker mentioned earlier was hired as a stock tender and, in emergencies, a Pony Express rider. When off duty he sometimes drank too much. At one of those times Moroni, aged six, was making a play wagon with wheels sawed from an elm tree, a wood that is tough and hard to split. The wagon was almost done when Frank came along and gave it a kick that somewhat shattered it. Brother was furious, and declared that as soon as he grew to be a man he would whip Frank for that act, a pledge he repeated a good many times in the next few years.

About that same time a row started one night between two teamsters of an emigrant train that was camped by our ranch. One of the men was waving a six-shooter and threatening the other, who kept backing toward his wagon. The canvas wagon cover was drawn over the end of the seat, and though the man with the gun didn't know it, the other fellow had a gun on the seat under the cover. With his hands clasped behind his head, looking defenseless as a baby chicken, he backed all the way to the wagon seat. There he grabbed his gun with his right hand, whipped it forward, and shot the gun-toter over the left eye. Before he could fall, he shot him again, over the right eye. As there was nothing but army law in the country then, nothing was done about the killing.

Only a short time before that killing, the great McCanles–Wild Bill killings took place at Rock Creek in July, 1861. A few nights after the killings Wild Bill stayed overnight at our ranch. All three of us boys—Hervey, eight; Moroni, six; and myself, past four—followed him around all evening, admiring him for his great and heroic deed. And it was said that Ben Holladay tendered him a lifetime pass over his lines for it.[16]

16. In 1859 David McCanles built the Rock Creek station, which he later contracted to sell to the stage company. In early 1861, Horace Wellman and his wife were installed as stationkeepers, and twenty-three-year-old James Hickok was hired as assistant stock tender. Wellman was to turn the payments for the station over to McCanles; and on July 12, McCanles, accompanied by his twelve-year-old son, his cousin James Woods, and a neighbor, James Gordon, all unarmed, called at the station, presumably to collect, since the final payment was then past due (in fact, no payments had yet been made), or to repossess the station. After a brief exchange between Wellman's wife and McCanles, Hickok stepped to the door and, without provocation, shot and killed McCanles. Hickok and Wellman then killed Woods and Gordon, but the McCanles boy escaped. Hickok and Wellman were acquitted after a mock trial, and the story of the affair was inflated to heroic proportions with McCanles cast as the villain. See *Nebraska History* for Spring, 1968 (Vol. XLIX, No. 1), which is devoted almost completely to the Hickok-McCanles affair.

III

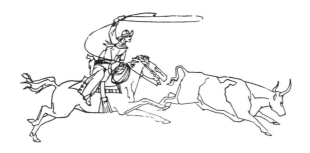

THE INDIAN RAIDS OF 1864

IN 1863 MY PARENTS went back to Marengo, Illinois, for a visit, leaving three of us children in Beatrice, Nebraska, with the Tinkham family to board and go to school. When Father came back that spring, he right away left for Denver with a bull freight outfit. He took the oldest Tinkham boy, Tom, with him as a teamster.

When the outfit reached Denver it was pressed into service by the government to deliver army goods on west to one of its more distant outposts. This would make the return trip very late, so, as Tom wanted to go to school at home that winter, Father in some way got him released from the outfit.

Stage travel was expensive, and Tom and his family very thrifty, so the boy decided to walk home. The Indians were, on the whole, still peaceful in 1863, although a few roving bands now and then committed depredations. For this reason there were always soldiers patrolling the stage routes, which was a good thing for Tom, for a lone footman would seem to be easy prey to such Indians.

So Tom set out, with a rifle slung across his shoulder and a cap-and-ball six-shooter as a side arm. Sure enough, he hadn't gone far, only about to Cedar Creek, when a small band of renegades espied him and began circling to get in an effective long-range shot. Tom managed to hold them off with an occasional long-range shot of his own until a patrol troop hove in sight and scared them away to the hills.

A couple of days later Tom sighted a bear at short gun range. The bear was sitting on his haunches and looked so tempting that Tom took a shot at him, wounding him just a little. Of course, the bear charged him, and he made for the nearest tree, which was a small one. Now Tom was only a farm boy on the tame order, and not yet an experienced plainsman, so he dropped his rifle in order to climb the tree faster. He still had his six-shooter, but it was of such small caliber he was afraid to upset the bear any more by shooting him with it, so he sat for several hours in the tree. He was a mighty cramped and hungry boy before a freight train came in sight and the bear lumbered away.

Late one evening he neared Fort Sedgwick, south of present Julesburg. A rough point of land came down to the Platte River there, close to an island separated from the mainland by a narrow channel. He came to the point just as a deer with its tongue hanging out dashed off the island in front of him. He brought his rifle up and downed it at the same moment that a pack of buffalo wolves bolted out of the island brush.[1] It didn't take the wolves long to finish off the deer, and then they came after Tom, who was heading for the fort at his best speed. Now and then he dropped a wolf to keep the pack back, as they'd stop to eat each one he killed. On the three-mile dash from the island to the fort he killed about five wolves before his shots finally alerted the soldiers at the post. Supposing Indians were after someone, a small detachment of cavalry came rushing to his rescue, and none too soon.

Tom had almost reached Fort McPherson, south of today's town of Maxwell, Nebraska, when he came onto a small band of decrepit old buffalo bulls that had been whipped out of the main herds by young bulls. It was the custom of such old residenters to form small sympathetic bands that would not turn aside for man or the Devil.

1. Buffalo wolves followed the bison herds, feeding on the carcasses of fallen animals.

But of course young Tom had to try his luck on an old bull, because he wanted to be able to say he had killed a buffalo on his way home. As was to be expected, he only wounded the bull a bit, drawing a little blood and causing it to charge him. The rest of the band smelled the blood and came along, keeping right on Tom's heels until he dived into a gulch so narrow the buffaloes could not get their heads into it to gore him. They pawed the ground all around him until dark, then bedded down above him. It was a chilly night and Tom had only one blanket, so he lay in his ditch and shivered until morning, when the buffaloes got up, stretched, and wandered away.

While in the vicinity of the fort, Tom saw a soapweed plant in bloom. His mother was very fond of flowers, so he dug up the spiny plant with its long spike of white, bell-shaped flowers and packed it in a horse's nose bag. With the dirt on its roots, it must have weighed five to eight pounds, but he carried it the rest of the way home, nearly three hundred miles.

His last adventure happened near Hungry Hollow, just east of Fort Kearny. There he bedded down for the night, wrapped in his blanket, with his dunnage bag for a pillow. Hours later something cold sniffed at his ear and woke him up. He reached up to slap it away—and was doused with skunk perfume. Wearing only his underwear, he hoofed it into a nearby stage station and bought a cheap pair of trousers and a shirt from the stock tender, then buried his old clothes and went on home. When he recovered the clothes, some two weeks later, the smell was almost, but not entirely, gone. Now we always considered some of Tom's tales about his trip pretty far drawn—all but the last one, that is—for the smell still on his garments when he got them back proved that story was the real stuff.

When the Union Pacific started to build its line west from the Missouri River the next year (1864), the old Sioux Chief Red Cloud saw that his hunting grounds would be doomed if the road was ever finished. So, thinking to discourage the westward development of the country, he started what he thought would be a body blow to the settlement of the west.[2] He began to send his warriors east in small squads, pretending they were heading for St. Joe to trade. About every twenty-five miles one of these bands would leave the stage road and drop off to the south of the Republican. There they all. went into camp to await the day, Sunday, August 7, 1864, set for the great Sioux raid.

The attack was to begin at noon all along the Ben Holladay stage line from Big Sandy, near present Fairbury, to the American Ranch on the South Platte River,[3] a total distance of 325 miles. Every white in the region was to be killed and every station and ranch laid waste. The Sioux in this area had not been on the warpath for years, so old Red Cloud's plan was a clever one. A band of Indians was to ride into each of the stations and ranches about noon that fateful Sunday, when the ranch hands would be relaxed and off guard, not even wearing six-shooters. It would seem that the Indians were just dropping in for a visit, as they did all the time, and they could slaughter scores of unarmed people with their bows and arrows and war clubs. On the whole line that Sunday the Indians did destroy about one-third of the stations and ranches, kill about one hundred people,[4] and carry off into captivity at least five women and two children, one a baby.

On the west end, at the American Ranch, it so happened there were several large wagon trains encamped. This ranch was located on splendid grass and water, making it a fine place for travelers to

---

2. Almost nothing had been done toward the actual building of the railroad by 1864, so it was not a primary cause of the Indian depredations. Indian discontent had reached a critical stage by 1863 and 1864, largely because of the government's ineffectuality in its dealing with the Indians. The tribes involved in the raids in the Platte Valley at this time were the Brulé Sioux, the Arapahos, and the Cheyennes. Mr. Lemmon is in error in implicating Red Cloud (at this time about forty-three, and thus not really so old) in the attacks; his band of Oglala Sioux were not involved. See James C. Olson, *History of Nebraska* (Lincoln: University of Nebraska Press, 1955), pp. 119, 141–142, and *Red Cloud and the Sioux Problem* (Lincoln: University of Nebraska Press), pp. 16, 25.

3. The American Ranch, near present Iliff, Colorado, was owned by John Morris, who was killed in an Indian attack on the ranch in January, 1865.

4. Other sources put the number of white persons killed in the raid at from thirty to forty. See Leroy R. Hafen, *The Overland Mail* (Cleveland: Arthur H. Clark Co., 1926), p. 353; Addison E. Sheldon, *History and Stories of Nebraska* (Lincoln: University Publishing Co., 1914), p. 139; and Olson, *History of Nebraska*, p. 141.

spend Sunday and wash up. But on the north side of the river that summer, only a few miles from the ranch, there was a big camp of Sioux, Arapahos, and Cheyennes. These Indians, who had prepared for the coming attack by accumulating hundreds of horses (so every warrior would have several changes of war ponies), struck the American Ranch at the appointed time. Although the battle there lasted for three days and nights, it was something of a draw. About twenty men were killed on each side before the Indians gave up and pulled back to their camp; where they stayed for several weeks, as not enough troops could be gotten together to dislodge them.

Down at our end of the line the Comstock family, neighbors of ours, were pretty well involved in the raid. E. S. Comstock, the head of the family, kept the Oak Grove station, two and a half miles east of today's town of Oak. His oldest son, Jim, was in charge of the Little Blue station, about six miles on west at the foot of the Nine-mile Ridge. His second son, George, had the Thirty-two-mile Creek station, twenty-eight miles farther west. A younger son, Ansil, also lived at the last station. On the day of the raid, E. S. Comstock, who had been visiting George at Thirty-two-mile Creek, started home at daybreak on an old white pony. By some miracle he did not meet any of the raiding parties on his ride of over forty miles. Just after dark that evening he rode into the Eubank ranch, only five miles west of his own Oak Grove ranch. He found the buildings in ashes and dead bodies all around.

Everything was quiet by then and there was nothing he could do. Forewarned, he went on east, circled to the north, and came down on his own place from the hills. Although the ranch was surrounded by Indians waiting for daylight to finish the siege, he managed to slip through their cordon and reach his buildings, where he found the bodies of two men, Marsh Kelley and Jim Butler, in his smoke-house. There didn't seem to be any living people around, or anything he could do there either, so he slipped away. The Indians then came in at daylight and burned the station. As there had been no oppor-tunity to remove, or even to bury, Kelley and Butler, their bodies were burned with the smokehouse.

The story of that day, as Comstock learned it later, was this: Shortly after he left Thirty-two-mile ranch that morning, his son

Ansil and a hired man, Mike Connely, had gone Sunday horseback riding with the two Artist girls from Dewitt. A short way to the east they had come onto the smoking remains of a small wagon train.[5] The drivers had been killed and scalped, the bull teams run off, and the wagons burned. The four young folks burned the wind back to the ranch, spread the alarm, and then joined the exodus for Fort Kearny.

At Jim Comstock's Little Blue station a large wagon train was encamped that day. Joining forces with the ranch people, they fought and whipped the Indians detailed to attack at that point. Then, as soon as they could pull out, everybody there had joined in the stampede to the fort, and on down the Platte to the Missouri over a route that was not raided. The Indians came back and burned the Little Blue station to the ground, too.

At E. S. Comstock's own ranch, Marsh Kelley, a part owner in the Joe Roper ranch, seven miles to the west, and Jim Butler had been passing by on their way to St. Joe for supplies. They had stopped in for a visit, and the fight had started when one of the visiting Indians suddenly shot Kelley in the back with an arrow. Kelley, who was out in the yard, staggered into the house with the arrow sticking through him. He tried to climb the stairs, and met the youngest Comstock boy, age twelve, coming down. Handing him his six-shooter, he said, "Harry, fight as long as you live." Harry then ran down and shot an Indian, probably the one that had just shot Kelley.

Camped just in front of the ranch that day were the two Ostrander brothers and a Mr. and Mrs. Julian. The men were killed in the fight and Mrs. Julian was taken captive. The rest escaped. Later, when it was safe to return to the ranch, the charred remains of Kelley and Butler, along with the bodies of Julian and the Ostranders, were gathered up and buried.

At the Eubank ranch, near today's town of Oak, Joe Eubank was killed and scalped in plain view of his wife, who, with her son

---

5. Probably the Simonton and Smith wagon train described in Frank A. Root and William E. Connelley, *The Overland Stage to California* (Topeka, Kansas, 1901), p. 354.

Arthur, her daughter Isabelle, her baby, Willie, and the neighbor's daughter, Laura Roper, were captured by the Indian band that carried out the attack there. In all, thirteen of the Eubank family were either killed or carried off that day.[6] John Comstock, son of George and grandson of E. S., later became my brother-in-law, so I heard him tell all this many times.

Our family, however, completely escaped the raid. Earlier in the summer Father had taken Mother, Hervey, Moroni, my five-year-old sister Alpharetta, and me to Marysville, Kansas, where Mother was to put us in school for the winter. Father had then headed for Denver and Pikes Peak with a wagon train of mining machinery. His load included a large quartz-mill boiler that he hauled on two coupled-out wagons.[7]

He was near Julesburg on the day of the raid, and was forced to abandon his train when his Negro bull whackers deserted in the face of the Indian scare. Although his machinery was not burned with the wagons, he still lost it all, as by the time he could outfit and get back the next spring, it had been moved on to the mines by local freighters—who also collected the freight charges. The claim for this loss as well as losses due to other Indian depredations suffered by my father can still be found on file in Washington, D.C. The claims were disallowed on account of insufficient proof as to the exact tribe of Indians who did the depredating.

When we left for Marysville, Father had put the Liberty Farm in the hands of one Charlie Emery of Beatrice.[8] But no lives were lost there on the day of the big raid, either. This was because the Indians were a few minutes late in attacking our ranch, and the stage, dashing along under the whip, got there in time to bring news of the raid. Of course everybody hopped aboard and rode to Buffalo

6. "On August 7, 1864, a war party of Cheyenne and Arapaho attacked the Eubank ranch on the Little Blue River near the 'narrows' of the Oregon Trail. . . . Laura Roper, Mrs. William Eubank, Jr., and two children, Isabelle Eubank and an infant boy, were captured and four persons killed" (Mollie Dorsey Sanford, *Mollie: The Journal of Mollie Dorsey Sanford in Nebraska and Colorado Territories 1857–1866* [Lincoln: University of Nebraska Press, 1959], p. 190 n.).

7. Wagons with the reaches lengthened out.

8. James Lemmon sold the farm to Emery for three thousand dollars. Emery made a down payment of three hundred dollars but failed to make any other payments, and Lemmon repossessed the farm the following spring.

station, four miles west, where two large wagon trains were camped. The bull whackers with the trains, together with the people on the stage, whipped the Indians out.[9]

As refugees from all points began coming in, everybody joined the exodus to the east, abandoning ranch buildings, wagons, and livestock. The Indians then went in, burned everything, and drove off the ox and mule teams. All of our buildings at Liberty Farm were burned, too, except for a string of coarse log corncribs that wouldn't burn well.

Another queer little story came out of the big raid of 1864. For a few years before that summer there had been a white peddler covering the Holladay stage line from St. Joe to Julesburg. He carried notions to peddle to ranch people, and beads, knives, cheap jewelry, and beaver traps to trade with the Indians. The peddler seemed to be on very friendly terms with old Red Cloud and was freely admitted to all the Red Cloud villages. For this reason he was

---

9. The famous race of the stagecoach against the Indians took place on Tuesday, August 9, two days after the initial raids. How the Liberty Farm occupants escaped the Sunday raids may perhaps be explained by the following statement which Ed Lemmon made in another account printed in the Belle Fourche *Bee*: "They [the Indians] did not have enough to attack every ranch simultaneously, which gave some of them the chance to assemble, as was the case of Liberty Farm assembling with Buffalo Station four miles west." He also mentioned that on Tuesday, August 9, the warriors were "cleaning up the line." Sheldon, *History and Stories of Nebraska*, pp. 139–140, and Root and Connelley, *The Overland Stage to California*, pp. 363–365, relate the story of the great "race for life," both giving its date as August 9. The latter source took the story from the Omaha *Bee* (no date given) as follows: The driver of the stage was Robert Emery, brother of Charlie, who had heard a rumor in Atchison that Liberty Farm had been burned and the family massacred. In the face of such news, no other driver would take the stage west that day except Robert, who wanted to find out what had happened to his brother. He left Atchison with nine passengers, two of them women, and made the trip without incident until nearly into the "narrows," a very narrow ravine on the bank of the Little Blue River. Just before driving into the ravine, Emery saw about fifty Indians ahead of him. He turned the horses instantly—two more rods and he could not have turned around—and whipped them back over the trail with the Indians in hot pursuit. Amid a hail of arrows, the coach sped on for about three miles. An ox train of twenty-five westbound wagons saw the stage careening eastward and hurriedly corraled, leaving an opening into which Emery drove his stage.

When the stations were rebuilt in 1865, a new one was located at the west end of Nine-mile Ridge and given the name of Buffalo Ranch (Root and Connelley, *The Overland Stage to California*, p. 256). This is likely the site Mr. Lemmon refers to as Buffalo Station.

called Red Cloud Tom, and that was the only name I, or anyone else, knew him by. However, the whites in that whole region suspicioned that he also peddled guns and ammunition, and maybe firewater on occasion, to the Indians. That, they said, was the real reason he could come and go among their villages as he pleased.

After the big August raid, Red Cloud Tom's peddler wagon was found gutted just east of the Pawnee Ranch, and thereafter he was seen no more in Nebraska Territory. It was naturally supposed he had been attacked by some Sioux who did not know of his friendship with Red Cloud, and that when they learned of it they were afraid of punishment by the old chief and so hid the body and did not report killing him. And there the matter was dropped, as the peddler was not any too well thought of by the whites, especially after the raid.

In the spring of 1865 Father sent Bill Ike to our Liberty Farm to build a cabin and start cropping the land again. My brother Hervey, twelve years old, went to the farm with him. When my folks had made the visit to Illinois the spring before, they had brought a new hired girl back with them. Her name was Barbara Allen, and she was much admired by the stage drivers, stock tenders, and other help. When she saw how popular she was, she took the stump and announced she wanted it understood she had not come west on a husband hunt. But within a year she was married to Bill Ike. This hired girl was the subject of the famous ballad "Farewell to Barbara Allen." [10]

One day while Bill, Barbara, and Hervey were at dinner in the new cabin they saw two Indians slip out of a draw, jump on the team that was picketed on good grass about a hundred yards from the door, and take off. Bill and Hervey grabbed their guns and fired several long-range shots at them, but couldn't see that they made

10. The English and the Scots both claim the original ballad, which dates back to about 1666, and both versions were brought to America by early settlers. Hundreds of variations have spread across the United States since then.

any hits. For quite a while this team had been given up to be the finest on the whole line, and Father had even refused five hundred dollars for them on several occasions. So Brother, who had taken the precaution to picket his pony near the door, was soon on his way to Marysville to report to Father, who was getting ready to start for the Little Blue with a strong crew to help with rebuilding the burned-out ranch.

Bill Ike cut loose from us soon after Father pulled in with the new crew. He then built himself a ranch about twenty miles on east of us, where he and his wife lived until June, 1866, when the stage was pulled off the line to Kearney, which at that time was the end of the Union Pacific railroad. After that Barbara deserted him and he went, in a manner, to the wild by joining Bill Rowland, the squaw man, up in Crow Indian country.

As a friend of Rowland's, Bill was admitted freely to all the Indian camps. On one of their wandering trips in western Montana, near the upper navigation of the Missouri and about halfway between the Yellowstone and Missouri Rivers, they visited a Sioux camp. There they saw several well-built log cabins filled with goods that would have been of little use to Indians. The village chief, Bill said, though he seemed to be a Sioux, was Red Cloud Tom, the peddler. But when Bill called him by that name he never batted an eye. This chief, he said, had two young wives and a few small children who showed their white blood plain as day.

Bill's party stayed there several days and Bill tried all kinds of ways to catch Tom off guard, but only once did he come near to unbosoming himself. And then, before he admitted anything, he caught himself and closed up like a clam. Through Rowland, Bill asked all kinds of questions of the other Indians, but they all declared the chief was a full-blood Sioux. Bill concluded that very likely they were honest in this belief, and that Tom kept so well disguised that not even his wives knew his true identity. From what Bill could learn, the goods in Tom's stores were kept for exchange with other traders on the upper reaches of the river, and when he went on trading trips he scrubbed off his paint, changed from Indian to white man's clothes, and so kept both sides from discovering who he really was.

When Rowland's party finally reached a fort, Bill Ike reported his discovery to the commander. But that officer told him they had all they could handle without chasing will-o'-the-wisps. Just the same, Bill was always certain he had found Red Cloud Tom.

As for the banner team of bays that was stolen from our farm that spring, they were seen a few weeks later in St. Joe, pulling a circus wagon. Some of Father's friends, who knew the team well, questioned the new owner as to where he got them, and were told he had bought them from an agent of Jack Morrow's.[11]

This Jack Morrow had a big road ranch just above Fort McPherson on the South Platte River, and there was nearly always a good-sized Indian camp close by, with visiting Indians coming and going at all times. It was suspicioned that many were hostiles, keeping posted on the movement of troops and civilians. Most of the time big bands of mules and heavy work horses were kept under herd at Morrow's headquarters, ready to be traded to needy freighters and emigrants.

As very little stock was branded in those days it was hard to prove ownership. And Jack always saw to it that this stock, which it was said was stolen from passing trains, was not brought in to be traded or sold until long after the dispossessed owners were gone from the region. (I can't recall that an animal was ever recovered from Jack by its rightful owner.) It was also said that Morrow doled out more firewater, guns, and ammunition to hostiles than all other traders on the Platte River. Anyway, as the circus was moving east every day, Father concluded it would cost more than the team was worth to follow and try to recover the horses, for they were unbranded, and ownership would be hard to prove outside his own district.

This same Jack Morrow later furnished foot beef on contract to the Standing Rock, Cheyenne, and Brulé reservations, and it was told that he put eight hundred steers around a hill twice, so they would be counted as double that number. When the receiving agent saw how small the herd really was, he recounted the steers and then put expert trackers out to scour the country. When he could find no

---

11. Jack Morrow was born in 1831 and went west from Pennsylvania. His ranch was about twelve miles west of Cottonwood Springs (Fort McPherson). He died near Omaha in 1876. (Root and Connelley, *The Overland Stage to California*, pp. 208–210; and the Omaha *Daily Bee*, July 7, 1876.)

trace of the missing steers, he charged Jack with the shortage. But Jack stood pat and refused to reimburse the Indian Department. Later, when his heirs put in a claim for seventy-five thousand dollars against the government for property destroyed or stolen by the Indians, the claim was allowed, about 1880, and collected by them.

Just east of Morrow's old ranch site there used to be a crude wooden marker at the head of a grave. The name on it was that of a Mrs. Thurman who had been Jack's housekeeper. It was said that she was killed by the accidental discharge of her own derringer in the hand of Jack Morrow, that she had picked it up from her trunk while airing her clothes and, at his request, had handed it to him. I saw that old headboard many times while passing the spot on roundups and buffalo hunts. It was of special interest to me because this same Mrs. Thurman had once been one of Mother's hired girls at Liberty Farm. She had been very competent, but just a little shady of reputation.

After Father had the rebuilding and cropping started on our Liberty Farm ranch, he went west again. He passed through Fort Laramie on this trip, and there he saw four Indians hanging from tripods made with upended wagon tongues. They had been hanging for several days, and Father wanted to know why they were hung. This is the story he was told: After the August raid of the year before, the minor Sioux chief who had captured Laura Roper, Mrs. Julian, Mrs. Eubank, and baby Willie and Isabelle Eubank, had traded Mrs. Eubank, Willie, and Mrs. Julian to a Cheyenne chief, who had taken them north for the winter. Not long before Father came along, Mrs. Eubank and the baby were brought in to Fort Laramie under a trade agreement and turned over to the commander, who let the four Indians who surrendered them leave with their trade goods. But when Mrs. Eubank told of the atrocities she had seen these same Indians inflict on their captives, the commander sent a detachment of cavalry out to bring them back. He had then hung them, and let them dangle for the friendly Indians camped nearby to see and report to the hostiles.

This made Father angry, for he knew such treatment would stop all surrender of white captives, and he told the commander so. He was right, for the return of Clara Kelley of the Mandan region in the late seventies is the only one I can recall. Of the others captured in that August raid, Laura Roper (who had been one of Mother's hired girls), Isabelle and Arthur Eubank, and a Connie Marpie who was taken at Plum Creek, had been surrendered to troops from Fort Lyon, Colorado, late in the fall of '64.[12] But only Laura ever came home again.

As far as I can learn, the United States government was, so to speak, bankrupt because of the Civil War and couldn't furnish transportation home for the captives. The neighbors (including my father) who could afford it subscribed to a fund to bring Laura home. The four of them had been kept at the Planters House in Denver, and when Laura left the three younger children there, it was the last that she or any of our people ever saw of them. Father always thought that the other three were adopted by families who became so attached to them that they would not even answer inquiries.[13]

Soon after the theft of the banner bays Father brought the rest of our family back to Liberty Farm, where I got to know Jack Wilson, one of the crew hired to rebuild and crop the place. Jack was an easterner who had left home to find his fortune in the Golden West. He landed in Pittsville, Missouri, in the fall of 1864, and while wintering there fell in love with Miranda Pitts. There were so many people by the name of Pitts in this place that (so I was later told by Charles Hoffman and Reuben Cook of the W G Cattle Company of Fall River County, South Dakota) at an 1880 election six hundred adult Pitts men voted at one polling precinct.

When Jack hired out to Father in 1865 to go up into Nebraska where the big raid had taken place only a few months before, Miranda had begged and pleaded with him not to go to a country where so much murdering and scalping was going on. But Jack went anyway. Not long after he came to Liberty Farm the eastbound

---

12. Laura Roper, Isabelle Eubank, and Danny Marble, who had been taken prisoner in the Plum Creek raid, were turned over to Major Wynkoop from Fort Lyon on September 11, 1864. Mrs. Eubank was released by the Indians in May, 1865. See Sanford, *Mollie*, p. 190 n.

13. Mollie Sanford, in *Mollie*, p. 190, reported that Isabelle Eubank was adopted by a Dr. Brondsall of Denver.

stage rolled in one morning and the passengers got off to breakfast at our place, as usual, before going on. One of the men finished eating and stepped outside the dining room. When he chanced to see a prairie chicken sitting on a fence post about fifty yards away, he pulled a gun and shot the chicken, off-handed. This was a splendid shot with such a gun—a .36 Colt cap-and-ball—and Jack right away asked what he would take for it. As I recall, he bought the gun for seventeen dollars and considered it a great bargain.

While tending the crops at Liberty that spring and summer (1865), we had to keep a constant lookout for roving bands of hostile Indians. We had two men cultivating in the cornfields, and for their protection we kept a guard stationed at each end of the field. Hervey, a very good shot already, was one of the guards.

On the Fourth of July, Hervey stayed at the house to celebrate with Moroni, Alpharetta, and me. The field was two and a half miles from the house, but Jack, the other field hand, and their one guard got ready to leave for work as usual. Jack hadn't been able to buy a second gun, so Hervey told him he had better take one of his guns along. As these were all cap-and-ball guns that had to be reloaded after each shot, it was customary to carry two. So Jack went off to the field with his own gun and one of Hervey's.

That afternoon Father, who had just gotten back from the west, and Mother went out horseback riding—and that was the situation when sixteen Indians attacked the farm. They struck first at the cornfield. In the shooting there one Indian was killed, though none of our three men could say which one killed him. With all the shooting going on, they unhitched from their cultivators as fast as they could, jumped on the horses, and streaked for home. Both of Jack's horses were of racing blood, but the mare he was riding was the faster of the two. She got a foot-long crease under her belly from an Indian's bullet, but kept her feet, and Jack hung on and they all came in safe.

When they told us what had happened, Hervey jumped on his Blackhawk-Morgan race pony and lit out to try to find Father and Mother. But he hadn't been gone long when they came home. It seemed that the Indians, after giving up on chasing the field hands, had spied Father and Mother off to the northwest, on the other side of the Little Blue, and had tried to cut them off from the ranch. But it took them so long to cross the steep-banked stream that our parents had made it home with time to spare.

Naturally, Mother was worried about Hervey when she found out he'd gone to try to warn them, but Father told her there wasn't an Indian pony in the country that could come near the racer, and that Brother would be all right. Which proved to be the case, for though the Indians saw him and tried to head him off, he, instead of trying to ride around the hostiles as they expected him to do, had ridden straight away from home to the north and had soon outrun them. By then it was getting dark, so he swung to the east and came in to the stage road below Buffalo Station, four miles away, and then came whistling on home as if nothing out of the ordinary had happened.

That summer, too, we had a strange experience with a boy who had been captured by Indians when he was so young that he didn't know he was white. That had happened down in the Smoky Hill country of central Kansas. Two white women who were taken prisoner by Indians in the 1864 uprising saw this boy, who seemed to be about fourteen years old, and decided he was white. They told him this, and finally convinced him by pointing out that a lot more of the camp drudgery was put on him than on the other boys of his age.

Not long afterward he came to blows one day with another herd boy over the unequal division of labor. In the fight he struck the Indian boy over the head with a loaded quirt.[14] The boy fell, and he thought he had broken his skull. The white women then warned him that if the Indian boy died, the tribe would torture and kill him. So, while herding the ponies the next night, he picked the best one of the bunch and headed northwest toward Fort Sedgwick. By then he was so scared that he rode the pony to death and had to walk the last part of the way, pulling into the fort on the fifth day. All he had to eat the whole time was an old crow that had died of an arrow wound and which he picked up on the way.

An officer at the post took charge of the boy and took him along when the troop moved east a short time later. The officer mounted

14. A quirt with a shot-filled handle, very hard and heavy.

the lad on a fine pony and gave him a .36-caliber gun and unlimited ammunition, so of course he was soon dashing ahead of the command, shooting any kind of small game that ranged near the road. Barnyard chickens were something the boy had never seen, and when they came to the W. W. Hackney farm, thirty-five miles west of our ranch, he began slaughtering the chickens in the yard. When Hackney tried to stop him, the boy threw down on him. The officer rode up just in time and explained to the lad that these were tame, owned fowl and not to be killed.

The troops reached our place near noon. We were about to sit down to dinner, so we invited the boy to eat with us. He was willing, but the officer cautioned us to be careful with him, as he was not yet broke from the wild. While we were eating, he saw our big black Newfoundland dog and said, "Shunka-ute-waste" ("Dog good eat"). When he wanted the sugar, he pointed to the bowl and said, "Chehumps," meaning "sugar."

It was about five years before I heard the Sioux tongue spoken again, but those two sentences were forever impressed on my memory. And I will never forget the way that boy mounted his pony after dinner and dashed away toward the soldiers' camp, a mile east on the bend of the river, without ever touching the bridle reins or the saddle horn, just guiding the pony by knee pressure and the swing of his body. Though we were all good riders, my brothers and I looked on at that exhibition with plain envy. Before he left, the boy told us, through an interpreter, that he was in on the American Ranch fight the year before. He said he had tried as hard as he knew how to kill the whites, as at that time he supposed he was a full-fledged Sioux.

When the officer reached the East with the lad, he advertised for his parents. A couple finally came forward and established a partial claim to him, though nothing definite could be proved. This couple was allowed to take him and give him a home, but the East was too tame for him and he soon deserted, went west again, and hired out as a government teamster at Fort Laramie. After that I heard no more of him. And, as far as I could ever find out, the two white women who persuaded him to quit the Sioux camp were never redeemed from the Indians, nor did I ever learn who they were.

By the spring of 1866 the Union Pacific rails had been laid as far west as Kearney. This made a good market for grain at that point, as it was needed for feed for teams working on railroad construction. So Father, Jack Wilson, and a man named Maurice Law started for the end of the track with all the corn we had on hand, leaving the ranch in the hands of Hervey, Moroni, and myself. Hervey was thirteen at the time, Moroni, eleven, and I was nine. Mother was there, of course, and Alpharetta, my seven-year-old sister, and the hired girl, Clara Roper, a sister to Laura who had been captured by Indians two years earlier. Two thirteen-year-old neighbor boys came over, and we carried in a good supply of water. Then Mother helped us gather in all the axes, shovels, picks, crowbars, and mauls. We had plenty of guns and ammunition, and if the Indians did attack, Mother and Clara could load while we boys did the shooting.

Well, the grain haulers had been on the road only a few hours when Father noticed prairie fires starting up in different places in the vicinity of our ranch. He knew they meant several bands of Indians trailing or keeping track of each other by means of the fires. His outfit was near Spring Ranch, the next station west of ours, when Father first saw the fires. Since he knew that a company of infantry was still stationed at the ranch to protect the mail, he hurried there and had the officer in charge pile about twenty soldiers and some saddles into a government wagon behind six or eight mules. Then they all flew for our place.

When they got there they found us surrounded by Sioux and, in a manner, under siege. The Sioux had been chasing a band of Pawnees when they stopped off to attack our place, but Father and his band of soldiers soon drove them off, which was a big relief to us boys. The Indians then made for their favorite rendezvous in the big timber on Liberty Creek, two and a half miles from the ranch.

Now we had at Liberty Farm a good many half-broken colts, and a lively time was had by all getting those infantrymen mounted on the colts. But when they were all on and looked like they might stay, Jack Wilson, riding the swift mare of the cornfield race of the year before, led the way to the timber. On nearing it, the officer ordered a charge right in after the Indians; but Father, on Hervey's race pony, rode into the lead and literally forced the men back. Then he told the officer that if they charged into that thick growth of trees and brush, the Indian bows and arrows would do a lot more damage at close range than the soldiers' guns, and that with the timber swarming with Indians, not a white man would come out alive.

While this argument was going on, Jack Wilson had singled out a lone Indian, run him down on the racing mare, and shot him. He then went to support the main body of soldiers, and before he could get back to scalp his downed Indian, others had raced from the timber and taken away both the body and the horse. To make a long story short, we drove off the Indians, and that ended hostilities for a while, as far as we were concerned.

The Maurice Law with Father that day had been his assistant wagon boss on the trip west with the mining machinery in 1864. When Law was getting ready to make that trip, which was just before we left Liberty Farm for Marysville, he overlooked a fine silver slip-case penholder and gold pen. For safekeeping until we all came home again, Mother put it in her Chinese camphorwood trunk, which we took with us.

Some of the boys got to trading at school that fall, as boys will, and I filched the penholder, took it to school, and traded it off. That evening my brothers told on me, and Mother sent me straight off to retrieve it. Loaded with all my worldly goods, I set out. And it took every last thing I had to get it back, for it had been retraded in three parts. During the summer of rebuilding at Liberty Farm, someone told Law about my sacrifice to get the penholder back, and he said, "Well, Ed, I will now make you a present of it." There was a place on the side of the case for the name of the owner, but somebody had already scratched the name Liberty Farm there.

At about this same time Father had a percentage partner [15] by the name of John Hiles. John was a good man, but he had a roving nature and would every now and then take off for as long as six months at a time. When he came back he was always loaded with second-hand jewelry, which he would dole out to Mother, Sister, and the hired girls. For us boys he'd have silver rings, and sometimes

---

15. A partner who did not furnish a share of the equipment, but received a stipulated percentage of the profits in return for his work and/or influence.

cheap silver watches. This made Father think he was mixed up in some kind of a shady business, but we never found out what, if any. A little later that summer Hiles left us, and we, in appreciation for all the gifts he had given us, wanted to give him something in return. I gave him the penholder with the gold pen and the name Liberty Farm on the side.

IV

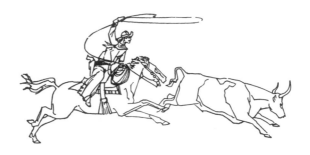

MOVING ALONG WITH END-OF-TRACK

T HE COMING of the Union Pacific to Kearney led to the abandonment of the Ben Holladay stage line from there on east, as the railroad naturally took over the mail and passenger traffic to that point. The troops were then pulled out of our territory and put to guarding the railroad construction workers, leaving road ranches and stage stations to the mercy of the hostiles. With the troops gone and freight and passenger traffic at an end, there was no longer any business for the ranch and station keepers. So practically everybody from east of the Hackney ranch, near present Hebron, to Kearney joined the U.P. construction crews.

Father, who had eighteen choice teams and a good deal of equipment, was the first to join the railroad outfits. The Comstock family followed suit, and then the Metcalf brothers, Ute and George, and a good many others. Ute Metcalf had kept the Spring Ranch station, and George, much younger, had worked for him.

Before abandoning our place, Father homesteaded the quarter where the buildings stood and stored most of our unperishable goods—such as flooring, doors, windows, roofing, and some furniture—in our big root cellar, padlocked the door, and sealed it with well-packed dirt. Most of the other ranch owners did the same before they left their places.

Because of his many good teams, Father got a job delivering ties ahead of the track layers.[1] One night that summer he camped his outfit on the bank of the Platte River near big Brady Island, so that the river made one side of his wagon corral. During the night some Indians slipped off the island into the corral and tried to stampede the horses and mules. The night guards, awake and on the job, fired at them and woke the whole camp. Jack Wilson, one of the crew, took the lead in the chase that followed, and three Indians were killed. When morning came and they got a good look at the dead men, one of Father's men said it looked to him like one of them had the features of a white man. So Father sent to a road ranch for some whiskey and they washed the paint off the fellow's face with it. And sure enough, he was a white renegade who sometimes worked for Jack Morrow.

The next year (1867) on Lodgepole Creek, near Sidney, Father and his outfit were again attacked by Indians, and then again when they were on their way to the Black Hills,[2] west of Cheyenne, to cut cedars for ties. This last time there were thirty or forty wagons in the outfit, and five or six cook wagons, with a total of more than fifty fighting men. A big band of painted warriors swooped down on them in broad daylight and began circling the train. Their plan was to force the train to corral, miles from water, and then lay siege to it. But Father was too wise to be taken in that way. He ordered part of his men—about one man to each two wagons—to stay with the train and keep it rolling, while the rest joined the outriders to fight the Indians. By this means they drove the raiders off.

As the track laying moved west, the end-of-track towns moved too, getting bigger and wilder all the time. The winter of '66–'67 was spent at or near North Platte City, the winter of '67–'68 at Cheyenne,

1. Tie logs were cut in the canyons bordering the south side of the Platte Valley from the east end of Brady Island as far west as North Platte City.
2. The present Laramie Hills or Sherman Hills, not to be confused with the Black Hills of South Dakota.

and the last winter at Benton, in present Wyoming, which was then a part of Dakota Territory. At Julesburg the track laying was held up for a while and that town, said to have had a temporary population of four thousand sheltered residents, became the toughest on the line. Benton was even tougher, though, when the tracks moved on west and it was the end of the line for a while.

As our family moved along with the camps, we saw plenty of exciting happenings. One day a long-haired gent rode into town and went into a barbershop. He sat down in a chair, laid his gun on his lap, and said, "Give me a shave, and damn you, if you cut me I'll kill you."

The barber began stropping his razor. "If I cut you," he said, "I'll see the blood first and I'll cut your throat from ear to ear before you can move." There was no blood drawn, so there was no shooting. But I've often wondered if that exchange was real, or just a grandstand play between friends.

In the fall of 1867, Mother, Moroni, Alpharetta, and I stayed in Beatrice, Nebraska, for a while. When Father came after us in December, he left Hervey, who was fourteen by then, in Cheyenne to collect the last payment on a small tie contract delivery, which finished up the work for that season. As I recall, it amounted to about $260, which Hervey turned over to Aunt Sallie Milligan.

Aunt Sallie and Uncle Joe Milligan had a camp in the west edge of Cheyenne, where most of the freighters boarded while laying up for loads. Aunt Sallie, who was a trusty for everybody, doled out the money to Hervey as he needed it to pay the teamsters, who mostly spent it visiting the entertainment emporiums of the town. In taking care of this bit of business, Hervey saw a lot of the underworld and came to know sundry and all.

Before Father left, Hervey, while prowling around one day visiting other camps, stopped in the camp of one Ed Hammond. Ed had been our neighbor on the Little Blue, where he was known to be considerable on the rustle. Just as Hervey stepped in, Hammond discovered that some of his flashy ivory harness rings were missing. He right away began to lay it onto that "damn Lemmon outfit" for taking them. About that time he felt something tickling his ribs from behind. Hervey was doing the tickling—with one of his Colt's Navy

.36 cap-and-ball guns. "You just walk right over to our camp and say that to Father," he told Ed.

Hammond tried to beg off, saying he was just joking and that he had put the rings away himself, to keep them from being stolen. But Hervey marched him to Father and ordered him to repeat his charge. Hammond did, but still said it was a joke and that he'd known all the time Brother was listening. So Father slapped his face a few times and told him he was just joking, too. Hammond must've thought Father's joke was flavored with too much elbow grease, for he said, "I'll crack no more jokes like that soon."

When we got back from Beatrice, Father established us in Cheyenne. The next morning I went out to see the town with Hervey. One of the first places we went to was a dance and drink emporium, with all sorts of painted girls around. Brother saw a teamster he wanted to talk to, and left me by the door. In a minute a buxom painted girl stepped up to me and said, "You little snot-nose, you get out of here or I'll sit on you and smother you."

Big as she was, she could've done it, and I was sure looking for Brother. He saw my uneasiness and came right over. When the girl asked him who the snot-nose was, he said, "He is no snot-nose, but my kid brother that I'm very proud of. And he is almost my equal with a gun, even if he does look young." That being the case, the girl said, I was welcome and then some.

After that we walked over to the northwest part of town. Pretty quick we heard some shooting and rushed to the spot. We were just in time to see the end of the notorious Pat Mullaly fight in which five men were killed. The fight was between two freight outfits, and Pat, too, had been a neighbor of ours on the Little Blue.[3]

~~~~~~~~~~~~~~~~~

3. "On the night of September 16, 1867 an event occurred in the northwestern portion of the city, . . . the killing of Pat Mullaly and 'Limber Jim.' Of the latter but little was known at the time, for he was a comparatively new comer in the city. Pat Mullaly, who was at the time of his death one of the members of the special police force of fifty-eight, had been in Cheyenne from the very first and had many friends among the people of the city. . . . on the evening of September 16th, Pat Mullaly, Limber Jim and two females went up to the saloon of 'Lead Beader' for the purpose, as Mullaly expressed it, of 'setting up the wine.' The door was closed but it was at length forced open by Mullaly, who with 'Limber Jim' close behind, entered the house. As he did so, a shot fired by some party from under a bed in an adjoining room, . . . took effect in Mullaly's

On my second day in Cheyenne, Hervey and I were sitting with a crowd of other boys on some boxes in front of a grocery store. The boys had been admiring Brother's two Colts, which he wore in scabbards on a belt, which also held his bullet pouch, cap box, and powder flask. Hervey had taken off the belt and one of the boys was holding it, when along came a dandified gambler with the look of the East all over him. The gambler reached down and gathered up the belt, guns and all. "Those are not very nice playthings," he said, and walked off a few doors and went into a saloon. There he handed the guns to the barkeep, who recognized them and asked where he got them. "Oh, from a small boy," the fellow said. Then he stepped to the door and pointed out the boy.

"Those guns don't belong to him," the barkeep said. "They belong to that one," pointing at Brother, "and he has a permit to carry them. If you think he can't handle 'em, you just wait a minute until he calls for them, which he will. And when I hand 'em over you'll see how quick they get into action. Why, there's not a faster or a straighter shot on the frontier than him, not even Wild Bill Hickok or Jack Watson. He could dust the ashes off your cigar and never jar your lips, or clip a fly off the leader's ear on a four-horse team and never touch the ear."

―――――――――――

side or breast and killed him almost instantly. 'Limber Jim' turned to retreat and as he did so he was shot in the back by someone in the building, but not before he had fired one shot from a revolver wounding 'Lead Beader,' the woman who kept the house, in the right arm. He ran about fifty yards from the house when he dropped dead in a pile of lumber. Several shots were fired in all and inside of five minutes after the first one was heard there were as many as twelve hundred people around the place. . . . As soon as it became known who . . . had been killed the crowd resolved itself into a mob, and not only the building in which the shooting took place, but others adjoining, were burned to the ground, the flames lighting up the entire city. The city witnessed a reign of terror for the balance of the night and in some places where the people were fortunate enough to have cellars, they resorted to them as shots were being fired in all directions. . . . Some three miles east of the city were camped about 400 graders and word was sent to them by the mob to come up and help them burn the town. As soon as this was known word was sent to the military authorities at Fort Russell . . . asking for assistance. In reply to this call three companies of infantry came down on the 'double jump,' and were soon followed by the companies of cavalry. The arrival of the troops put an end to all further rioting for that night." ("History of Wyoming, Written by C. G. Coutant, Pioneer Historian, and Heretofore Unpublished," *Annals of Wyoming*, XII [October 1940], 324–326.)

By that time Brother was coming through the front door of the saloon, but the gambler was already going out the back one. When the barkeep asked Hervey how it happened he didn't interfere when the gambler took the guns, he said he had seen the fellow get off the train the night before and that he shrieked so loud of the East that he thought he'd just leave him to learn Cheyenne's ways from older fellows of his own kind. A few days later the gambler saw Hervey, rushed up to him with outstretched hand, and said, "Please shake, boy, for you certainly sized me up to a finish. I've gotten my eyeteeth cut to the tune of about five thousand dollars since then, and I've learned not to look on you young looking westerners as unfit to protect yourselves. Please shake again."

While our family was living in Cheyenne in 1868 it got to be a fad for all the town boys to have whips to pop along the streets. Each boy tried to have the best whip, and to be better at using it than anyone else. Moroni and I had got hold of two extra-good whips that we were mighty proud of.

One day we were downtown and Moroni was popping his whip when a freighter, who was loading out at a hardware store for Cache la Poudre, was about ready to pull out. He noticed Brother's fine whip and asked to look at it. Moroni handed it up to him, and the freighter yelled, "You damn little thief, you stole this from Jim Moore's barn, where I stabled my team last night." With that, he started to drive off, but Brother grabbed the bits on his leaders and held on. The freighter whipped out his six-shooter and ordered him to let go, which of course he did. Then we heeled it for home and got our guns.

We knew the road the freighter would take, so we took a cutoff, reached the road ahead of him, and hid behind a cut bank. When he came along, Brother ordered him to wrap the lines around the brake, put up his hands, and just let the team mosey on. With a big laugh, the freighter said, "Now, boys, I was just testing your nerve to see if you had the same stuff in you as your father, for I know him well."

Moroni said, "That's all right, but just toss that whip over, and keep your hands up till you're out of six-shooter range." Which of course he did.

[49]

When Father came home, several months later, we told him about the freighter, but couldn't tell him his name, as we didn't know it. All Father said was, "Boys, in this country the best man wins, and you had a right to get your property back."

During this time there were hostile Indians all around town, so the Cheyenne boys organized a company of boy militia. An eighteen-year-old fellow named Bell was our captain and Moroni was first lieutenant. We drilled at night at the city race track, about a mile and a quarter northeast of town. We knew there were hostiles camped on the head of Lodgepole Creek, about twenty miles on beyond the race track, so while we did our practice shooting with blanks, we kept eight guns loaded with solid shot handy.

One evening just at dusk a lone horseman came loping toward us from the direction of the hostile village. The captain gave the usual command to halt. When he gave it the third time and the rider still paid no attention, he ordered four of the boys to fire on him with the loaded guns. They did, and the rider swung a trifle to the left but kept on going toward town. The next morning a dead man with a couple of bullet holes in him was found just south of the freight yards, under the nose of a gray horse that looked like the one ridden by the man our boys fired on. He was never identified, but it was believed he was a spy from the hostiles, looking over the lay of things. After that we were not allowed to go out at night for quick-shoot practice. But the mayor, when chastising us, admitted that we likely had saved some freighter the loss of his team to the Indians.

About that same time, a long-haired gent rode into town and stopped at a hardware store and gunshop, where he bought a Winchester and a lot of cartridges. He filled the magazine and chamber, then stepped to the door and said, "I guess I'll try her." Then he drew a bead on a man on foot across the street, about a block and a half north, and touched the trigger, shooting the man through the head. The stranger jumped on his horse and rode out of town in the direction of the hostile camp. It was never known whether or not he even knew the man he killed, but likely he didn't, since he was probably a renegade from the camp. At that time there were a good many such men among the hostiles, mostly deserters from the Confederate armies.

Before leaving off with what I remember of old Cheyenne, I must tell about Apple Ann. When we first came to the town in 1867, we saw a kind of shriveled up little woman, maybe about thirty years old, peddling apples. She had a pleasant way about her, though she scarcely ever tarried to talk, for she was all business and seemed to be on the go almost day and night. She had a regular stand where she sold raw apples and apple pies, but she also put in a lot of time peddling on the street, at public gatherings, and in front of McDaniels theater before and after shows. She often peddled in front of the leading gambling and dance houses, too, though I can't recall ever seeing her go into either one, or McDaniels either, likely because she begrudged the price of admission.

Apple Ann was respected by all, and I don't believe the roughest tough in the place would've dared offer her an insult—because I'm sure if he had he would've been strung up without mercy. By the time we left Cheyenne in the fall of 1870, Ann was beginning to invest in real estate bargains, although she still lived in a little room behind her shop. It was nearly twenty-one years before I went back again, and I had hardly stepped on the street before I ran onto old Apple Ann.

I was then a bad cripple and at first she didn't recognize me. But when I reminded her of some of the scrapes I'd been mixed up in, back in the old boom days, she remembered me well and insisted I come down to her emporium and have a piece of apple pie. She said she had just made it from a new recipe, which she considered fully up to the day. So I did, but she wouldn't let me pay for it—and R. S. Van Tassell told me later he believed that was the only time she was ever known to treat anyone. I think she must have had a tender spot in her heart for me because I had helped rid the town of Red Pat and Mormon Ann. Some of us boys did that by composing a little song that we sang on the streets, causing the pair to leave pronto.

This Mormon Ann was a daredevil, quick as a panther and almost as dangerous, with a cool nerve that was second to nobody, unless it was Calamity Jane. She hung out with the bandit element of the town, and could handle a six-shooter with the best of them. Her favorite pal was Red Pat, a big, broad-shouldered badman with bright red hair and keen bright eyes. He was said to have been a prize fighter who had broken a man's neck in the ring, and so had had to come west.

Many bad deeds were traced to these two, but never with enough proof to do anything about them. Their favorite spot was a beer garden on Crow Creek, on the west side of Cheyenne. The place was kept by a Swiss doctor and had so many outbuildings and dark crannies that all kinds of crime could be hidden there. Mormon Ann was supposed to lure men with money into dumps like that one, then help take their money, and maybe their lives.

In 1868 a band of vigilantes, headed by A. C. Beckwith, set out to clean up Cheyenne, and Red Pat and Mormon Ann's names were high on their list. Our boy militia heard of it and made up a song that was pretty hot. It may have been us boys singing that song on the streets, or because they heard their names just about topped the vig list, or both, but they got out of town in a hurry about then.

The last time I was in Cheyenne, in 1904, Apple Ann was still doing business on the streets, and I was told by Van Tassell that she owned a good many residential buildings in the city. She must have been right at seventy years old by then, and everyone still regarded her with the greatest respect.

In the spring of 1868 Father took Ute Metcalf into partnership with him in the tie-hauling business. Ute, the former keeper of the Spring Ranch stage station, had a poor reputation, a good education, piercing black eyes, and a winning personality. He played a good hand at poker and drank champagne as if it was water, and these accomplishments put him on good terms with quite a lot of army officers, and so helped him get good government contracts.

At this time, with the tracks nearing Rawlins Springs in Wyoming Territory, some good government hay and wood contracts were about to be let, which caused Father to deem it a good idea to take Ute in as a percentage partner. Just before the new contracts came up for bids Father was finishing up a tie contract, worth about twenty thousand dollars, in Rawlins. Leaving his new partner in charge of the work, he came to Cheyenne for a short visit with us. A few days later, Hervey, who had stayed in Rawlins with the teams and equipment, wired that Ute had finished the tie contract, collected the money, and absconded. Father took the first train out and was soon on Ute's trail.

The first night out he stopped at a ranch and saloon. He had taken his favorite hand gun, the old self-cocking .50-caliber derringer with the revolving barrels, which he handed over to the barkeep when he went into the saloon. A bystander asked to look at it, as it was an unusual weapon. Taking the gun in his hands, the fellow carelessly cocked it. Father at once reached over and took the gun, explaining that it was stiff-springed and it was unsafe to let the hammer down. So Father let it down, just to show him, and the gun went off, shooting his left forefinger. The shot tore out an inch of bone and made a horrible sight of his hand. He jerked out his jackknife and was about to cut away the mangled remains when a discharged soldier stopped him, saying he had seen many such fingers get well, and they beat having no finger at all. So Father left it the way it was —and the soldier was right. After it got well it was better than none.

Father kept right on after Ute Metcalf, though. And over in the Bear River country of southwest Wyoming Territory he was told that his man had tolled a wealthy mine promoter into an isolated region to show him a rich mine prospect, and had there murdered him for his money. (In those days speculators carried their money with them, since there were no banks.) For this crime he had been convicted and hung, Father was told, so he quit the chase and came home.

And there he found that Ute had left all the hands unpaid, and also the grocery and feed bills. Consequently, Father had to sell off most of his teams and equipment to pay his creditors. By the time he had settled everything he had only three teams and wagons left, out of the eighteen he had started with.

While Father was headquartered at Rawlins Springs he ran a little store in connection with his commissary, and had a lot of knick-knacks such as candy and nuts in the store. The workers, when loafing, often played cards for these dry treats. One of the workmen was Ute's brother, George Metcalf, who weighed two hundred pounds and was a top hand with his fists.

One day he and Hervey were playing cards and Hervey caught him cheating. When he accused him, George raised up from his side of the table and said, "I'll just slap your jaws for that." But Hervey flipped out a Colt's and said, "Not so fast, George. Just sit down and drop your arms back and let your coat slide down on the floor. If there aren't any cards in your sleeves, you can slap me, but don't slap too hard, for I've seen you cheat at cards before, and I don't think I'm wrong now." George did as he was told, and one of the other fellows shook his coat and some cards fell out of a sleeve. George was a hale-fellow-well-met all right, and not afraid of man or devil, but he knew when he was in the wrong.

Well, Father soon managed to get a tie-hauling contract in line with the small outfit he had left. His teamsters were Hervey, an old friend named Millspaw, and himself. They were to cut ties in a thick stand of timber, and Father went in ahead of the others and, in a manner, cleared a road. He loaded his wagon with the ties he had cut in making the road, and started back. On the way out he came onto a yoke of oxen hitched to a wagon and blocking his way. There didn't seem to be a driver around, so he picked up the whip from the wagon and started to swing the team out of his way. But at that the driver showed up, swearing, and ordered Father to leave his team alone.

Father tried to tell him he had that road coppered, but the bull driver was shedding his coat and getting ready to fight. So Father shed his own coat and got ready to accommodate him. The bull whacker squared off and told Father his outfit was going to haul the ties out of this timber. Father said he had a good signed contract and would haul the ties. The bully said not so, that he had a big Missouri outfit and intended to haul all of that district. Then suddenly he took his team and left, without pushing the matter any further.

The next day Father, Brother, and Millspaw went into the timber, loaded their wagons, and started back. They were strung out about a hundred yards apart, with Father in the lead, Brother next, and Millspaw in the rear. Down the road a ways Father swung around a bend just as sixteen armed men stepped out of the brush and lined up across the road in front of him. The driver of the day before rushed up, grabbed him by the heels, and yanked him off his load.

Father fell beside the wagon, and some ties fell off the load on top of him. Then every man that could get near enough began pounding him.

Hervey hove in sight just then, jumped off his load, and rushed into the fight just as Father managed to get onto his feet. Both of them went to whaling away at the nearest man, and it happened they both landed on the same fellow. Now this fellow had a brother in the fight, and this brother, yelling that no two men could tap his brother at the same time and get away with it, lammed Hervey over the head with a Winchester and knocked him under the wagon.

Hervey crawled out with his six-shooter in his hand. He flirted it back to use the downward cocking stroke, but the first brother, who was behind him, grabbed it and wrenched it away from him, skinning his trigger finger pretty bad. By that time Millspaw was coming around the bend. He jumped into the fight, too, but being an educated man of commanding and forceful language, he managed to get the attention of the leader of the other outfit and make him understand that Father had the legal right to haul those ties.

The boss asked Father to show his contract, which he did, and so peace was restored—except that the fellow who had Brother's gun wouldn't give it up. "When we meet again, one or the other of us will have it *and* its mate, which I'm sorry I didn't carry today," Hervey told him. Well, it seems that the fellow soon heard of Brother's record with a gun, so he quit his hauler job and lit out for the Bear River country to cut ties.

As soon as Hervey could get away, he went after him. All Father said to him before he left was, "Don't shoot him in the back." Brother told him he wouldn't, that he hadn't been brought up that way. But when he came home again he had only his one gun, and we couldn't ever get anything out of him about what had happened. Even if he had had the second gun he wouldn't have dared show it, as that would have been proof he had killed the man who had taken it.

Another affair that happened in the Bear River camps had to do with a Mrs. Bictoll, who before her marriage had been another of Mother's hired girls at Liberty Farm. In the migration from the Little Blue to Union Pacific construction work at Kearney, the Bictolls went along. They had two children by then, a boy six and a girl five, and Bictoll put his few teams to work on the grade while his wife cooked for the grading crew.

Late in the fall they were in camp west of Cheyenne, near Sherman Pass, and James Daugherty, an expert hunter, was furnishing wild game for the camp. All the so-called camp buildings were tents set above frame skeletons. These buildings were used for food storehouses as well as for the cook and mess halls. Dogs couldn't very well be kept out of such flimsy affairs, so, since grub supplies were expensive and hard to get, no dogs were allowed in camp. None, that is, except a valuable hunting dog that belonged to Daugherty, who had taught him not to touch any food except what his master gave him with his own hand. He had trained him this way because he sometimes put out poisoned meat for gray wolves, and of course didn't want to lose his dog.

One evening when supper was about ready, Mrs. Bictoll went to the grub tent for sugar, leaving her five-year-old Emma to watch the kitchen. While she was gone she heard Emma scream. She rushed back to find Emma flown, and what she took to be a big black dog in the kitchen. The animal had upset several pans of biscuits, overturned the slop bucket on the floor, and was trying to eat a hot roast it had pawed out of the open oven. Mrs. Bictoll grabbed the ax from beside the door, slammed the dog over the head with the flat side of it, and ran him out of the kitchen. A minute later the men began coming in for supper. "You'll be in luck if you get anything to eat here," she told them. "A big black dog just about finished up everything."

Daugherty came in just in time to hear that, and asked, "Which way did he go? I'll have to kill him before he damages any more grub." Mrs. Bictoll told him he had gone off up the mountain, so Daugherty grabbed his rifle and took after him. There was enough snow on the ground to leave a good trail, and back at the mess tent they soon heard a shot.

"I might as well've killed him in the first place," Mrs. Bictoll said, "for Jim never misses." In a little while Daugherty came to the kitchen and asked the cook to come out and see if this was her dog. She stepped to the door, took a quick look, and said it was.

"Well," Daugherty told her, "that happens to be a grizzley bear."

At that the woman fainted and fell backwards into the arms of the nearest man, who happened to be the walking boss on that crew. At the same time, her husband came around the corner from the corral where he had been tending his teams.

"You damn scoundrel," he yelled at the walking boss, "I've been suspicioning this for some time—and now that you've got her you can just keep her."

Now Mrs. Bictoll weighed something over two hundred pounds, so the boss yelled back, "Don't be a fool. Come and get her before I drop her, for I'm sure overmatched." When Bictoll made no move, the boss, getting madder by the minute, hollered, "For gosh sakes, take this livestock off my hands."

The rest of the outfit finally made Bictoll understand that his wife had fainted from fright after whamming a grizzly bear with an ax. Once that was clear, he declared he was going to whip the boss for calling his wife livestock. But the boss refused to fight, and Mrs. Bictoll was finally carried to her tent, where Daugherty, a good friend of the family, was left to care for her while Bictoll, with the help of Emma, gathered up the supper and fed the crew.

Now Mrs. Bictoll was a good cook and the men didn't want to lose her over any family ruction, so they decided to give her credit for killing the bear that had messed up the supper. Accordingly, they told the story that way to Bictoll, and to her when she revived enough to understand. Of course, Bictoll ever afterward took great pride in telling anyone who would listen how his wife killed a grizzly bear with an ax.

This same James Daugherty practically made his home with our family from about 1863 until the railroad was finished in 1869. He was over six feet tall and weighed a trifle over two hundred pounds, with not an ounce of fat on him. When hunting he always wore moccasins, and he could stalk either game or Indians as well as an Indian could. He was as perfect a man, physically, as I ever saw, and was the very best offhand 18 [?] rifle shot I ever knew. I used to watch him practice holding his big 18 Sharps rifle on a target, off-hand, until I'd get so nervous I'd have to look away.

One time, while he was furnishing meat for the Carmichael and Brooks construction crew on the U.P., he thought he'd make a change in the meat line for the outfit. So he set out to bag a couple of grizzly bears he had sighted. He was slipping up on the bears when he saw what seemed to be some mountain lions stalking game at an angle to the path of the bears. In trying to get a better look at the lions and their game, he moved a little from his windward stalk of the bears. That gave them his scent and they hurried away.

Daugherty then saw some deer in a thicket, and concluded they were the game both the bears and the lions were after. Although he had no use for the lion meat, he decided to shoot them anyway. From where he crouched behind a down tree, he took a dead rest across the log and fired at the head of one of the lions. That lion flattened out— but the other one stood upright and dashed away. He drew dead center on its back, about where suspenders would cross on a man, and pulled the trigger.

Then he ran to look his lions over. He found a pair of Indians wearing lion skins, supposedly for charming deer, as it is said this can be done the same way a cat charms a bird. The Indians had threaded curved sticks into the skin of the lion tails so they could curl them over their backs and wiggle them in a bewitching way that was supposed to catch the eye of the deer. Daugherty scalped the Indians and took the lion skins, which he had tanned, with the heads stuffed in such a way that the eyes were wide open, in the best staring condition for charming results.

V

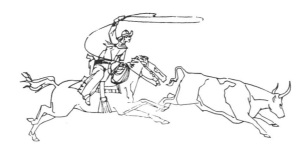

COWPUNCHING AND CARRYING
THE MAIL

A FTER THE Union Pacific railroad was finished in May, 1869, our
family had to look for other work. Hervey right away got a job
with J. W. Iliff,[1] the cattle king of the north, as a trailer. That is,
when any cattle strayed far off their regular range he followed them
until they were recovered. As I was quite a hand with horses and
guns, he had no trouble getting me a job there, too.

I made my headquarters at the ranch, twelve miles southeast of
Cheyenne. Though this was my first cowpunching job, I actually
worked mostly as a courier between the ranch and Fort D. A.
Russell,[2] where Iliff had contracts to furnish beef. As I was only

1. John Wesley Iliff was born in Ohio in 1831, the son of a well-to-do farmer.
By the time of his death in 1878, nineteen years after he went west, his $750
stake had pyramided into $1,500,000. His brand was the reversed LF, and the
town of Iliff, Colorado, is in the center of the region where his cattle ranged. See
Nellie Snyder Yost, *The Call of the Range : The Story of the Nebraska Stock
Growers Association* (Denver: Sage Books, 1966), pp. 69, 70, 388.
2. Fort D. A. Russell was built in 1867 on Crow Creek near Cheyenne to
provide protection for the Union Pacific Railroad. It was renamed Fort F. E.

thirteen years old, I could hardly stand the regular night-guard stint of a full-fledged cowpuncher, but I could handle the courier job fine, as I could scarcely be lost, either by day or by night, because I had an unusual sense of direction. In fact, during my fifty-three years of cowpunching I was never really lost but once, and that was on a Platte River island in brush fifteen feet high all around, with never a tree big enough to climb to get my bearings.

During my messenger service it was never necessary for me to fight Indians, for my fast, durable horses always carried me to safety, even though I did have to use my quirt on a couple of occasions. These fast horses were of Church Island stock and were mostly race ponies, as they were bred and raised by Brigham Young for cavalry use. They came into our possession this way: When our family left Utah, back in 1859, Father left quite a lot of property, mostly registered Shorthorn cattle, in the charge of a Mormon named Rideout. A short time later Brigham Young sent Rideout abroad as a missionary. The cattle were then neglected, and when Father went back after them ten years later, after finishing the work on the U.P., they were so much reduced in number and value that Brigham offered him fifty-two head of good horses off Church Island. The horses had become so wild from isolation on the island that we had to shoot seven of the leaders before we could make the rest take the ford through the lake off the island. As I said, these were all hot-blooded horses, nearly all racers, and the same stock from which Ben Holladay had gotten most of his Pony Express horses.

Father drove the horses to Cheyenne, where, that winter of '69 and '70, I was put to herding them at Chalk Bluffs, some twelve or fourteen miles south of town. I roomed and boarded with a bunch of wood choppers who had been teamsters of Father's. When the railroad work was finished, other jobs were so scarce that these men had taken up wood chopping as a way of eating steady, with Father furnishing the teams to haul the wood to Cheyenne.

A Mormon by the name of Rube Taylor had come with the horses as bronco buster and trailer. Now Taylor was what would be

<hr />

Warren in 1929. See T. A. Larson, *History of Wyoming* (Lincoln: University of Nebraska Press, 1965), p. 28.

called a conscientious objector today, since he didn't believe in killing people, but he was an expert trailer. Whenever I lost any ponies I sent word by the wood haulers for Rube to come out from Cheyenne and help me trail them. This happened quite often, for the horses seemed determined to go back to their native range, which was due west.

As the canyons from Chalk Bluffs led southwest, the horses would follow that course until out of the mountains. The trouble was, by following the canyons they came out in a direct line with a winter camp of hostile Indians about seventy-five miles away. On account of the poor flesh of its ponies, this village was almost inactive during the winter, although a few Indians would go out now and then, on foot, and mostly on horse-stealing trips.

One time when I missed some horses and sent for Rube, we packed our grub and bed on an extra horse and took the trail. The first day we made it to an old abandoned trapper's cabin, twenty-five miles out. A lot of people, Indians as well as whites, used the cabin as a stopping place because it had a fireplace, and also a bed pegged to the wall. We took our horses to a park some distance from the cabin, put the hobbles on, and left them hidden in the trees. Then we went to the cabin, ate supper, and went to bed, after putting our guns at the foot of the bed and our six-shooters at our heads. There was a three-paned slide window in the west wall, across from the bed, and we were hardly settled down when we heard a little noise at the window. It was bright moonlight, and we could see the faces of three Indians pressed against the three panes.

The Indians had probably intended to use the cabin for a night shelter themselves, but when they saw our tracks outside they came to the window to see if anyone was inside. Without making a sound, I picked up my six-shooter; but Rube reached for his gun at the foot of the bed, and of course made the bed squeak. The Indians disappeared in a flash. Naturally, we didn't make any other move until daylight, and by then there was nothing left of the Indians but their tracks, leading off in a westerly direction. We soon found our ponies and took them home, where I told Father and Hervey about Rube scaring the Indians away. They both said he'd made the bed squeak on purpose.

I know I could've gotten two of the Indians before they would've known we were there, and I might've gotten all three. Hervey, nearly seventeen and a tried frontiersman, sure did bawl Rube out for that foolish act; and later that fall, when Rube went to Texas with Hervey, he showed the same traits when they went on Indian chases. Hervey said he seemed to pursue as hard as anyone, for he was a fine tracker, but he never managed to kill any Indians.

Though I wasn't quite thirteen years old, I had the best chance of my life to get an Indian that night in the cabin. In the really bad Indian days on the Little Blue I had been too young to do much Indian fighting. But I do remember that in June, 1866, when I was nine, Mother had me pacing the river bank armed with a shotgun loaded with buckshot, guarding our shallow river bank well to keep the Indians from cutting us off from water. This well was a substitute for our inside well that had caved in. As we were then getting ready to abandon the farm and go on railroad construction, we hadn't cleaned out the well or rebuilt the stockade after it had been burned by the Sioux in '64.

Hervey, as I've already mentioned, was a trailer with Iliff's outfit and spent most of his time on the trail with a pack horse. One day, while following an estray trail that led toward Denver, he was overtaken by about seventy-five Crow Indians, all warriors mounted on their best horses. Although he knew quite a few of the Indians, they told him they would have to take him along, as they were after a bunch of Southern Ute horses their scouts had located north of Denver, and they couldn't take chances on his betraying them. Hervey explained that he was only trailing a bunch of strayed cattle. They said they didn't doubt him, but they took away his Winchester and took him along anyway. Later, on his promise to be good, they gave the gun back to him, because they had heard of his expert marksmanship and wanted to see him pick off some antelope at long range.

They were about three more days reaching the Ute camp, for they traveled slow so their horses would be fresh to go into battle with the enemy. As they neared the camp, the Crows offered Hervey a small band of horses if he'd take a leading part in the upcoming fight and pick off, at long range, the Ute leaders riding the best horses. But Brother would have none of it, since the Utes were his friends, too, and if riled could do him much damage in his riding for Iliff.

When quite close to the Ute camp, the Crows hid in some timber to eat and rest their horses. The camp was located in the outside opening of a large park. In front of the village six herders were holding about three hundred war horses, and farther back in the park they had five or six hundred head of stock horses. The Crows detailed fifteen of their men to dash in and dispose of the herders and drive off the war horses. The rest of their braves then lined up to meet the charge of the main body of Ute warriors, which looked to be about the same size as their own force. They figured that the Utes, with their war horses gone, would have to fall back on the work horses for mounts, and so expected to be able to dash all around them and strike from any angle. Even so, they took the precaution to put six flankers on each side, to handle any Utes that might happen to have a few good horses in the stock herd.

The raid was a complete success as far as the horses were concerned, and the Crows could then have run off and left the Utes. Instead, Hervey said, they sent the captured war horses on ahead about twenty miles, while the rest stayed to whoop and fight the Utes for about two hours. About a dozen men were killed on each side, and quite a few wounded. Most of the time the Utes and the Crows were all mixed up, but it was plain to Hervey that the Crows, on their trained war horses, had the best of it, as they could dash in and deal a blow and be gone before the Utes could hit back. Most of the fighting was done with war clubs, tomahawks, and bows and arrows. The few guns on hand were used to pick off any Utes that tried to run around the Crows to catch the stolen horses.

Hervey said the battle ended as suddenly as it started. The Crows then gathered up their dead and wounded, put them on travois, and went on their way rejoicing. Hervey had stayed the whole time on a lookout hill, watching, and when some of the Utes rode over to see him, after the fighting, he told them how he happened to be there. They didn't seem to blame him at all, but shook hands warmly before they rode off. He went back then, picked up his cattle trail, and recovered most of his estrays. My only part in all this was following up and helping him take the cattle back to their home range.

In 1870 an expedition of some forty men was fitted out in Cheyenne for the Big Horn country which, by the treaty of 1868, was forbidden to the whites.[3] Father had a wagon and some equipment in this expedition, and riding with him were Hervey, myself, and three other men. We had gotten only about one hundred miles out when troops from Fort D. A. Russell were sent out to bring us back. The expedition went into camp, and then tried to talk the troop commander out of it, parleying for time to telegraph Washington. But Father knew the delay might well cause the outfit to get winterbound, so he drew off and headed us for the Jackson Hole, now a part of Yellowstone Park, which was, and still is, the very wildest part of the United States.

The purpose of this expedition was to mine placer gold. And to give some idea of the roughness of the country, I need only say the canyon where we stopped was so deep that the men had only five hours of daylight bright enough for mining each day. And the blueflies and mosquitoes were so bad we had to build stables and keep our horses inside both day and night. After Father got us established there, he went back home to Cheyenne.

This wild piece of country was practically ruled by the Shoshoni Indians, and by a notorious band of robbers that made its headquarters in Rawlins Springs. This outfit stole a lot of Shoshoni ponies, which they sold to miners and trappers, and the Shoshonis, in turn, did all they could to break up the robber gang.

Brother, being the best hunter in our party, was delegated to keep us in fresh meat. One afternoon he wounded a deer. He didn't want to leave it to the wolves and lions that were thick in that country, so

---

3. Under the treaty of 1868, the United States government agreed to abandon the Powder River posts and to set aside as a reservation for the Indians the area from the Missouri River on the east to the Big Horn Mountains on the west, and from the northern boundary of Nebraska on the south to the 46th parallel on the north. In addition, the Indians were given hunting rights on lands north of the North Platte River and on the Republican River. See James C. Olson, *Red Cloud and the Sioux Problem* (Lincoln: University of Nebraska Press, 1965), p. 73; and Larson, *History of Wyoming*, pp. 31–32.

he kept after it until night came on and he had to make camp and build a ring of bright fires all around himself to keep wild animals from attacking. After quite a while he got the wildlife so bluffed off that, by leaning his back against a tree inside the fire circle, he could take cat naps.

While so dozing, he all at once had a feeling of danger. He jumped up and leaped behind the tree, just as an arrow whizzed into the trunk, right where his head had been. He waited behind his tree, out of the firelight, and soon a voice called out to him that there had been a mistake, that they had taken him for the leader of the bandit outfit. This was all in Shoshoni, which Brother spoke and understood. Hervey called back that another mistake would be made if they tried to rush him, for, besides his Remington rifle, he was carrying a Colt .45 that would suit their range even better than the rifle. But the Indians kept insisting they meant no harm to him or his party. Then they asked him to take them to his main camp, where they hoped their story would be believed.

Brother agreed to this, provided they would walk ahead of him and out of arrow range. In this manner they came into the camp, where the Indians told their story again. They even offered to take our horses to their camp (which was out of the roughs, where flies and mosquitoes were not so bothersome) and care for them until we were ready to go home. We agreed to this, as it would be better for the horses and also relieve us of the work of cutting hay for them. We felt safe in doing this because, since the summer of '64, the Shoshonis had not warred on any whites except the robber gang that was all the time stealing their horses.

When we got back to Cheyenne from the mines, that fall of 1870, Father had decided to head back to our old stand on the Little Blue and see how things were there. In our return party, besides the six of us Lemmons, we had five Iliff cowhands. One was Jack Wilson, our old hand. Jack had stayed with us to the end of the railroad work, and had then worked for a time as a cowhand for Iliff. Another of our party was Hank Manchester, who had been Iliff's head boss.

Mother and Sister rode in a four-horse carriage, which Father drove. Then we had a bed wagon and a herd of about seventy head of horses and mules, including the Brigham Young band from Church Island. Besides the remuda drivers, we had enough men so that five riders could stay quite a distance ahead to guard against a surprise attack by Indians, for some had followed us all the way, hoping to catch us off guard and get away with our big bunch of horses.

Father always camped in a sheltered location, usually in a horse-shoe bend of the creeks we followed wherever possible. So we got along all right until we neared Julesburg. We were traveling down Lodgepole Creek and our outriders, quite a ways ahead, were rounding a bend in the creek. Just before they rode out of sight we pulled off the road to make camp in another sheltered bend. But when the riders rounded the bend up ahead, they saw a big west-bound wagon train in great confusion and dashed off to offer help.

A sizable band of Indians was trying to cut the train off from water, and when our men came up with the travelers they begged them to take command of their defense. Manchester said they would if Father didn't need them to protect his outfit. He sent Hervey kiting back to see, and Father told him we'd be safe as long as we were within gunshot hearing of the Iliff men, and that we would signal for them to come to us if we needed them. So Hank took charge of the defense of the train. He picked a few good men from its crew and, with his own men, fought the Indians off while the train moved on to a good camp beside the creek. This done, the defenders fell back to the camp, and right away Jack Wilson saw some familiar faces in the train crew.

They turned out to be the same folks he had known at Pittsville, Missouri, and when they recognized him they shouted for Miranda Pitts, who was with the train, and she came running. When she recognized Jack she simply swarmed all over him, hugging and kissing him and begging him not to let the red hostiles carry her off into captivity. Jack promised her they'd do it only over his dead body, and soon the rest of the train was putting on a big jollification in behalf of the lovers. While all this was going on, the Iliff men and the picked men of the train crew kept tabs on the Indians and finally drove them off.

The outcome of the affair was that some of the emigrants turned back, for they had seen enough of Indians to last them the rest of their lives. Among the turners-back were Miranda and her family, and Jack, of course, who shifted bed and baggage to their wagons. Jack and Miranda were married by the first minister they met on the road, so their story had a happy ending.

Miranda had been a very young girl when Jack had known her in Missouri. Now she was a beautiful woman of the Missouri-raised kind who could mount a sixteen-hand-high mule bareback, with the grace of a panther, and ride him to church. Jack's life of the past five years had made him into a handsome man that any girl could be proud of. And neither of them were the silly kind, for he had faced too many redskins and she had barked her shins and stubbed her toes on shinnery oak too often for that. Besides, Jack had a well-filled pocket and six fine I.C.U.S.[4] mules he had just bought at Fort D. A. Russell. Miranda's father gave them a good Missouri farm for a wedding present, and there they settled down and lived happy ever after.

It may seem strange that Jack had never once written Miranda since he had left her in Pittsville, five and a half years earlier. But it wasn't unusual, not in those days of poor mail service and constant moving about. And besides, when he made that trip east with us, Jack was finally on his way back to Pittsville and his sweetheart.

Well, we finished the trip to Liberty Farm with all our family, all the horses, and all of the Iliff cowboys but Jack Wilson. But when we pulled into our old farm dooryard we were met by a man named Ben Royce, who told Father the place was now his. He was an ex-soldier, he said, and had been mustered out of the army right there, so he'd filed on the claim Father had abandoned.

Father told him why he had left the farm four years before, and why he hadn't been able to get back any sooner. But Royce said it didn't matter, that he was legally contesting the claim and wasn't going to move off peaceably. Father told him he couldn't legally contest (or jump) a claim without either putting up his own buildings or giving the former owner sixty days' notice to remove the

4. Inspected and condemned United States (property).

improvements already on the land. The notices, three in number, had to be posted in conspicuous places for at least three months, he said, and since Royce hadn't done this, and had broken a lock and seal on private property besides, he could have him jailed.

All this time the Iliff cowboys stood by, offering to take Royce apart and put him off the place. But Father had noticed the small children hanging on to Royce and scared nearly to death by the cowmen with their six-shooters and rifles, and the tearful, frightened faces of some women at the farmhouse windows. So now he grinned and said, "Royce, if I really wanted to put you off I wouldn't need any help. But this ranch has no value to me, except that it's a good building site, so in the morning I'll go on east twenty-four miles to a school section that's more to my liking."5 When Royce got his breath he offered to pay for the improvements, but Father waved the offer aside. And when we went to the cellar where we had sealed up some of our goods four years before, we found the stuff all there and in good condition.

For that winter, then, we rented part of the old ranch and stage station on Big Sandy from Joe Tennis. And not long after getting settled in our new location, Moroni and Father went over to the settlement on Bacon Creek, near Dewitt. There Moroni saw Frank Baker, the stock tender and part-time Pony Express rider who had kicked his little wagon and smashed it nine years back. Frank had married one of the Artist girls (she had once been one of Mother's hired girls) and settled down there.

Moroni had never forgotten his pledge to whip Baker when he grew up—and now he was fifteen and almost full grown. With blood in his eye, he started for Baker, telling him to get ready to take a good beating. But Father grabbed him and held him back, though Baker said to let him come on, that he'd defend himself the best he could, as he knew he deserved the beating. But Father wouldn't let them fight.

The next spring (1871) Lawhorn and Hardigan, Texas cattlemen,

5. On February 10, 1873, Benjamin Royce received a patent to the quarter section first claimed by James Lemmon and on which the Liberty Farm buildings stood.

drove seven herds of cattle into southern Nebraska and peddled them out to feeders, mostly around Nebraska City. They held the cattle south of today's town of Oak for several months. As the country was settling fast by then, and the cattle stampeded almost every night, great damage was done to the crops. Because I had had some experience with cattle and with settlers and their customs, Lawhorn and Hardigan hired me to gather up the stampeded cattle and settle for the damages.

These herds were held close enough to each other that when one herd stampeded they all went, as the jar and rumble traveled through the ground, telegraphing the move to all the other herds. Sometimes the results were fatal. One night I was with a herd of three-year-old steers that stampeded. We were trying to head them when we heard another stampeding herd (four-year-old steers and up) coming toward us. As the running herds neared each other, the bosses of both bunches yelled for all hands to quit the lead and get out of the way. The two herds met head-on in a deep gulch. About one hundred steers were killed and a lot more crippled, but owing to the bosses calling us out of the way in time, not a single man or horse was hurt.

That stampede might be classed as one of Zane Grey's "Thundering Herd" tales, except that nobody was hurt. In fact, I was never in a stampede where a man or a horse was hurt—and I was in all kinds of stampedes in the fifty-three years I followed the Longhorns. But the bad part of that one was the big job we had skinning the dead cattle, and then the authorities made us bury the carcasses.

Later on that year I took a contract to carry mail from Kiowa across to and up the Republican River. This was the first mail contract ever let in that district. My route crossed diagonally from the Little Blue River southwest to the Guide Rock post office on the Republican, a distance of about twenty-three miles, then up the Republican by way of Red Cloud and Ulmstead to Riverton, which was then the outpost of settlement in that region.[6] At Red Cloud

6. The Rankin Colony, a group organized in Omaha in 1869, settled Guide Rock, but an Indian scare drove all but two of them away. Red Cloud, the first permanent settlement in the Republican Valley, was established in the summer of 1870 by a party from Beatrice under the leadership of Silas Garber, formerly a captain of the Iowa Volunteer Infantry and later governor of Nebraska (1875–1879). Riverton was founded in the spring of 1871 by a group known as the

and Riverton substantial stockades surrounded groups of cabins. By day the settlers worked on their nearby homesteads; at night they stayed in the stockaded cabins, for roving bands of hostiles still drifted through the country, rendezvousing on the Smoky Hill River to the south.

Naturally, at all the places where I stopped the talk was of Indians. Since I had been born and raised in the West, I was always on the alert, my gun hand in a manner hovering near my six-shooter, ready for a quick draw, when I was passing through or near places that would make good hiding for Indians.

On the Republican River, a few miles from Guide Rock, there was a deep runway that was bordered by cattails in slew water. In extra wet weather I had to go off my regular trail to get around this bog. One day I made my detour around the bog and was following the west bank of the cattail slew to get back on the trail. Because this stretch looked like a good place for Indians to hide, I always rode with my hand on my gun butt. All at once, only a few feet to my left, there came what sounded like an Indian war whoop. Out came my gun, and I took an unsighted shot at what I was sure was an Indian ambush. For a minute the air was full of feathers, and then I saw I had shot a sandhill crane. When stretching their necks, cranes are as tall as a man, and when disturbed they let out an awful squawk.

It was four or five miles on to my dinner stop at Guide Rock, and it took me the whole way to get my heart shoved from my teeth, where it hove at the sudden squawk of that bird, back to where it belonged. That was my biggest fright, though I've had others that lasted longer. But I soon found out that my shocks for that day were not over. About two o'clock I pulled in at Red Cloud, where Captain Garber was postmaster. He opened the mailbag, examined the registered mail, and found one number missing. He called this to the attention of the crowd at the post office, then handed the bag back to me, all the while looking at me in a way I didn't like.

I started on west, full of uneasy suspicions, for I was positive the postmaster at Guide Rock hadn't found anything missing—which

Thompson Colony, who had explored the valley the previous fall. See James C. Olson, *History of Nebraska* (Lincoln: University of Nebraska Press, 1955), p. 178.

[70]

led me to believe he was the one who had filched the missing package. Not many months earlier our east-end carrier, Ed Schuler, had robbed the mail right along for about three months. He was right then serving a ten-year term in the pen for it, and I was afraid the prospects didn't look good for me if there was a package missing. For the blame would have to lay between me and the Guide Rock postmaster.

But about five miles from Red Cloud, I looked back and saw the dust flying from the heels of a fast-moving horse. The rider soon caught up and told me Garber had found the package, a bundle of stamped envelopes from Washington, D.C., that was too bulky to go inside the registered wrapper. So my heart settled back to its rightful place again—but not for long.

The next morning a dozen well-diggers left Riverton (my overnight stop) at daylight to go to their digging on the tableland over northeast of the settlement. I waited until eight o'clock, regular departure time for the mail, then headed out. About nine o'clock I came to the north bank of the Republican, which was in flood, and found all the well-diggers there. They told me that shortly after getting to their wells they had been charged by a dozen Indians. They were all well armed, so, even though some of them had to ride bareback, they took after the Indians. Surprised at having the tables turned on them, the raiders broke to the south toward the Smoky Hill country. When they came to the flooded Republican they jumped their horses right in and swam across.

The well-diggers were boasting like everything about having wounded the hindermost Indian. They were sure, too, they had hit his horse, because it had floundered up the far bank, well behind the others, and disappeared behind a plum thicket. But when I asked them why they didn't swim across and investigate, they made all kinds of excuses—such as rheumatism, or cramps, or not knowing if their horses could swim. So I offered them my horse, which I knew to be a good swimmer. Then they said they thought I should go, as I knew the horse.

Since I had been boasting to them about being a frontiersman, I couldn't very well show the white feather now. I said I'd go if they would loan me a rifle and a pair of field glasses, and keep a close

[71]

watch on the far side of the river. If the Indian over there stirred, they were to pepper his position with lead, as their guns would easily reach that far. Then I dropped downstream to where there was no brush on the far side to hide an Indian, and swam my horse over. I landed on the south bank and rode up the little rise of ground beyond, where I could see the Indian pony standing with a drooped head. With the glasses I could see the dead Indian, face up, with flies buzzing over him. I rode on over and stirred the pony, which had a shattered thigh. Then I rode back and reported all this to the well-diggers.

On my next trip I found that they had gone up the river some twelve miles to get a boat to go after the Indian's remains. After that I sure twitted those fellows about their rheumatism and cramp symptoms.

That same year I was going west on one of my trips and had passed the Ulmstead post office by about eight miles. At that point there was a body of trees, about two miles long by three-quarters of a mile wide, that was known as the Big Timber. Flood water had cut off another eighty acres of small timber and brush, leaving a sand channel fifty to one hundred feet wide and over a half-mile long between the two patches of timber. The brush in this cut-off piece was covered with wild grape and hop vines, making a fine place for anything that might want to hide.

My mail route curved around this cut-off stretch of brush before lining up with the regular route again. One day, as I came near the east end of this detour, I saw some strange-looking dark objects near the sand channel. They looked like mounted Indians to me, so I rode back to Ulmstead and recruited a dozen armed riders and a rifle, because I carried only a six-shooter.

We hurried back to the place where I had seen the dark bodies, but even with the field glasses we couldn't be certain what they were. We rode to the west end of the channel then, but couldn't see as much there as from the east end. So we split the posse. My part went back to the east position to fire some shots at the objects and, if they were Indians, dislodge them and give the west-end posse a better look, and maybe a chance to shoot at a range of three or four hundred yards.

They proved to be Indians, all right, about twenty of them. They dashed across the sand channel and disappeared in the Big Timber, where we didn't dare follow them. The west posse had fired at least fifty shots at them as they ran, but we couldn't see a sign of a hit— no blood on the sand or anything. So I sure twitted that posse, too, for getting buck fever and missing with every shot.

VI

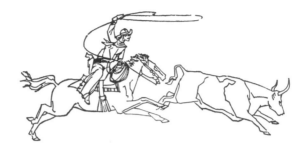

SOME ADVENTURES OF HERVEY
AND MORONI

WHILE I WAS having my experiences with stampeding long-horns and carrying mail through Indian country, brother Hervey was having some experiences of his own down in Texas. He had headed south late in the fall of 1870, shortly after we went back to the Little Blue. Another fellow, Ben Wilson, hit Texas about the same time and the two became fast friends, always hiring out to the same outfits.

They first went to work for Mathews and Johnson, Texas cattlemen, where Hervey was soon put to bossing trail herds. Then they got acquainted with the Taylor family, which was mixed up in a feud with the Sutton family. Since Hervey always hired some of the younger Taylor boys for his trail crews, he was soon welded in close with the Taylor faction.

The Taylor ranch belonged to old lady Taylor, who was nearing the end of her lease on life. Along about 1873 the old lady decided she would like to have one last big fling and have all her clan home for it. But, due to the feud with the Suttons, some of her boys were sort of on the run, though only one, Bill Taylor, was actually subject to arrest by a warrant held by the sheriff. The old lady tried to take care of this by going to the sheriff and asking him, as a favor, to stay away from her party so he wouldn't have to try to serve the warrant. He agreed to stay away and she went ahead with her big entertainment. But when the party was in full swing, the sheriff walked in with four deputies. When the shooting was over there were no law officers standing, or even breathing, to serve the warrants.

The above is all I was ever able to find out about the affair, although, years later, I talked to two old cowmen in the Lubbock, Texas, hotel in 1891. Both of these men were in on old lady Taylor's party, but when I asked them to tell me more about it they said they didn't talk about those old happenings. All Hervey would say about it was that the killings took place about ten in the evening, and by nine o'clock the next morning he and Ben Wilson were over a hundred miles away, and that they had changed horses three times at ranches owned by Mathews and Johnson, whose holdings reached far to the southwest. They didn't stop traveling until they landed in southwest Texas, west of the Nueces, where they hired out to Tipp and Clay Mann.

On their run from the Taylor ranch they rode most of the way through an unsettled, lonely region, breaking every rise of ground on their hands and knees, after anchoring their horses to the ground with dragging reins. With field glasses they scanned the country ahead for Indians or Indian sign. Then by hiding, and by dodging such Indians as they saw, they kept going. At night they hobbled their horses and hid them in heavy thickets, quite a long way from their dark campsites.

But one night, so Ben told me later, Brother insisted on making a fire at their camp. Then, he said, they sat by the blaze most of the night while Hervey told him of our Indian troubles on the Holladay stage line and on the Union Pacific construction work. Ben said Brother talked much of home and family, too, and he believed Hervey was so lonesome and homesick that he was actually itching for an Indian fight to ease his nerves. But though they had seen plenty of Indians at long range that day, none bothered them that night. Ben said Brother talked in a low, earnest voice, and that it was

[75]

the only time in the eight or nine years they spent together that he ever spoke of his relatives, or those early experiences.

That west Nueces country was, in a way, the far border of the Texas cattle country. Just back of this far-out frontier there was an older settlement. Several young cattlemen and their wives had ranches out on the border, but in times of danger retreated to the older settlement in the rear. The danger came from half-hostile bands of raiding reservation Indians, who were furnished such scanty rations by the government that, needing something to sell or trade, they stole horses. Consequently, these border ranchmen could look for raids nearly every time the moon was right—that is, light in the forepart of the night so they could locate the horses, and dark in the afterpart to cover their escape.

When such raids took place, the men sent their womenfolk and children to the older settlement while they took to the trail to try to get the horses back. The women, though, kicked against being sent to the settlement. They were all good marksmen, they said, and could take care of themselves. Finally six of these women, the two Mrs. Manns among them, made up a plan of their own for the next Indian raid. As the right time of the moon came near, they each began graining the best horse on the ranch. They knew that in every big bunch of loose horses there were always a few slow ones that held a driven herd back, and that a grained horse carrying a light rider could easy overtake such a herd.

So this time when the Indians slipped in and made off with a horse herd and the men made ready to go after them, the women said they wouldn't take refuge across the Nueces. All they wanted was one man to stay with them, they said, and they'd take care of themselves. They chose Hervey to stay behind while the rest of the ranchmen took the trail of the stolen horses. It was known to all of them that the Indians were almost sure to head for a water hole about eighty miles away. The ranchmen headed for it, too, hoping to catch the Indians there before they could divide the horses and scatter. The women waited only a little while, then, carrying a few extra feeds of grain for their horses, they lit out for the water hole, too, with Hervey in the lead.

They took a somewhat different route from the one the men

followed and, by pushing their grain-fed horses hard, reached the water hole first. The Indians were already there, and Hervey, under cover of the dark night, left the women and crawled on his hands and knees into the horse bunch. He picked out a horse that was one of his own pets, slipped a hackamore on it, jumped on, and charged the two Indian guards. He killed them both, then stampeded the horse herd toward the place where the women were waiting.

Of course the shooting and the noise of the stampede brought the Indians out in a hurry. They hadn't been set entirely afoot, so it wasn't long before the whole outfit—Hervey, the women, and the horse herd, with the Indians hot after them—ran into the rancher posse, which was just pulling into the water hole. Hervey gave out with the war whoop of the whites, letting the men know they were not Indians, and the women gave a yell of their own, so their men would know they were there. At that, Tipp and Clay and the others charged right through the whole shebang and met the Indians head-on. The women kept right on, heading the horse bunch for home, while Hervey, with fresh mounts for the ranchmen, waited beside the trail for them to finish with the Indians and catch up.

One of the Manns afterward claimed he hadn't been fooled at all, and that he had known all the time what those grained horses and the hand-picked man had meant. And besides, he said, the women had held some secret meetings and the children had sneaked in and watched them at target practice and heard them working on the yell they used at the time of the fight. His wife said they had only wanted to show the men they were not as helpless as the men thought; and another woman said she and her friends had sized up the situation from every angle and concluded that, if they had been captured, some of the Indian braves they had seen would make as good husbands as the ones they had, who exposed them to such border dangers.

Now this is an old and well-known story down in that part of Texas, but it was fifty-one years after it happened before I learned that it was Hervey who went with the women on the chase after the stolen horses. I was in Texas when I ran onto an old Texan who had known Hervey. I asked him about the "fairy tale," and he snorted, "Fairy tale, hell. Didn't you know Hervey was the one the ladies picked to be their guide?" Hervey, always a modest cuss, had never mentioned who the guide was.

Another time when the Indians had made off with a bunch of horses, Hervey and some of the other cowmen got onto their trail so soon that they overhauled them before they had gone far, catching up with them in a region slashed with deep gulches. The ranchmen were crowding them so hard that the Indians took shelter in the head of a canyon where a wide rock shelf stuck out over a deep hole or cave.

There was seepage water in the cave, and the Indians probably had a good supply of jerky along, so it looked to the ranchmen like they would have to lay siege to the Indians if they ever got them out. As they didn't want to take the time to do that, they decided to smoke them out. They gathered a lot of dry wood, piled it on top of the rock shelf, and fired it. When it was pretty well burned, they pushed it over the edge with long poles. But the scheme didn't work, for there weren't any back air holes to make a draft to pull the smoke into the cave. They were about to give up on that idea, when all at once the Indians began to yell and shriek and beg for mercy.

It turned out that, it being the fall of the year, all the rattlesnakes in the country had denned up in that cave. The fire on top of the shelf and in the mouth of the cave had thawed them out, of course, and the place was literally crawling with squirming, striking snakes. After raking the burning brush away and letting the Indians out, they found that none were seriously bitten, for they had huddled together, standing up, and their leggings had protected their legs. They were a much tamed bunch, though, and the posse turned them over to the state rangers. The Nueces frontier had a breathing spell from the raids for a while after that.

After 1869 the Sioux, Cheyennes, and Arapahos, all but a few small, swift-moving bands east of Kearney, gave up the Little Blue and Republican River country in Nebraska. This left the region pretty well open to the Otos and Pawnees for hunting buffalo, which were still plentiful just beyond the line of settlement. And also for now and then picking off a white hunter. Such killings were usually laid to the Sioux, who were not yet reconciled to agency life, and who found an occasional dead white man very consoling. After

Hervey went to Texas and got to know some of the noted frontiersmen and buffalo hunters, he heard that a hunter friend of his had
been killed in Nebraska by some Oto Indians under Chief Jim
Whitewater. As Hervey didn't get home again until the winter of
1875, when he came for a short visit, he didn't get to check into the
killing until then.

In the meantime, Whitewater and his band had gone buffalo
hunting. On their way home they camped near Fairbury in Gage
County, where Whitewater had too much to drink. The rest of his
outfit had pulled out and left him to his carousing, and then his
horse got loose and took out after the caravan. When the Chief
sobered a trifle and found he'd been left behind, he started out afoot
to try to overtake his band. After a while he overhauled two farmers
in a lumber wagon and asked for a ride. As he crawled into the
wagon he saw a bottle of whiskey, but when he asked for a drink
the farmers told him they didn't dare give one to an Indian. At that
he drew his six-shooter and killed them both. He then went on and
overtook his band.

Now Jim Whitewater was an outstanding Indian. A flashy dresser,
he spoke English as well as any white man. So as soon as the murdered
men were found, someone right away remembered seeing Jim riding
with them, and he was soon under arrest. The facts as given here
came out in the trial, and he was convicted, but given a light sentence
on account of the whites at Fairbury giving him liquor, which was
against the law. But not long after going to jail, Jim got religion and
was then either pardoned or paroled. He came back to his people as
their worshipful chief and, sometimes, their preacher.

It was about this time that Hervey came home. One Sunday he
went out prairie chicken hunting with a wagonload of us. Jim and
some of his band had been camped in the vicinity for a while, and
we met him and his family in a spring wagon, riding home from a
church service in the Kiowa schoolhouse. Jim was wearing a swallow-
tailed coat and a stovepipe hat, elegant as could be. As we were
passing him he held up his hand and said, "Don't you know Chief
Whitewater don't allow hunting on his domain on Sunday?"

Then Hervey said, "You're a fine specimen to be telling white
men what they should do. Right now you should be behind bars for

killing two white men, and a good friend of mine, too, that you and your band killed on the Republican and let the Sioux take the blame for. It would be a pleasure to give you a dose of the same medicine, and don't you think this shotgun is all I've got, for I've got a Colt's forty-five in my belt that I'd like to use on you."

The Chief said, "Since I've found my Lord I cannot become angry at such unjust accusations," and so saying he whipped up and headed for home. Right after that he broke camp and left our part of the country.

Of course Hervey had a lot of tales to tell about things that happened while he was away. In 1872, he said, he came up the trail with a herd. In the crew were two boys who had been schoolmates in Texas. One was quite a bit bigger than the other, and something of a bully besides, always running it over on the smaller one. One day, just north of the Red River, the big fellow had been more abusive than usual to the little one. That noon the two were on herd together, the big one on the side nearest camp. When they were relieved for dinner, he got to camp first and sat down to eat with his back to the herd. When the smaller one rode toward camp he had a loop already made in his rope. He tossed it over the big fellow's head, then whirled his horse and put the spurs to him.

The outfit was dinnering in rough country, and the horseman was soon out of sight over a hill. Then the fellows in camp heard a shot. A little later the boy rode back to camp, got down, and got himself a layout and ate his dinner. He went on about his work and none of the crew went to see what had happened or said anything about it, because they figured the big fellow deserved what he probably got. When they got back to Texas, Hervey said, and anybody asked about the missing man, they just said they didn't know what became of him. Which was in a manner true.

My brother Moroni went into the Black Hills of South Dakota early in 1876 by way of the Pine Ridge route. At that time there were five routes into the Hills: the Cheyenne, the Sidney, the Kearney (or Pine Ridge), the Sioux City, and the Mandan. Of the five, the

Mandan was the most exposed to Indian depredations, since it lay broadside to several Indian reservations and ran through an almost unexplored region. Next in rank for Indian danger was the Cheyenne route, which, especially in the Hat Creek region, was square in line with the meeting places of Sitting Bull and Indians from the Red Cloud and Spotted Tail agencies. The Sidney route was third, for it, too, was near the trail traveled by Indians absconding from both agencies. The Sioux City trail was fairly safe until it came about even with present Harney Springs, southwest of Scenic, South Dakota, which was a favorite hunting ground for Indians out after mountain sheep and ibex, game easy to get with a bow and arrow. This was the road followed by the Gordon party in 1875.

The Kearney route crossed over from the Platte, at Kearney, to the Loup and Elkhorn, then to the Niobrara. It crossed the country where the Pine Ridge agency now stands, then down White Clay Creek past the present town of Oglala, crossing the White River due north of that place. After crossing the Cheyenne River near the Custer County bridge, it led through Buffalo Gap to Custer, the boom town of the Black Hills gold excitement of 1876. This last was the trail taken by Moroni and his party. They did not meet any Indians, but when the Sheidley outfit I was with went in by the Mandan route in '77, nearly every campground had rifle pits around it, plain sign of Indian fights.

Moroni, however, considered the danger from Indians in that part of the country very tame as compared to our early years on the Little Blue and later, while building the Union Pacific. In fact, he often said he was annoyed more by road agents on those Black Hills trails than by Indians, since this was during the period of road agent industry when those fellows were making a regular business of hijacking mine clean-up gold.

One agent, known as Persimmon Bill Chambers, was pronounced the prince of them all, for it was said he never intentionally robbed a woman. That is, if he was sure the valuables she carried were her own he did not take them, but if he thought men had handed them to her for safekeeping he gathered them up, too. Also, he went so well disguised that it was hard to prove his part in the robberies, although nearly everyone knew who he was. For this reason he came and went in the Hills towns and rode into camps wherever he came across them, and was usually fed without fear or question.

Moroni was, at this time, a bull-freight team boss for Pratt and Ferris, one of the biggest freight outfits in the region.[1] He also had in his train ten yoke of cattle and three wagons of his own. After a while he sold his own outfit to Johnny Timmons, in Deadwood, for $2,700. He put the money in a gold belt around his waist, turned the rest of the train over to his assistant, and headed for Sidney, on horseback and alone. Somewhere in the Horsehead country of Fall River County he saw Persimmon Bill riding alone up the trail toward him. Now Persimmon Bill had many times been fed at his train; but while he was still at long Winchester range, Moroni got off his horse and pretended to be setting his saddle back, all the while keeping the horse between Bill and himself.

When Bill came nearer, Moroni pulled his Winchester from its scabbard, dropped it across the saddle, and ordered the outlaw to put up his hands and ride up in that position. Bill did so, but said, "Rone, what do you want? Have you turned from bull boss to a law officer?"

"No, not by a damned sight," Brother said, "but I happen to have a little hard-earned dough on me that I don't want you to have."

And Bill said, "Why Rone! You don't think for a minute that I'd eat your grub, as I've done many times, and then hold you up, do you?"

Brother told him no, he didn't, but he just wasn't taking any chances. So they traded the latest news, and then Bill started to ride on. "Now just keep your hands up till you're out of gun range," Moroni told him. And Bill did, but laughing like it was all a big joke.

----

1. Pratt and Ferris, owned by Colonel James Harvey Pratt and his brother-in-law, Cornelius Ferris, engaged in extensive freighting of supplies from Sidney north to the Indian agencies in the early seventies. After the discovery of gold in Black Hills they hauled thousands of tons of supplies to the gold towns. In 1878 they went into ranching, and their headquarters were located on Spring Creek, a mile west of the Nebraska-Wyoming border, on the old Red Cloud agency site. See Nellie Snyder Yost, *The Call of the Range: The Story of the Nebraska Stock Growers Association* (Denver: Sage Books, 1966), pp. 82, 85.

Shortly after that Bill disappeared from the Black Hills. Some thought he'd been killed while so well disguised that he was not identified. But shortly before Captain Willard,[2] onetime treasure coach guard, died, he told me that Persimmon Bill, after accumulating a good deal of gold, just quit the road and went back to his old home, where he took back his real name, married, and settled down to lead a respectable life.

2. Captain A. M. Willard was the first deputy sheriff of Lawrence County, South Dakota. (Bob Lee and Dick Williams, *Last Grass Frontier: The South Dakota Stock Growers Heritage* [Sturgis, S.D.: Black Hills Publishers, 1964], p. 54.)

VII

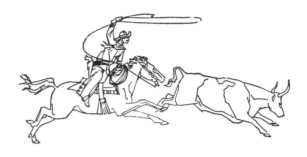

BLOOD AND THUNDER
ON THE RANGE

E ARLY IN 1877, Tom McCumpsey and I headed for Ogallala, the
greatest cowtown in the West at that time.[1] Tom's family had
lived on the Big Blue, not far from Lincoln, until the father, Richard
McCumpsey, had mysteriously disappeared, never to be heard from
again by the family. That was around 1874, about a year after my
mother died. So the widow and her sons, Jim, Tom, Ed, Johnnie,
and Wilbur, moved into our home near Kiowa and Mrs. McCumpsey
kept house for us. Most of the boys made their home with us, too,
for the next three years or so. At that time Father was traveling with
his race horses, and Tom went with him as a rider until his weight

---

1. Ogallala, formerly a Pony Express station, became a way station on the
Union Pacific in 1869. As the Texas cattle trail shifted west, the U.P. built
cattle pens and loading chutes near Ogallala in 1874 in an attempt to recapture
the huge cattle shipping trade it had enjoyed at the other end-of-trail towns.
Seventy-five thousand cattle were shipped from Ogallala in 1875, more than one
hundred thousand the next year; and it remained a major shipping point for the
next ten years. See Nellie Snyder Yost, *The Call of the Range: The Story of the
Nebraska Stock Growers Association* (Denver: Sage Books, 1966), pp. 54, 55, 56.

debarred him. Then he came home and the two of us headed for Ogallala. We went to work for Sheidley brothers, a big cattle outfit located between Big Springs and Sidney.[2] Dave Clark was the company manager.

Now, while Tom wasn't much of a marksman, he thought he was pretty good with his fists, which was a dangerous idea in a country where six-shooters usually settled all arguments. So I persuaded him to go home and practice hitting a target, and also to see what he could do about temper control, because I had about all I could do, in my crippled condition, to take care of my own differences.[3] Tom took my advice, then came back the next spring to hold down a job with the [Oelrichs brothers'] WH outfit on the North Platte River, due south of Lusk, Wyoming. He made a fine cowboy in short order, for he was already a good rider and roper, being schooled in those accomplishments by Hervey and myself. On his first roundup he learned to spring from his bed at the first touch of his relief man for night guard, and to be prompt at relieving day herders. Also to swallow his grub whole, roll his bed in the morning, carry his full share of water to camp, and cut his share of wood for the cook.

But Tom also discovered that a cowboy's wage was a slow way to get rich, so in the early days of Belle Fourche's claim to being the greatest cattle shipping point on earth,[4] he opened a saloon there. Tom White, the most noted character in town, was his partner. One day they had a difference. Then McCumpsey said to White, "I will not take back anything I've said, and I'm not afraid of any man on earth." So the two Toms stood there, a few feet apart, both armed, eyeing each other without the flick of an eyelash, until the tension

~~~~~~~~~~~~~~~~~~~~~~~~~~

2. In the late seventies, Ben, Bill, and George Sheidley established their ranch headquarters between Big Springs and Sidney, although their office was in Kansas City. They had been in the cattle business in Texas before the Civil War and, after the war, put herds on the trail north. (*Ibid.*, p. 77.)

3. While Lemmon was working for Lawhorn and Hardigan near Nebraska City in 1871, his horse fell with him, breaking and crushing his right leg. The next year another horse fell with him, breaking the same leg again, and killing the horse.

4. Belle Fourche was the world's largest primary cattle-shipping center for a few years during the early nineties, its outbound shipments totaling 4,700 carloads in 1894 alone. See Herbert S. Schell, *History of South Dakota* (Lincoln: University of Nebraska Press, 1961), p. 250.

got so tight that friends stepped in, turned them around, and took them home. Both are now buried in the Belle Fourche cemetery, although McCumpsey lived to see two of his sons drowned in the Belle Fourche River.

The two little boys, aged four and six, were playing with other boys on the river bank. When the little one slipped in, the other, as brave as his father, jumped in to try to save him. Both were washed downstream to the riffle at the mouth of the Red Water, where their bodies were later recovered. Poor Tom was never the same afterward.

In the meantime, I stayed with the Sheidley outfit for a few weeks, then went to work for Major Seth Mabry.[5] We were finishing up the general roundup in June when there came a rush order for beef to complete a delivery for a man named Low, who had the beef contracts for the Red Cloud and Spotted Tail agencies on the White River. A lot of Low's beeves had strayed during the winter. The roundups had not advanced far enough to gather the cattle needed to make up the delivery by July 1, the expiration date on his contract, so he had called on Mabry to furnish about nine hundred head to make up the difference.

I was with the ten-man crew that, under Bill Campbell, a Texan, was to deliver the beef. We left the main roundup near the mouth of Pumpkin Creek, south of the Platte River, and moved the herd north. We were camped at Snake Creek when a government courier overhauled us. He brought an order to top out [select] one hundred of the choicest beeves and deliver them posthaste to a soldiers' camp at the mouth of Lance Creek on the Cheyenne River.

This camp of about three hundred cavalrymen had been established to intercept Indians plying back and forth between the Red Cloud and Spotted Tail agencies and the Sitting Bull Indians, who were then on their way to Canada. This was just a year after the Custer massacre, and there had been so much travel by both Indians and the cavalry that all the game had been driven off and the camp was out of fresh meat. The courier brought us a rough

5. Mabry, a Texan, maintained his headquarters ranch at Boiling Springs, on the Niobrara. See Yost, *The Call of the Range*, pp. 94–95.

pencilled map of the trail to the camp. It showed a course from Snake Creek toward the far southwest corner of the Black Hills, about 160 miles away. Upon breaking the divide north of Snake Creek, the courier said, we would have the Hills in plain sight.

We topped out the beeves and got an outfit together: a pack of grub, bedding for three men, and nine fast horses. Then Campbell said, "Ed, it's up to you to boss this delivery." I was the youngest man in the outfit, only one month past twenty years old, and I asked him why he picked me, as there were plenty of older men in the crew. He said it was because I knew more about Plains Indians, and because it was well known that I was best at trail finding and would not lose my directions, either by day or by night. When the rest of the boys sided with Bill, I gave in. Bill then told me he had given us the fastest horses in the outfit, so that, if Indians got after us, we could abandon the cattle (which would be paid for by the government anyway) and save our scalps by outrunning the redskins.

We hit the trail, making about twenty miles a day, and came to a point I judged was about sixty miles from the soldier camp. From there I sent one of my two helpers on ahead to locate the camp. I gave him orders to break every rise on hands and knees and scan the country with field glasses. If he saw a little smoke, such as would be made with a few dry twigs, he was to give it a wide berth; but if he saw a big, dark blue smoke, like that made by green ash saplings kindled with dry fuel, he could take it for granted the fire was made by whites who weren't trying to hide, and he could ride in with safety. He reached the cavalry camp all right, late on the first day out, and stayed overnight. He started back the next day and met us about noon, as we had been moving ahead in the same direction he had taken. He then piloted us back to the government camp.

When the officer in charge asked one of my men to point out the boss so he could give him a receipt for the cattle, he pointed to me. The officer looked me up and down, and then said it was a damn shame to have to put a stripling of a boy in charge of such an important undertaking. But my helpers, who were several years older than I was, spoke right up and told him he'd have a hard time trying to lose me on a dark night or to fool me about the habits of these northern Indians. They seemed to be proud of the fact that I had handled the job so well.

We laid over a day at the camp to rest our horses, and the commander pointed out a tree between the forks of the Cheyenne and Lance Creek where, he said, he had hung some Indians a year earlier. Years later, Mary Crawler, said to be the only real squaw who took part in the battle of the Little Big Horn in 1876, was giving the full details of the fight. She told of killing two wounded soldiers herself, shooting one and stabbing the other. She said she did it because some soldiers had hung an uncle of hers on Lance Creek a little while before the battle. Mary had been only seventeen then.

On our way back to join our outfit on the Running Water [Niobrara], we ran into a large band of Indians about thirty miles from the Red Cloud agency. They were going our way, so we slowed up and rode along with them for a few miles. Since I could speak a little Sioux, I explained our trip and told them we had a big herd of beef for them back on the Running Water. When we reached Fort Robinson, which was located alongside the Red Cloud agency, we learned that only the day before troops had had a fight with that same band of Indians on Hat Creek, where they had killed eleven and turned the rest back from a try at joining Sitting Bull in Canada.[6] We remembered then that we had seen several Indian police among them, put there by the troop commander to see that they behaved and went back to the agency.

After delivering the beef herd, we went back to Ogallala for another herd of Indian cattle. On the way down I sold my boss, Bill Campbell, a fine horse. He still owed me a balance of twenty-four dollars, so he told me to meet him after dinner at Tucker's saloon and he would pay me. But when I got there they were just picking up Bill's remains to take to the undertaker. It turned out that he had barely enough money on him to cover his burial, so of course I never got my twenty-four dollars.

The shooting came up over a cowboy by the name of Moy. This

6. After the Battle of the Little Big Horn, the Hunkpapa Sitting Bull had fled to Canada with his followers.

Moy had asked Bill to pass him the hash at the Gast Hotel dinner table. Hash (as it's called in cowboy lingo) is not looked upon very highly, as it is supposed to be made of all kinds of refuse. As Bill passed it to Moy he told him he looked like a hash man. They had both been drinking and Moy right away wanted to fight. Neither had their guns, so Bill apologized and thought the matter was settled. But Moy accosted him again and Bill got rid of him again, but the third time he accosted him, Bill told him if nothing would do him but a fight, to go get his gun.

Bill went back to the hotel and got his Smith and Wesson, then walked across to Tucker's saloon. His gun hadn't seemed to be working right, so he went to the back of the long saloon and began working the cylinder. Then, with his back to the door, he shot off the gun into the floor. Moy had rushed over to Louis Aufdengarten's store, where he had a brother. He ran up to him and jerked out his six-shooter, but the brother took it away from him. When Moy told him he had to shoot it out with Campbell, the brother told him he was too drunk to do any shooting and that he would do it for him. The Moys came in at Tucker's front door just as Bill pulled off his shot into the floor. The sober Moy began shooting while Bill's back was to him, but Bill whirled and walked toward him, both of them shooting.

They were fifty or sixty feet apart when the shooting began, and after Bill had fired his five shots he rushed in, grabbed Moy around the neck with his left arm, and hit him over the head with his empty gun. While he was doing that, Moy shot him through the heart. Bystanders said Bill struck at least three more blows after he was shot. Moy was shot through the shoulder and at least three by-standers—old man Gast, a trail herd owner named Butler, and his pointer,[7] whose name I have forgotten—were wounded by stray bullets. The Moy brothers skipped right out for Texas, but Bill's friends down there ran them out and they took out for the northwest, probably Canada.[8]

~~~~~~~~~~~~~~~~~~~~~~

7. The man who rode in the lead of a trail herd, pointing the way.
8. Captain James Cook, the well-known Agate, Nebraska, ranchman, was a witness to the shooting, his account differs somewhat from Mr. Lemmon's. According to Cook, he and the two Moy brothers, whom he describes as neatly

Our outfit was in camp with a herd of beeves, that fall of 1877, only two and a half miles from where Sam Bass, Joel Collins, and five others pulled off the Big Springs train robbery nineteen miles west of Ogallala. At daylight the next morning some officers came by and took a good look at us—and no wonder, for somebody had gotten away with seventy thousand dollars in the first holdup of a Union Pacific train. Of course everybody was under suspicion for a while.

Joel Collins had a twin brother, Joe, who was as homely and as honest a man as you would ever meet, while Joel was as handsome as they make them. In 1876 Joe had given Joel a present of six hundred cows. Joel trailed the cows to Custer City, South Dakota, and peddled them out to butchers, then used the money to finance a dancehall and gambling house in Custer that winter. By spring he had gathered about him five gamblers and dancehall men. The six of them rode down to Ogallala during the summer, where they spent some time gambling and laying plans to rob the Union Pacific passenger train. The seventh man in the holdup crew was not from Custer City.

The outfit robbed the train about ten in the evening. By half-past eleven they were back in Ogallala in their usual places at the gambling tables. They had all ridden Heart-branded horses belonging to Major Mabry, who knew nothing about it, although some of his men must have. Six of the men were soon identified by M. F.

---

dressed trail hands, were at table in the Rooney Hotel. Bertie Gast, the waitress, was taking their order when the drunken Campbell, wearing "a big six-shooter and a belt full of cartridges," came in and sat down at the table. The Moys ordered beans, and Campbell commented, "Just what I thought, a couple of damn Yankee bean-eaters." He continued to carry on in abusive language, though the brothers tried to quiet him because a lady was present. Failing, they left the dining room and went into the hotel office, where Campbell followed them, keeping up his "string of abuse." The Moys then went to Tucker's saloon, where they had left their guns, intending to get them and leave town, but Campbell followed them "so closely that they were forced to protect themselves." All three began shooting at once. Campbell was killed, and the Moys fled through a side door, mounted their horses, and rode into the South Platte River at full speed, headed south. Cook lists the same three persons wounded: A Mr. Gastman, shot in the groin; Butler, shot in the knee; and the pointer, Monroe Hinton, who got a bullet through the thigh. See James H. Cook, "Early Days in Ogallala," *Nebraska History*, XIV (April–June 1933), 88–89.

Leech, an Ogallala merchant, who recognized a mask found at the site of the holdup as a piece off a length of cloth he had sold one of the men a day or two earlier. These six were all run to earth and died with their boots on.

Collins, and I believe Burns, were killed by soldiers, only a few days after the robbery, at Buffalo Station in Kansas. It was told that they were resisting arrest and had to be shot, but it was the general opinion the soldiers shot first and then ordered the surrender, for both the outlaws went down with loaded guns, though both were known to be quick on the draw. Collins was betrayed by a letter addressed to him, which fell out of his pocket when he pulled out his handkerchief in the station. After his death the letter was taken from his body. It was from Bertie Gast, of Ogallala, and inside was the poem "Will You Love Me When I'm Old?" which was later made into a song. Jim Berry was killed near his home in Missouri, after he had bought his family a two year's supply of provisions.

Sam Bass organized a terror of a band and made it hot for Texas for a while before he was killed at Roundrock. I have forgotten who the other two were. The seventh man was never identified, but I have always been sure I knew him. I had worked for him on the agency trail drives only a short while before the robbery, and he was as fine a boss as I ever worked under. Shortly after the holdup he showed up in Texas, where he bought a small herd of cattle; and you who have read *The Life of Sam Bass* will note that Sam often visited a certain ranch down there.[9]

That summer, too, I came near meeting George Metcalf again. One day, while turning cattle back from the Battle Creek settlement

9. According to Charles L. Martin, in *A Sketch of Sam Bass* (Norman: University of Oklahoma Press, 1956), pp. 12–29, Collins and Bass bought five hundred steers, largely on credit, and drove them to Kansas. They sold them there and went on a spree, then rode up to Deadwood, with eight thousand dollars in their pockets. After a few months they ran out of money and organized a gang with Bill Hefferidge, Jim Berry, Tom Nixon, and Jack Davis, for a time stealing horses and holding up stages. During one of their holdups they killed Johnny Slaughter of Cheyenne, a popular stage driver. Going to Ogallala, they laid careful plans and, on September 19, 1877, held up and robbed the Union Pacific train of sixty thousand dollars in gold from the express car, and money and watches from the passengers. Accounts other than Lemmon's do not mention Joel Collins' twin brother Joe or a seventh member of the holdup gang.

in the Black Hills, I passed within a half mile of a chicken-hunting party in a spring wagon. Just after that I met a ranchman and asked him who the hunters were. He told me the leader was George Metcalf of Rockerville. George left the hills soon after that, but a little later I became well acquainted with Sam Oliver, who had been a partner of George's in the hide-hunting business. Oliver told me George was a prince of a fellow, and how he had once made a quick trip with him to Billings, Montana. While they were there a snappy, black-haired, black-eyed fellow had followed them around until he got a chance to talk to George alone. After they left Billings, Oliver said, George told him the stranger was his brother, Ute, who he had thought was hung, years before, for killing a mining speculator.

When I told Father this, he said he could well believe anything about Ute Metcalf; and I know that if he could have gotten his hands on him, even then, he would have torn him to pieces. For I remember one time, while we were on the stage line, a bully came from the far West just to get Father into a fist fight to see if he was really as tough as he was reported to be. Father told the fellow there was nothing to fight about, but the bully was determined, so they went at it. Father, who was more scienced, was keeping the other fellow off with ease—until he grabbed a short bench made of a split log with pegged legs and began swinging it right and left as he came at Father.

Father waited for the bench to pass in a swing, then jumped in and grabbed the man by the throat and choked him to the floor. Then he jabbed a thumb into his eye socket, forced the eyeball out onto his cheek, grabbed it with his thumb and forefinger, and started to pull it out. Then a bystander stepped up and said, "Jim, he deserves it, but don't pull that eye out," and Father let it slip back. No, I don't doubt but he would have mangled Ute Metcalf if he had ever gotten his hands on him. Even George, Ute's own brother, had told Oliver that Ute "deserved hanging, if not for murder, then for robbing old man Lemmon."

That December, just a few months after the Union Pacific train robbery, a cold-blooded killing upset the Platte Valley. Two brothers, Baggage and Andy Walrath, had a ranch between the Platte Rivers near Big Springs. The brothers had both worked for the Union

Pacific, running out of North Platte, and Baggage was so called because he had been a baggage man on the railroad. They had saved their money, borrowed some more, and gotten together about three thousand head of cattle to start their ranch. Their comfortable frame ranch house was about three and a half miles west of Big Springs station, and there Baggage took his bride, a somewhat wild girl[10] of the region, and a daughter was born to them.

In the winter, when all cattle were turned on the open range and there wasn't much to do, the brothers could well have handled the work left to be done on the ranch. But two fellows came along wanting work and the brothers took them on, letting them chore around and poison wolves in exchange for their keep. The first of the newcomers was a big, good-looking Wisconsin farm boy by the name of Charlie Phillips. Docia Walrath, who was much younger than her husband, was soon on very friendly terms with him. But when Harry Duboise (who turned out to be a deserter from Fort Riley, Kansas) came along, he wasn't long putting Charlie in the shade, for Harry was a flashy dresser and had a sharp line.

Not long after Harry pulled in, Phillips came up missing. No one thought much about it at first because Charlie, while poisoning wolves, had also poisoned a fine Newfoundland dog belonging to Andy Walrath. Andy had been in the East, delivering cattle and visiting relatives, but it was now December and he was expected home any day. Naturally, it was thought that Phillips had skipped rather than face Andy's wrath when he found out about the dog.

The day Phillips was officially reported missing, I left for a visit with my folks on the Little Blue. After spending eight years in Texas, Hervey had come home and I wanted to see him. While we were both at home Hervey met a girl we had known when we were

10. Mary Docia Nichols, the foster daughter of a North Platte man by the name of Purdy, who was said to be a lively, good-looking girl. Only sixteen at the time of her marriage to Walrath, she soon tired of ranch life, got a divorce, and returned to North Platte, where she married her foster father. This marriage didn't last either, and she remarried Walrath, broke up with him shortly after, and married Purdy again. During their second brief marriage, Purdy died under mysterious circumstances. The death was ruled a suicide, however, and Docia married Walrath again—for the third time within a year. (Information provided by John Carson, North Platte *Telegraph*, September 12, 1967.)

[93]

boys. Her name was Lizzie Slover, and Hervey fell in love with her right off and wanted to marry her. But another fellow there, Mike Cauley, wanted to marry her, too. This Cauley had heard, from Ben Wilson, something of the killings at old lady Taylor's ranch, so he wrote to Uvalde County, Texas, and got some of the records. He showed them to Lizzie, and she, of course, sprung them on Brother and told him she would not marry a man with a cloud hanging over him. So Hervey had to light out for Texas again and, by working through some friends there, get the old indictment against him quashed.

I was gone from my ranch job at Big Springs just twenty days, and the morning I got back to the ranch, Marion Cook, our foreman, thought we ought to go up and have dinner with Docia and Baggage. For Docia, besides being the only young ranch woman in the region, was a splendid entertainer After dinner Baggage, as was his custom, began clearing up the dishes and Docia and I went to the parlor. Marion took the little girl on his knee and stayed in the kitchen with Baggage. All Docia would talk about was the missing Phillips. She said she was changing her mind about what had become of him, and that she believed there was more to it than they had thought at first. I told her I wasn't interested and didn't want to get mixed up in it. When she insisted on unbosoming herself, I made an excuse to join the kitchen force. Then she tried to buttonhole Marion, so I said we had to be going, because something told me if we stayed we would be mixed up in it. As soon as we were on our way I told him I thought Docia was going insane over Phillips' disappearance. He agreed, and said he had never swallowed the dog story anyway.

The next day Mack Radcliffe, from the Sheidley ranch a few miles east of us, stopped in on his way up to visit the Walraths. Marion saddled up and went with him, and shortly after they reached the ranch, Docia got Mack in the parlor and began telling him her story about Phillips. Duboise had been away when I was there, the day before, but that day he was in the kitchen with Baggage and Marion. He must have overheard something Docia said, for he picked up a slate and wrote on it, "For God's sake take a tumble." Then he handed it to the little girl and asked her to take it to her mother. But Docia went right ahead and told Mack her story.

She said Duboise had told Phillips he was the unknown seventh Big Springs robber, and that he had ten thousand dollars of the Union Pacific gold buried in the sand between two clumps of trees about half a mile below the ranch. He said that if Phillips would go down there and help dig up the loot, he could have half of it. When the two men left the house, Docia said, she followed them, keeping north of the railroad grade, which was about seventy-five yards north of the clump of trees. When they reached the trees, she heard Duboise say, "Charlie, I believe I saw someone peeking over the grade." Phillips turned to look, and Duboise stuck his six-shooter against the back of his head and pulled the trigger. Docia had then watched while Duboise drug the body to the river bank and pushed it over. If Mack would go to the clump of trees, she said, he would find dried blood on the sand and a trail in the sand to the river bank.

Mack, all excited, got Marion and left. They went where she told him to go, and there they found everything as she had said they would, except that her shoe prints were on one side of the trail in the sand. Mack and Marion then rode fast to our ranch, which was near the Big Springs station. Mack went there and wired for the Sidney sheriff, and Marion sent a courier to get a search party together. Marion and I hurried back to the scene of the murder, where we found more signs that showed Docia had helped drag the body to the river. They had drug it by the heels, and when sand accumulated in the crotch they had flipped him over. Several feet to the right of where Phillips fell, we found the print of the Winchester he always carried to shoot wolves, and all along the trail we picked up cartridges that had sifted out of his pockets.

But it took us two days to find the body. They had drug it across a wide river channel, then across a small island, and dumped it into the water on the far side. Except for one hand and a bloated spot in the middle of the stomach, the body was completely covered by sand and water. That spot on the stomach was as black as coal, but the rest of the body was as well preserved as if it had been embalmed. The clothes had been stripped off, all but the underwear, and the shirt had pulled up when they drug him, uncovering his stomach. We had brought a coffin along to the river, and after the coroner had looked the body over, we put it in the coffin. By the time we got back to the ranch with it, the sheriff had arrested Duboise. Sheriff Beason then started for Big Springs in a wagon, with Duboise sitting on the coffin in the wagon bed back of the seat. He kept spitting tobacco juice on it until Beason called him down. The body was later shipped to Sidney for burial.

At the trial Docia told so many different stories that she was indicted, too. The Walraths stood by her, though, probably on account of the little girl, but in clearing her they also cleared Duboise, whose picture in all the papers resulted in his being identified as a deserter who had shot a lieutenant. He was taken back to the fort for trial, but as the officer had only been wounded a little, he got off with a ten-year sentence.[11] Baggage kept the little girl, but turned Docia from his home after making her promise never to visit or bother the child. Although the court decided otherwise, I am still convinced that affair was as cold-blooded a murder as ever came directly to my notice.

Here, I will drop back and finish my story about Hervey. He came home in a little while and married the girl, Lizzie Slover. Nearly sixty years after he made the trip to Texas to fix up that indictment, I had a letter from his daughter, who lived in Corvallis, Oregon. By then Hervey had been dead for many years, and Lizzie had just died at the daughter's home. In going through her mother's things, she wrote, she had found the exonerating letters, which she sent to me, asking what they were all about. And that was the first I knew of how Hervey got himself out of that old trouble. According to the letters,

---

11. The Omaha *Herald*, as quoted by Jack Best in the North Platte *Telegraph*, September 12, 1967, carried this account: "Today the guilty people were taken in the presence of the corpse. The icy water had prevented decay and there was a striking life-likeness in the features. Mrs. Walrath threw herself on the corpse and covered the dead face with kisses and called him her 'darling Charley.' Duboise stood by the body, spit tobacco juice on the coffin and refused to recognize him." According to the same story, Docia was tried first, before Judge William Gaslin. "After twenty-four hours the jury returned a verdict against Mary D. Walrath of second degree murder. The jury were starved into rendering some verdict, so compromised upon the lighter one." Although Docia took the stand, Duboise did not, and the jury, more sympathetic than they had been in Docia's case, returned a verdict of not guilty. The *Herald* also identified Duboise as a deserter from the Third Cavalry, then stationed at Fort Laramie, where he had been a bugler.

it had been easy, since the papers made it plain that Texas had no money to spend to bring back and prosecute old offenders of long standing. Although Brother was, at the time, right there in Texas, the authorities didn't know it, as he was working through friends— otherwise they might not have been quite so anxious to drop the whole business.

VIII

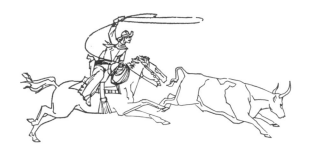

THE LATE SEVENTIES

W HEN I FIRST came to western Nebraska, that spring of '77, the manager of the big Bosler brothers' outfit[1] on the North Platte was Tom Lawrence. Before going to Boslers', Tom had owned a small herd of cattle, maybe twenty-five hundred head, and his brand was the Bar L on the left ribs. Tom also owned a horse he had trained himself. This horse later became famous as the "Bosler Blue," for when Tom turned his stock into the Bosler pool and took the management of the ranch, Old Blue was transferred with the rest.

If an animal was branded as a calf, as most of them were, when the calf was grown the brand would be as much as eight inches long, or high, and easy to see. So Tom had trained Old Blue to recognize his Bar L brand, and about the time I was on the Platte the horse was

---

1. James, George, Joseph, and Hiram Bosler had a large ranch on the north side of the North Platte River with a 150-mile river-front range on which they ran more than forty thousand head of cattle. They bought Texas cattle, wintered them on the Nebraska range, and sold them to the Indian agencies. See Nellie Snyder Yost, *The Call of the Range: The Story of the Nebraska Stock Growers Association* (Denver: Sage Books, 1966), p. 78.

at the pinnacle of his fame. In fact, the Bosler men would bet all kinds of money that a dummy could be put on Old Blue, and the horse, with only a rope around his neck, could be put into a roundup where Bar L cattle were fairly plentiful and he would cut out that brand. He would strain his neck to get a look at the critter's left side, and then bring the right animal out of the herd. He was absolutely the only horse I ever heard of that could be depended on to cut out an animal of his outfit's brand all by himself.

But Lawrence and Tom Parker, a part owner of the Bosler outfit, could not hitch [get along together], so Tom sold out for seventy-five thousand dollars and went to New Mexico, where he and Dick Head stocked up a big range, with ranches at both Watrous and Wagon-mound. Of course, when Tom sold out of the Bosler concern, Old Blue was forever lost to him.

While I was working out in that part of the country I got acquaint-ed with the Wiers, an Irish family that was practically running the whole town of Julesburg, just over in Colorado.[2] The family had settled there when the railroad was built through in '67. Besides the old folks, there were five boys and one girl. The old man bossed one crew of a double section outfit, and his oldest son, Joe, bossed the other one. Together the family ran a general store, the blacksmith shop, an eating house, and a feed barn, and the old lady also had a ladies' goods emporium. The daughter had married Sam Mathews, boss of Mabry's Heart ranch on the Niobrara, and two of the younger sons worked for him. Charlie Wier, next to the youngest, looked after the family's fine herd of Percheron horses that ranged north of town, and the youngest boy sometimes helped him.

There were two section houses in the little town. One was run by a Negro wench, the other by an Irish woman who could, if needed, handle a shillelagh to perfection. There was also quite a large schoolhouse, where all kinds of meetings and entertainments were held. As St. Patrick's Day came around, a big dance party was advertised. It was to be in the schoolhouse, of course, and the Irish

~~~~~~~~~~~~~~~~~~~~~

2. Today's Julesburg was Denver Junction at that time. Old Julesburg, first known as Wier, was located about eight miles west of Denver Junction, on the south side of the South Platte River near Fort Sedgwick.

lady of the one section house was on the reception committee. The Negro housekeeper from the other one was fixing the supper. Both ladies had babies about the same age.

At the schoolhouse one of the cloakrooms was fixed up for a place to put the babies while their parents danced. Old lady Wier, who was somewhat past the dancing stage of life, was to look after the babies. After supper that night, while the dishes were being cleared away—a job that kept all the women busy—Andy Wier, one of the sons who worked for Mathews, came into the cloakroom. A playful cuss, he brought with him some lampblack and some white enamel, and told his mother what he had in mind. Mrs. Wier, about as playful as Andy, fell right in with his plan and helped him blacken the Irish lady's white baby's head, hands, and arms, and enamel the same parts of the black baby. Then they switched all the outer garments and left the babies sleeping.

When the dance broke up, near daylight, the switch went undiscovered in everybody's hurry to get home. Later on in the morning, after the men had all gone to work, the mothers found out what had happened. Now these two ladies were not the best of friends at any time, so each laid the counterfeiting onto the other and, at about the same time, each grabbed a baby by the hind leg, so to speak, and started for the other, swearing vengeance. The section houses were quite a ways apart, so both babies were minus some skin when the mothers met, about halfway between. The Irish woman, not being as huskey as the Negro, had gathered up a shillelagh on the way. They dropped the babies and went at it, and the fur flew for a bit.

Their shrieks soon brought a crowd and they were pried apart, but not before both were in such bad shape they had to be shipped to Sidney for repairs at the hospital. And when Andy saw what he'd done, he lit out for the Niobrara and the Heart ranch, and didn't show up in Julesburg again for almost a year. By then the smoke had settled. This stunt was pulled off long before Owen Wister came to Wyoming and gathered local color for *The Virginian*, and likely it was where he got his idea for the exchange of babies in his book.

What happened to ten-year-old Charlie Wier a couple of years later came near being on the tragic order. Charlie had his own special saddle for his job of herding the Percherons, but one day when he was told to bring in the horses his seven-year-old brother was riding the saddle. Charlie then had to use one belonging to an older brother. He couldn't reach the stirrups, so he crowded his toes through the straps just above the stirrups. He had to run the horses to get them turned toward home, and was going at high speed when his horse fell. As it struggled to get up, Charlie's foot slipped all the way through the stirrup strap and he slid out of the saddle, pulling the stirrup over the saddle seat. When the horse got on its feet again, Charlie was hanging, head down, on the off side of the horse. And so he hung for many hours.

The saddle had long, stout leather strings and the boy now and then wrapped them around his hands and pulled himself up as far as he could. He was never able to get back in the saddle, but by holding himself up until his arms gave out he kept the blood from settling in his head and killing him. The saddle had been cinched so tight that after some hours the horse began to bloat. Sometime in the night it laid down and rolled, trying to relieve itself. Although his leg was broken at that time, Charlie was able to get hold of the bridle and hold the horse down. He still couldn't get his foot out of the stirrup leather or get back in the saddle, but he did get some rest. Toward morning the horse managed to get up again, with Charlie still hanging from the saddle, but a search party found him a few hours later. He had been caught in the saddle seventeen hours by then, but he got over it in good shape and grew up to be one of the best wagon bosses in that region.

In the late fall of 1878 I was caring for about seventy horses belonging to George Green,[3] who had gone east with his last shipment of beeves for that year. He had stayed to visit at his old home near Tiffin, Ohio, his first visit home since he had run away as a boy, thirty-one years before. Green's ranch was on Rush Creek, about thirty-five miles northeast of Sidney, Nebraska, and he had some four thousand head of cattle on his range. As they had all been

3. Green was the first ranchman on Rush Creek.

turned out to the four winds for the winter, all I had to do was look after the horses.

One evening early in November, the Tusler brothers'[4] outfit came along, branding late calves, and camped their mess wagon under a hill by our spring, about 150 feet from the ranch cabin. They were riding grain-fed horses, so they put two of their work horses in the stable, picketed six of their leaders out about seventy-five yards in front of the cabin, and left the fifteen head of loose saddle horses with them. The grass was extra good right there, as we had kept the cattle thrown back to save it for winter horse feed. Just before the outfit came along, I had brought in and penned a dozen cow horses that seemed determined to range too far away. At dark I moved the rest of my seventy head from where they had grazed that day to a gulch about a mile from the cabin. I took these precautions because it was well known that Little Wolf and his band of Indians had escaped from the Indian Territory, far to the south, and were on their way north, raiding the country for horses as they went.[5]

After supper all but two of the Tusler hands came to the cabin to play poker. The other two, an old rheumatic named Jess and the Negro cook, stayed in camp. They were sitting by their fire when they heard the horses out on the flat nickering. Figuring the loose ones were straying away, they went out to see. They came up just in time to see three Indians getting on three of the picketed horses that they had just cut loose. Jess and the cook were unarmed, so they ran for camp and their guns, yelling "Indians!" at every jump. By

---

4. The Tusler brothers ran some two thousand cattle and one thousand horses under the 66 brand. Their ranch was located on the Sidney trail into the Black Hills. See Yost, *The Call of the Range*, p. 86.

5. Little Wolf was chief of a band of Northern Cheyennes who had taken part in the Battle of the Little Big Horn but were later forced to surrender and were sent to the Southern Cheyenne reservation in Indian Territory. In September, 1878, Little Wolf, along with Dull Knife and Wild Hog, led a party of an estimated 89 men and 146 women and children in an attempted escape. They traveled north, raiding horse herds, and split into two groups after crossing the North Platte River. Little Wolf's band reached the sandhills and passed the winter there in safety, but Dull Knife's party was captured and confined at Fort Robinson. On the night of January 9, 1879, Dull Knife and about 30 others of his group were killed in a second escape attempt. In all, some 50 whites and 75 Cheyennes were killed in the uprising. (Frederick Webb Hodge, *Handbook of American Indians North of Mexico* [New York: Pageant Books, 1959], I, 253.)

the time we got outside, the Indians had rounded up the loose horses and taken off. I yelled at Henry Tusler to help himself to the horses in the corral, then I rushed off to see if my cached-out bunch was all right, and to take off the bells I had carelessly left on three of them.

By the time I got back, the Tusler men, riding my horses, had located the trail of the stolen horses by lantern light. It led a trifle east, then dropped into a gulchy draw that ran along Rush Creek. The night, dark and moonless, was foggy besides. So we split into four pairs and rode ahead about a quarter of a mile apart, but it was too dark to keep our course, except by the wind. We could have passed within a hundred feet of the horses and Indians, if they were bunched up and quiet, without even knowing it, so we signaled for everyone to go back to the ranch.

At the first peep of day we were out again, ready for a long ride. Less then three-quarters of a mile from the cabin we found where the Indians had penned the horses in a natural corral between the steep walls of the gulch. We could see by the sign that they had just moved out, showing that the night had been so dark that even the Indians hadn't tried to travel. We followed, and every few miles we could see where they had bunched the horses and changed to fresh mounts. Of course, as our horses tired and slowed down, they kept getting farther ahead of us. We followed them about fifty miles, and by then we were getting into strictly Indian country, where it seemed a good idea to turn back. Back at the ranch we found signs showing that the Indians had camped for at least a day in the gulch where they had penned the horses. They had killed a yearling heifer and jerked some of the meat, and had cut up part of the hide and made ropes, but had left those when they found picket ropes on the horses they took.

The man who rode with me that night as we tried to follow the trail was Ike Low. By morning light we could see where we had ridden along the top of the gulch wall, not over fifty feet from where the Indians were hiding with our horses. We had even got down and lighted matches to see the trail, and it was mighty lucky for us we hadn't done that right by the wall, because naturally they would've picked us off if they had thought we saw them. Probably the only reason they didn't was because it would have brought the rest of our men down on them and stampeded the horses besides. But if a horse had nickered or in any way given them away, they no doubt would've got us, since up there on the top of that bank we were skylighted for them, while we couldn't see them at all, down where they were in that black gulch.

If the Tusler outfit hadn't come along that evening, I'd sure have lost the horses I had in the stable and corral. And some three weeks later, when the same Indians were rounding up Sheidley's and Bill Paxton's horses, they played out three of the Tusler horses and left them on Paxton's range. Those Indians nearly cleaned all the horses out of our country that winter, stripping the herds of Paxton, Sheidley brothers, Bratt, Keith, and Theopstone Barnhart.[6] The next spring the Little Wolf band was captured north of Fort Keogh, [Montana]. We sent men up to the fort to get our horses, but only about half of the Paxton, Sheidley, and Barnhart horses were ever recovered, and none of the rest.

By 1879 I was working for Barton and Dillon of North Platte.[7] For a while I was stationed at a line camp on O'Fallons Bluffs, just south of the present town of Sutherland. With me was a little Englishman who was pretty choicy in the language he used. One day we were passing the widow Randall's ranch, northwest of North Platte city on the north side of the North Platte River.[8] Mrs. Randall,

---

6. William Paxton, a Kentuckian, had his Keystone ranch headquarters on Whitetail Creek, near the town of Paxton, which was named for him. His Ogallala Land and Cattle Company had ranges and cow camps throughout northwest Nebraska and bordering states. John Bratt, an Englishman who had come to America in 1864 at the age of twenty-one, had a large ranch, with headquarters south of the South Platte River and a little east of the town of North Platte. He later served two terms as mayor of North Platte. M. C. Keith's range was east of the forks of the Platte River. See Yost, *The Call of the Range*, pp. 40, 71, 72, 74, 125.

7. Guy Barton had been a partner of M. C. Keith before he went into partnership with Isaac Dillon. Barton later served as a Nebraska senator. (*Ibid.*, p. 71.)

8. Mrs. A. W. (Helen) Randall, the widow of Alexander Randall, at one time governor of Wisconsin and a former postmaster general of the United States,

the first lady rancher in that section, had about eight hundred head of fine cattle. It seemed she wanted to buy some registered Shorthorn bulls, and when we stopped for a drink she came out and tried to talk to my friend about them. But this embarrassed the Englishman and he kept changing the subject. (In those days bulls, stallions, and pretty legs were taboo in mixed company.) Finally she stamped her foot and said, "Never mind about that, I want to talk about bulls."

When she still couldn't get any satisfaction out of him about bulls, she turned to me and asked what I knew about Shorthorn bulls. I had never seen the lady before, but I told her my father had driven seventy head from the famous Van Meter herd of Fremont, Ohio, across the plains to Salt Lake City in 1853, and later had shipped a carload from Marysville, Kansas, to Bountiful, Utah. Well! After that Mrs. Randall didn't know the Englishman was around. She was bound we should stay for a meal so we could go over Shorthorn bulls thoroughly, which we did. Many years later I read in Jack Bratt's book[9] that she had shipped in a carload of Shorthorns from Ohio about that date. Very likely they were from the Van Meter herd, though this is just a surmise on my part.

At Barton and Dillon's headquarters ranch there was an old fellow that Barton had borrowed quite a sum of money from. Consequently, the old man almost ran the ranch. Now and then I would drop over to get a supply of grub and do a little visiting, but the old fellow always gave me rather a cold shoulder. The other boys noticed this, too, and finally one of them asked him why. This is the story he told: Early that spring two boys had come along to stay all night. They had quite a drive of bulls belonging to Russell Watts, a big neighbor to the west.[10] The bulls had wintered on the Medicine, some fifty miles southeast, and if they got an early start the next

was probably the first woman rancher in Nebraska. In the early seventies, after her husband's death, she went to North Platte and built up a ranch north of the river. (*Ibid.*, p. 109.)

9. *Trails of Yesterday* (Lincoln: University Publishing Co., 1921).

10. Russell Watts had come west from New York state in the late sixties to establish a large ranch south of the South Platte River. He maintained a large bull camp on the Blackwood, a tributary of the Republican, and also had range around Watts Lake in the sandhills. (Yost, *The Call of the Range*, pp. 75–76.)

morning, the boys figured they could make it on to Watts's ranch the second day.

One of the boys was Lame Johnny [Webster]. He was crippled about like myself, except that he always wore a high (built-up) heel on his boot. Johnny ordered an early breakfast, but the old man didn't like to be told what to do, so he went on about his work, feeding the chickens, milking, etc. So Johnny drew his attention to the fact that if they didn't get an early start they couldn't make it on in the next day. At that, the old man told him if he was in that big a hurry he could just go ahead and pull out. Then Johnny pulled his gun and told him he would give him just twenty minutes to set out some breakfast. Breakfast was ready on time, all right, but after that the old fellow had no use for Lame Johnny. So I had gotten the benefit of his dislike for a couple of months, but even after he found out his mistake he didn't apologize.

The next year, when my outfit moved onto the Cheyenne River range, Lame Johnny was already dead. The creek [named for him] where his grave and hang tree were located was on our range. He was hung by a posse of stage hands, and the place was about twelve miles north of Buffalo Gap, South Dakota, on the north bank of the creek and about thirty-five feet east of the road. As I remember it, the tree was an elm, and his body was dropped from the limb into a shallow, scooped-out hole below. The posse threw about two feet of rocks over him, and you could see pieces of his clothes under the boulders.[11]

---

11. On the night of June 9, 1879, two masked men held up the mail coach near Dry Creek, Dakota Territory, within fifty miles of Fort Meade. It has never been certain who the robbers were, although two men, John McDonald and Fritz Staurck, were arrested for the crime. They were convicted and sentenced; but shortly afterward another man, Frank Harris, confessed to the robbery, saying that he and Lame Johnny had held up the coach. At the time, however, Harris was charged only with horse stealing. John Furay, Special Agent for the U.S. Post Office Department, in a letter to A. D. Hazen, Third Assistant Postmaster General, gave this account: "About the time of the capture of McDonald and Staurck, there were . . . two fellows named Frank Harris and 'Lame Johnny' . . . who had been leading away some halters with horses in them. And the boys followed them also and one of them, Lame Johnny, got so badly strangled with a rope while the stage stopped to rest, as he was being conveyed to jail, that he lived only a few minutes." The pair had been arrested at Fort Robinson and were being taken to Rapid City for trial. See Agnes Wright

I had with me a boy named Smith, who was studying to be a doctor. One day when we were rounding up and he was off herd, he asked if he could have the day off and I told him he could. We were camped about twenty miles from Lame Johnny's grave, and that evening Smith came riding in with Johnny's skull in his slicker, tied on the back of his saddle. He also had several of Johnny's gold-filled teeth in a handkerchief in his pocket and, as I remember, the sole of the high-heeled boot. He showed the things around in a jolly way, but our manager, Dave Clark, ordered him to take the stuff right back to the grave and told me to fire Smith. I did, but learned later that he took the skull and teeth back east with him that fall. I always thought the boot heel and sole went with him, too, though I read, years afterward, that it was on exhibition in a showcase in Deadwood.

About four years after Smith took the stuff from the grave, Edgar Street and Maggie Frinke got married in Buffalo Gap. Right after the wedding they started for Rapid City and Deadwood on their honeymoon. They were riding in a spring wagon with another couple, while I rode alongside until we got opposite our ranch, for I had been one of the wedding party, too. When we came to Johnny's grave we found the limb he had been hung on stripped from the tree by lightning and lying across the mound. There wasn't any other damage to the tree, so the wedding party right away said it proved that Johnny was innocent of the crime they had hung him for.

Of course the story went the rounds and made good gossip. I didn't try to change their tale about the whole thing being a Lordly reminder to the hangmen that they had hung an innocent man, but I knew that if Johnny hadn't committed the crime he was hung for he was guilty of enough others to warrant the hanging. Johnny was a good cowpuncher and energetic to a fault, but he was a slick fellow with cards and had a sticky forefinger. The man, Beer, that he had worked for on Medicine Creek was a partner of Dave Rankin, the biggest cattle feeder Missouri ever knew. Beer used a beerkeg with four hoops on it for a brand.

Spring, "Who Robbed the Mail Coach?" *Frontier Times*, XLI (August–September 1967), 25.

The Dillon of the Barton and Dillon outfit was Isaac, a nephew of the great Sidney Dillon, president of the Union Pacific. Sidney had made Isaac a present of a half interest in the stock of cattle I was helping with, about twenty-five thousand head with not a drop of Texas blood in them. They had all been raised on the Platte, and were all branded with a C on the left hip, side, and jaw, with a double swallow fork on the left ear.

Two herds of those C's were the first cattle ever put on the Powder River range. Turned loose there in 1880, they were later sold to Frewen, manager of the 76 brand on the Powder.[12] I believe it was from this ranch that an Englishman got lost and was out three days. When they found him he was about famished for a drink of water, but he was also right on the bank of the river. The first thing he did was ask for a tin cup he saw tied on one of the boy's saddles. They asked him why he hadn't gotten down on his stomach so he could drink out of the river, and he said, "What! Drink like a beast?" It was said they just rode off and left him, without giving him the cup, and that he followed them on to the ranch, which wasn't far away.

Another story about that same Englishman concerned a boyhood friend of mine, Hank Devoe, of Marysville, Kansas. The Englishman, a very wealthy fellow, had an interest in several ranches. One of them was run by my friend Hank, and when the Englishman rode up one day and ordered Hank to take his horse and unsaddle him, Hank told him he was no servant and would not wrangle horses for any dude. The Britisher then roared, "I own an interest in this ranch and I will have you fired."

"I think not," Hank told him, "because when I saw what this ranch was drawing, in the shape of your person, I quit." He did, too, right when he said he did.

12. Moreton Frewen, a British aristocrat and uncle of Winston Churchill, came to Wyoming in 1878 with his brother and a group of friends to hunt, and stayed on to manage cattle companies in Wyoming and the Dakotas. His Dakota Stock and Grazing Company was spectacularly successful at first, declaring a 24 per cent dividend in 1884; but the next year a combination of unfavorable weather, losses to rustlers, and poor financial management led to its eventual bankruptcy. See Allen Andrews, *The Splendid Pauper* (Philadelphia: Lippincott, 1968).

While I was working down in that Medicine country, Ike Low, the fellow I rode with on the dark night the Indians stole the horses on Rush Creek, practically died in my arms after a gun duel in a roundup camp one morning. On his deathbed he asked us not to prosecute his killer, Charley Ensley, since he (Ike) had brought on the fight. When fighting the duel Ike was using my pearl-handled Colt .45. A few weeks later I sold the gun to a fellow named Oscar Phoebus. Shortly afterward, while flourishing the gun in Sidney, Oscar, who was somewhat lushed up, accidentally shot it off and killed himself.

That seemed to be an unlucky gun. I got it in Fort Sidney from an army officer who had ground the U.S. off and nickled over the place before selling it to me. At the coroner's inquest over Oscar it was discovered that the U.S. was ground off, though the number was still plain. It was through the number that the gun was traced to the fort, where it was still on record. I was told the officer nearly got court-martialed for its disappearance, and that if it had been traced to me I might have been in trouble for buying government property. I could have pled ignorance, and likely I could've made it stick, as I was so young.

IX

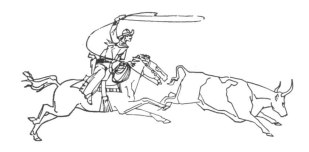

SOME GUNMEN AND OTHERS

D URING THE SUMMER of 1880, when the roundup was working
up the Niobrara, near the present town of Cody, Nebraska, a
man rode up on a very tall sorrel horse. The horse was branded
U.S.I.C., meaning "inspected and condemned by the U.S. government." The fellow was riding an old U.S. McClellan saddle, and
across the front of it he carried an old army Sharps rifle. He also had
a Colt's six-shooter and a beltful of cartridges, mixed for use in both
guns. He was wearing a slouch hat that had gone to seed, with a long
lock of his hair sticking out of a hole in its crown. He had about a
four months' growth of hair and beard on his head and face, and a
wild, hunted look in his eyes. He bore no resemblance to a cowboy,
and we wondered if he was a detective in disguise, looking for some
of the outlaws and absconders that worked with roundups.

When the fellow asked for the Seth Mabry outfit, we pointed out
Johnson, the manager of Mabry's crew, and he rode up and said,
"Crawford, don't you know me?"

The manager said, "No, and I don't think I want to." That set
the man laughing. Then he went ahead and told Johnson (whose
right name was Crawford) a story about some boyhood prank they

had been mixed up in, down in Texas. At that, Johnson recognized the shabby traveler as an old friend, Billy Carter. Johnson told Carter to go to camp and get the wrangler to cut his hair and give him a shave, and when he came in for dinner he would fix him up with a better-looking outfit. When Billy rode out to the meeting place for the afternoon circle, I don't think a one of us could tell he was the same fellow that rode in on the U.S.I.C. horse.

We soon found out why he had looked so wild and dilapidated. It was not that he was in disguise, but because of isolation and exposure while on a long and roundabout ride from Rawlins Springs, all the while dodging pursuit. He had left Rawlins in a hurry, and under pressing circumstances. It seemed that a Chinese laundryman had been robbed by the rounders of the town. When he resisted, they beat him so bad he died. Billy had been hanging around with that bunch, so he was rounded up with them. The citizens' mob that undertook to deal with the gang picked out Billy and three others and marched them to a patch of timber where there were trees big enough to be used as ready-made scaffolds.

But there happened to be quite a few in the crowd that weren't in sympathy with hanging Billy. They tried to talk the rest of the mob out of it, and in so doing crowded the hangmen so close they did not take time to bind his hands before hustling him under a tree and putting a rope around his neck and over a limb. Just as Billy's feet cleared the ground the rope holders slackened up a bit so they could give a harder pull. And Billy, bracing his toes and jumping into the air, grabbed the rope as high up as he could, then slipped the noose off his neck and ran. At the same time some of his sympathizers managed to make a sort of a path through the crowd into the timber, where a girl was waiting with a gun for him. And so he got away. He said he traveled by night and laid up by day, and all the time he could still feel that ticklish sawgrass rope around his neck, so it was no wonder he looked so wild when he showed up at our camp.

A few days later, while we were rounding up the Si Funk place on the north branch of the Niobrara, the first circlers came in and started a monte game on a spread blanket in the hay yard north of the stables. Billy had several bets down when someone hollered that a dozen cavalrymen were coming down the road. Billy grabbed the money roll in front of him, jumped on his horse, and was off for the sandhills to the south. He didn't even slow up for the river, which was about twenty feet wide, and his horse took it in one jump and didn't even break his stride. When the sergeant rode up with his troop, he said, "That fellow must think he is escaping from us, but he needn't worry, for no trooper ever sat a horse like that. Anyway, I'm not looking for Texas outlaws, but for U.S. army deserters." Billy stayed out for a night, then one of Mabry's men found him and told him it was all right for him to come on in.

Scrub Peeler was another of the old-time gunmen I met on the Niobrara my first summer in that country. He was one of the best cowhands and most likable fellows I ever knew. This is how he got his name: Back in Texas a man named Peeler was head trail boss for Captain Millett, who usually drove from seven to ten herds north every season.[1] Peeler made the herds up in Texas and, after getting them moving on the trail, plied back and forth between them, attending to supplies, watering places, good grazing, etc.

Now the Millett outfit, one of the toughest in Texas, was proud of its reputation and worked hard at upholding it. When a new hand showed up, the Millett boys always put him through a plenty rough initiation. One day a runt not much, if anything, over five feet tall showed up and asked for a job. Peeler told him their requirements were high and that he'd have to be a thoroughbred to meet their needs. It seemed that the little fellow had an idea as to the "requirements" and suspicioned that some of them might not be in line with actual cattle duties, so he was not altogether taken by surprise. He was tried out on bucking horses, then at roping, then wrestling calves and tailing steers down from horseback. But when the sport got rougher the runt suddenly jumped back, clearing a space in front of him. Then he jerked out his six-shooter and declared himself.

When the boys started to surround him so someone could get at him from behind, he whipped out another gun and covered them

---

1. Captain E. B. Millett drove his first trail herd north from Texas in 1866. See Mari Sandoz, *The Cattlemen* (New York: Hastings House, 1958), p. 56. Mari Sandoz also confirms Lemmon's assertion that the Millett outfit was a tough one (*ibid.*, p. 222).

from two directions. At that, Peeler stepped up and said, "Boys, I guess we'll call the little scrub one of us, for it looks like he can meet our requirements. Let's just christen him Scrub Peeler." It turned out that the little fellow could more than fill the needs of the Millett outfit, which ran the MV and JAC brands. Before long he had two notches on his gunstock, which caused him to change base to the north, where he wound up working for the Newman Brothers' outfit [2] on the Niobrara, near the present town of Rushville.

A while after I met him he had six-shooter trouble with one of the Janis boys and killed him. Scrub headed right out for Canada, though he would have been acquitted if he had stayed around, for he gave Janis the first shot, which was pulled off in such a hurry that it missed. I never again heard of Scrub Peeler, because of course he changed his name. As he was still a young man, he would soon change to be a different character, too.

A couple of other bad men who made history in some of the early cow towns were Charles Reed and Bill Bland. These fellows were trail-herd drivers, too, and about 1874 or '75, when one of the trail delivery points was Fort Scott, Kansas, Bland and Reed hit the town. Bland got into a poker game and had words with one of the cutthroat gamblers he was playing with. Another of the gang, a man who was not in the game, shot and killed him. Reed, a two-gun man, then whipped out both guns and shot as long as he could see a gambler to shoot at. When his guns were empty he ran to his horse and absconded for the north country. I am not sure whether it was six or seven men he left dead and dying, but it was said to be the biggest one-man killing ever recorded in a house quarrel.

By 1878 Reed was making Sidney, Nebraska, his hangout, and by then he was a full-fledged gambler, too. His reputation as a killer had followed him from Kansas, and he also had a solid girl, or one he supposed was solid. But one evening he found a man named Loomis

---

2. Kentucky-born E. S. (Zeke) and H. L. Newman in 1877 established their ranch, one of the first in the area, in the valley where Antelope Creek runs into the Niobrara, about twelve miles southeast of present-day Gordon, Nebraska. Most of their cattle were delivered to the Pine Ridge reservation for issue to the Indians. See Nellie Snyder Yost, *The Call of the Range: The Story of the Nebraska Stock Growers Association* (Denver: Sage Books, 1966), pp. 94, 95.

in her room with her and deliberately shot and killed him. Up to then Sidney had been such a wild and lawless town that the better element, headed by a man named Carne (who later ran a saloon in Custer City), organized a strong vigilance committee. Within a few minutes after the killing of Loomis the vigilantes had Reed surrounded. He gave up without resistance, saying that though they had him surrounded he could still kill several of them; but as he had been in the wrong in killing Loomis, and had done enough killing anyway, he had no wish to take the lives of respected citizens who had families depending on them.

They led him to a telegraph pole and put a rope around his neck. One of the hanging party climbed the pole and cast the rope over the top crosstie. But when the fellow started to make ready to draw him up, Reed said, "Boys, that is rough work on such delicate hands as most of you have, so if you will allow me I will save you the trouble," and he coolly climbed the pole. Then he said, "Pull up the slack, and good-by," and he jumped into eternity. It was said there was much sniffling and wiping of eyes as his neck popped, for he was a lot like Scrub Peeler, a man well liked by all.

In July, after the roundup was over, the Sheidley Cattle Company (Flying V brand; Dave Clark, manager; and myself as straw boss) located on the Cheyenne River at the mouth of French Creek in the Black Hills. While we were making our first trip north that summer, we threw the herd off the trail near the mouth of McGulligan Canyon at noon. After dinner I rode out to relieve a man on herd, and as I was riding back toward the tail of the herd I could see a man about half a mile away, cracking rocks together, or so it looked. I rode on over to see why he was doing that. When I came up he gave me a sharp look, then said, "Boy, I'm going to take a chance on you." (I was twenty-three years old, but looked younger.)

It turned out he was cracking boiled beef bones with rocks and eating the marrow. When I asked why he didn't kill a calf if he was that hungry, he said he would have, only he'd have to build a fire to cook it. "If you'd been hounded like I have for the last month, you wouldn't want to give yourself away with a fire, either," he told me. Of course he put up the usual spiel about how he'd had no chance to prove his innocence. So I told him I'd go back to camp and get the cook's ear and have him slip a sack of grub over the river bank for him. This was done, and I didn't see the fellow again until the next season, when I came onto him in a cow outfit on White River. His name was Bill Miller, and he was a splendid cowhand.

A couple of years later he came riding into our WG ranch on the Cheyenne at daylight. His horse was worn out, and he had a note to me from an old Sheidley boss. The note asked me to trade Miller a fresh horse for his jaded one. I supposed he had been mixed up in some shooting scrape and I sort of hesitated. Then he said, "Ed, I've got to have a fresh horse, and I don't want to add another crime to my list to get it. I've been riding through your horses all morning, and I see a lot more of 'em to the east."

Just then Sam Brown rode up on a big eleven-hundred-pound bay horse, and I asked him how he stacked up. Brown said good for service, but no cow action. "How does he strike you?" I asked Miller.

"To a T," he said, and threw his saddle on him and rode off to the east. I supposed he would turn toward Canada, the usual trail for absconders, as soon as he was out of sight. But I was mistaken. Two or three years after the town of Lemmon was founded, a traveling man came up to me and said, "I met an old friend of yours over in Minnesota." He wouldn't tell me the "old friend's" name, but said that while he was talking to him the man pointed out an old bay horse in his pasture and said, "Tell Lemmon that old horse practically earned me this farm. It's the horse he traded me, a long time ago, and for several years now I've given him his time in [retired him to] that pasture." Of course, the old friend was Bill Miller.

Ike Dillon was another cowpoke who got on the wrong side of the law. Ike worked for the Keystone when H. A. (Lon) Godard was manager. Lon put him out in a line camp with a fellow named Alex Mervil. The camp was by a spring, south of the Cheyenne, where Bill Hudspeth is now located. Pretty quick Ike decided to start a brand of his own by branding sucking calves—only he killed their mothers so there'd be no comeback. Alex didn't think much of that way of getting a start, and that worried Ike. So one day, after he'd branded a calf, Ike shoved his six-shooter under Alex' arm and said, "Now, damn you, Alex, you shoot that cow," which Alex did. But

Alex was still scared Dillon would kill him to make sure his thieving was well covered, so he went to Lon and spilled the works. Dillon was fired but never prosecuted.

A couple of years later Sam Bell was riding the badlands south of Battle Creek, in the most isolated part of that region, when he saw a man driving a herd of about two hundred black Percheron horses. Sam headed over that way and the driver dropped back, but when he recognized Sam and saw that Sam recognized him, he rode back and had a talk with him. The driver was Ike, and he was headed toward the Missouri to cross at Labeau, another isolated place. And that was the last we ever heard of Ike Dillon. Sam never gave any reason for not reporting him; I guess it was just the old way of not betraying a friend.

Then there was Dave Malasky. While the rest of the crew went back to Ogallala for another herd to fill out an Indian contract in 1877, I rode herd with Dave on eighty-two leftover steers. He was about the most companionable puncher I was ever planted out with. But soon after our stay together he went back to his old home in San Antonio on a visit, and while there killed two men and a painted woman in a dancehall. A stray bullet got the girl.

Dave came back to Ogallala then and bought into a saloon, where, together with Luke Short and Bat Masterson, he was walked up on in a poker game by U.S. marshal D. B. Ball and some deputies. Ball then wired Texas that he had three of their bad men and killers. He got a wire right back, to the effect that Texas had no money to bring back and prosecute absconders, and to turn them loose if they would promise to stay out of Texas. They promised. But the urge to go home soon got too much for Dave. He wasn't in Texas long, though, before he killed two more men, and then lit out for Mexico. I was told that he killed a man in just about every important town on the way. It was said that he'd ride in and ask for the town's bad man, then hunt him up and get a shooting match out of him. In a manner, it was dog eat dog, so no one paid any attention.

When I was in Mexico on my wedding trip, some twenty years later, I was told by an old friend of both Dave's and mine that he was then captain of a strong band of bandits near Chihuahua. Still later I heard that he had lined up with Pancho Villa.

THE NORTHERN NEBRASKA
AND DAKOTA AREAS THAT LEMMON KNEW BEST

And finally, there was Mack Stewart, a great cowman. I turned more than seven hundred head of beeves over to him for the Sitting Bulls at Standing Rock in 1881. At that time he was as fine-looking a man as you'd ever lay eyes on. Eighteen years later I found him in the pen at Chihuahua, a stooped, gray old man serving a twenty-year sentence for killing a Mexican soldier or policeman, I forget which. Mack said he killed the Mexican in self-defense, but Mexican law said not. While I was visiting him there I gave him a fifty-dollar bill, and then sent him five dollars every month until he got out, five years later.

After moving the Flying V herds to the Cheyenne and getting settled at the mouth of French Creek, we cut down to a winter crew of four: Sam Bell, John McKnabb, Sam Cousier, and myself. Bell and McKnabb rode line on something like four thousand Flying V cattle that ranged along the Cheyenne, mostly on the reservation, as the river made the boundary line. I rode line on a couple thousand head along French Creek, where I was not so much exposed to Indians.

Small bands of Indians were nearly always roving around, hunting deer and antelope. Due to the Indians being restricted to their reservations, game was a lot more plentiful off the reservations, on range where they were not supposed to hunt without a permit. But permits were not easy to get, and they did a lot of trespassing off their own range, and so didn't like to meet up with us cowboys. We didn't know this at first, and Sam and McKnabb came in almost every day with stories of being shot at by Indians. I was also coming across a few small bands of Indians, but none had acted hostile, and I kind of doubted their stories. Then one morning when it was McKnabb's turn to bring in our little remuda, he came dashing home in about twenty minutes and said he'd been shot at in a stand of timber on the government side of the line, about a mile and a half east of the ranch, where the horses were grazing.

After breakfast he and Sam both went out, and within a half hour came back on the run with only about two-thirds of our horses. They had been shot at, they said, in a deep canyon a little farther away and to the north, up Nasty Creek. I wanted to find out the facts about the hostiles before going out on my own line ride, so I said we should all go out and have a look. But Sam said he hadn't lost any Indians, and since he had one of the best horses in the bunch, he'd take his chances on outrunning them if they tried to cut him off from the ranch. Cousier and McKnabb agreed to go with me.

Armed with Sharps carbine saddle guns and six-shooters, we rode directly north to high ground. Just as we broke the rise we saw an Indian about a mile away on the far side of a deep draw. He was down off his pony and busy at something. We rode straight for him, but when we came to the gulch, which was about seventy-five feet deep and two hundred yards across, McKnabb balked. He said he hadn't lost any Indians either, but he did offer to stay where he was and come across to our rescue if we needed him. So Cousier and I went on. When we came close to the north rim of the canyon we drew and cocked our carbines. By then we were about 150 yards from the Indian and could see he was skinning an antelope. We rode a little closer. He stopped skinning and picked up his rifle. Then he sat flat on the ground, crossed his wiping sticks to make a gun rest, and put his gun barrel in the fork.

We rode on toward him, and if I'm any judge, he was more scared than we were. As soon as we were within sign-making distance he held out his hand, palm first, in token of friendship. We answered in like manner. He then explained, by signs and words, that the shooting the boys thought was aimed at them was really aimed at deer in the brush. As we got it from the Indian, the shots that had seemed to be at Bell and McKnabb that morning were from off the landslides, where the slides tipped back. They had been shooting at deer on the slide fronts, and the bullets had carried upward, so that the ones the boys thought were whizzing over their heads had really been hundreds of feet above them. He also told us they had been trying to dodge the riders because they (the Indians) were off the reservation and were afraid the boys would report them.

We told the Indian their hunting was none of our affair, and that we wouldn't say a word if they didn't kick about a few of our cattle crossing the river onto the reservation. He said that was no affair of theirs and the grass over there was plentiful. So ended our fears of the Indians—until ten years later, the year of the great Messiah craze and the uprising of 1890–1891. And by then the Sheidley Cattle Company had moved to the Moreau River country, well to the north. After our peace powwow the Indian, who had one of the finest rifles I have ever seen, wanted me to take the gun and go across the draw three or four miles and kill another antelope, which I did. By leaving himself unarmed he was showing he trusted us.

During those first years in the Black Hills, cowboys, out of work when winter came to the range country, got jobs in the mines if they could. A cowboy I knew, Kirk Willey, went to work in the Home-stake at Lead City. He boarded with a couple of Cousin Jacks, as the Cornishmen were called. A near neighbor to the Jacks had a shoat he was raising in a small pen that was partly roofed over for a winter shelter. The owner of the shoat didn't try very hard to keep it in its pen, since when it got out it ranged around in the neighbors' slop and garbage, and so foraged most of its living.

Of course it had lived off the Cousin Jacks a good deal, too, so they looked on it as partly theirs and were looking ahead to the dark night when it would be of butchering size. About that time there came along an old prospector, just back from the mountains, with a cub bear he had trained to perform on the streets of the towns, after which he passed the hat around. He was making out pretty good with the bear, and that evening in Lead City, as dark came on, he went look-ing for a place to shut up his bear. The owner of the shoat, who had that day done his butchering, told the old miner he could put the bear in the empty pen. Now this turned out to be the night the Cornishmen had decided to butcher the shoat themselves. Slipping over to the pen, one climbed in to hand the hundred-pound pig over the fence to the other, who waited on the outside. Right away there was a terrible racket and fuss in the pen.

"Gotnin', Jack?" the outsider called over the fence.

"Gotnin', hell, he's gotnin' I," the insider panted back. And when he finally got loose and scrambled out of the pen, he looked like a cyclone had "gotnin'" him.

Most of the settlers, cowboys, and the like who didn't have jobs in the mines, lumber camps, or with cattle outfits had a hard time

[119]

keeping alive, especially in the winter. So it seemed to me that the cattlemen, who didn't contribute much to the actual support of the country, could well afford to spare an occasional beef to the hard-up settlers—but only for home use, and not for peddling to the Hills towns, as sometimes happened.

One day about the middle of that first winter, when there was a good eight inches of snow on the ground, Pink Ayres and I were out seeing to the condition of cows with late calves, picking out the ones we should take in and dole out our scant supply of hay to. About twelve miles from our ranch we came, late in the afternoon, to the mouth of Little Cedar Creek on the Cheyenne River. Now this twelve miles was, as the crow flies, across badlands that were hard to travel in slippery snow. On the other hand, by a roundabout trail of good footing, it was nearer twenty miles home, so we decided to take the badlands route.

About four miles from the ranch, just south of French Creek, we rode up on a fresh-butchered Flying V spayed heifer. Only the saddle, or hind quarters, had been taken. This, with a fresh wagon track leading away, showed that someone had left in a hurry. I sat there on my horse, making up my mind whether or not to follow the track, but Pink jumped off his horse and started to turn back the hide to look at the brand. I asked him what he was doing, and he said, "Why, I'm going to look at the brand."

I told him to get back on his horse and tend to his own knitting. "If we trail that track," I said, "it will likely lead to your own brother-in-law's ranch, and we both know his pantry is near empty. But it's a shame to leave so much good beef to the wolves."

I fired off a few shots from my gun and left the shells around the carcass to keep the wolves away. Then I told Pink that after supper he might ride up to his home, and on the way he could stop at his brother-in-law's place and mention the heifer, and what a waste it was to leave all that good meat out there. I never followed up, myself, to see if the settler came after the beef, but I heard later that none of it went to waste. The brothers, Pink and Lon Ayres, were two of the most honorable and respected men in Custer County, and the son of the brother-in-law later stood very high in the forestry service.

The next spring, after wintering our Flying V saddle stock and work horses on the divide between Battle and French creeks, Pink and I were casting the herd to the spring range on the South French Creek tableland. The first day of the drive we missed about 25 horses from our bunch of 160 head. The next day we picked up the balance and were casting them across at the mouth of French Creek. Near the ranch belonging to Sam Bell, Gus Haaser, and Alex Webb, we were traveling a narrow trail along a landslide on the north bank. Suddenly a maverick came in from the side and ran square into the lead of the loose horses, butting them right and left and frothing at the mouth. He kept this up until the close-packed bunch of horses turned him, then he ran off up a side gulch.

When we came to the Bell, Haaser, and Webb ranch, where we were going to change horses for the ride home, I got off my horse to let down the bars to the corral. I noticed that a couple of the lower bars were already down, and I thought the maverick had probably been penned there and had rubbed them down and got out. When one of the ranchmen rode up, I told him the bars were down and that the yearling must've got out there. He began to laugh. "No," he said, "that maverick wasn't in the corral. He was tied down in a draw a little ways back, with a hot iron just about on his hide. But when I saw you coming, I thought you might be stock detectives or the sheriff, so I turned him loose. He's a fine maverick, and now I'm going to follow him up and finish my job."

Two years later this same Sam Bell found good evidence that a settler had butchered a Flying V cow near today's town of Fairburn. As I had been with the company longer and had more years of cattle experience than any of the other boys, Dave Clark asked me to go see about it. I found the butcher was the father of a big, hard-up family, so I told Clark I didn't want to appear against him, and if compelled to do so, I would jockey my evidence so as to clear the settler. In the end I shamed Dave out of prosecuting.

No more than six years before that, no range man ever butchered his own cattle. But after the Wyoming Stock Growers Association met in the spring of 1880 and agreed that any members of the Association who butchered, or allowed others to butcher, any but their own cattle would be blackballed, a big change came about. I hadn't heard of the new rule yet in July of that year, when I cut an O Bar calf into our herd to butcher that evening. But Dave saw it and made me drive it back about two and a half miles and put it beside its mother on Big Cottonwood, ten or twelve miles north of Fort Robinson.

X

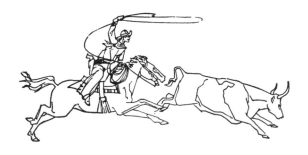

TRUE EXPERIENCES AND
TALL TALES

I N 1881 WHAT WAS called the "Bull Union" took place. That was
the time all the freighters from Pierre to the Black Hills struck for
higher freight rates, and all outfits were tied up for about five weeks.
With all hands idle, funds soon ran low and the teamsters were doing
almost anything for money. On Bad River, just off Fort Pierre, there
was a big scaffold, or Indian burying place. The Indians never
buried their dead in the ground, but put the blanket-wrapped bodies
up on fourteen- to sixteen-foot-high platforms held up by trees or by
poles set in the ground. So this burial place on Bad River turned out
to be one way for the boys to pick up a little cash.

The bodies were always wrapped in one or two good blankets, so
Smokey Thomas and Dick Wickett paired off to swipe the blankets
which, if they weren't too dirty, could be sold to cowboys for a
dollar apiece. The boys had taken several blankets one night, and it
was Smokey's turn to climb the scaffold and unwrap an Indian who
had just been scaffolded. He climbed the pole at the foot end of the
platform and slashed the binding cords. Just then Dick, on the

[123]

ground waiting for Smokey to toss down the blanket, happened to notice a leftover pole. It looked about the right length to reach the dead Indian.

Just as Smokey stripped the head and shoulders bare, Dick stuck the pole under the back of the corpse's head and raised its gaping face right up in front of Smokey, who let all holds go and fell off backward in a dead faint. Dick dived for cover, for he expected Smokey to be mad as blazes when he came to and figured out the trick that had been played on him. But in the end Dick had to come out of the brush and carry water in his hat to dash on Smokey's face to bring him to. And Smokey was so ashamed of fainting from fright that he agreed to keep still if Dick would. So the stunt had been eleven years a secret when Smokey finally told it.

It was during that Bull Union strike that I met Alva Ayres again. He had been freighting into the Black Hills over the Pierre route until the strike, and while that was on he spent his time breaking in some young work oxen. Buck Williams had traded him the new stock for some broken-down old bulls, and I was called on to counter-brand the young stuff for him. I hadn't seen Alva or his brother Curley (Silvin Bishop Ayres) since the fall of 1870, when we left Cheyenne. The brothers had freighted over the Holladay stage line as early as 1862, and had kept it up until the railroad was finished in 1869. With the opening of the Black Hills they had transferred to that region, first on the Cheyenne route, and then the Pierre.

We talked over the old days, remembering the time Alva had lost all his freight stock to the Sioux, and some of the stunts Curley, the wit of the train, used to pull. Once when they were camped on the west side of Crow Creek at the edge of Cheyenne, Curley had pulled in from a wood-hauling trip to the Black Hills of Wyoming, twenty-five miles west of town. It was winter and the campfire was so close-packed with warmers that he wouldn't get within warming distance. So he reached in his overcoat pocket and gathered a handful of Spencer .50-caliber cartridges and tossed them in the log fire. That widened the circle in a hurry and gave him full use of the fire. The fact was, there wasn't much danger from the explosion, unless the butt of a cartridge had happened to lodge against a log, but most of the fire circlers didn't know until afterward what caused the blast. So they hadn't wasted any time getting out of there.

Since at that time the outfit didn't have a regular cook, every man put his name on the bottom of his tin plate and washed it or not, as he pleased. I was fooling around their camp one day when Curley was the last to come in to the grub pile. The others already had their plates filled, but Curley couldn't find his, so he began tipping the others over, looking for his. He had dumped them all before it was discovered that his plate had been mislaid among the other culinary stuff. The outfit belonged to Alva, and Curley was only working for him, so of course Alva threatened to charge Curley with eight meals at seventy-five cents apiece.

From freighting on the Cheyenne–Black Hills route, Curley went on to the Coeur d'Alene country and I lost track of him. Another brother, George, married Katie Towle of Beatrice, Nebraska. Katie was the daughter of the postmaster there, and I well remember when I was a kid visiting there that Katie used to be in charge of the post office window when she was no more than ten years old. After leaving Beatrice, George walked to the Black Hills in 1876, where he tried logging, then placer mining. After that he hired out as a clerk in Richard C. Lake's Rapid City hardware store.[1] He later bought Lake out and became an important man in Rapid, and then a member of the House of Representatives from 1927 to 1929.

In the early eighties there were a good many stage stations and road ranches on the Pierre–Black Hills route. One was run by a family of French descent, and the missus, who helped with the outside work, was a lot darker than the average Frenchwoman. Bands of Indians often visited the ranch, trading away clothes of the coarse, substantial kind issued to all northern Indians at that time. The missus, as well as ranchers and freighters, wore this government issue clothing. Now this woman, being so dark and mingling so much with the Indians she traded with, and also wearing the same kind of

1. Richard C. Lake, one of the partners in the Lake, Tomb, and Lemmon cattle company of the 1880's, lived in Evanston, Illinois. He was a well-known financier and later managed the great Masonic building in Chicago.

clothes, was twitted a lot by her husband about her resemblance to a squaw. This sometimes made her temper boil.

One morning when a party of Black Hills Sioux was breaking camp, a squaw went over to the house to visit and trade a little. The missus, being short of dish aprons, traded her out of a wrapper that had a belt with a slip buckle. Then she remembered that her ten-year-old son had let his hat blow away in a South Dakota gale, so she asked the squaw if she had a boy's hat for sale. The squaw said she did, that it was almost new and she'd send her own boy over with it for a dollar. The boy came as the caravan was leaving, left the hat, and hurried away to catch up.

The missus put on the Indian wrapper, and with it the Indian smell. Then she looked out where she had scattered some grain for her chickens and saw a crow chasing the chickens away and eating the grain. She ran out to shoo it away, but it hopped onto her shoulder and began stroking her cheek with its beak. Then she remembered that the squaw had told her not to let her boy shoot her pet crow while it was hunting birds and rabbits around the place. The crow stayed on with the family, but wouldn't have anything to do with anybody but the missus, causing her husband to say it was because she looked so much like a squaw that the bird couldn't tell the difference. The Frenchman kept this up until she lost her temper and grabbed the rolling pin. The mister ran for the door, but looked back as he went through it, and the weapon caught him just over the eye.

Now the missus had just washed the wrapper, except for the belt, which was hanging on the kitchen wall. When she saw the gash she had cut in his head, she repented and tended to the wound. The only wrapping she could lay hands on in a hurry happened to be the belt, so she wound it a couple of times around his head and buckled it to hold the bandage in place. Well, the crow took up with him right off. At first the man thought it was the blood smell that drew the bird. He tried to brush it away, but it stayed right there on his shoulder, stroking his cheek. Then the missus turned the tables and twitted him with looking like an Indian, for he wasn't very light either. When the wound healed and they took the bandage off, the crow quit the man and took up with the boy, who was wearing the hat.

About three weeks later the boy was out with the crow. All at once it stuck its beak up, sniffed the west wind, and flew away. The whole family grieved over its loss the rest of the day, because they had come to think a lot of it. But about ten the next morning the Sioux caravan pulled in again, and with it the crow, dividing its attention among the whole band. The Indians said the bird had come to them the evening before, about ten miles to the west. But whether it was the crow's keen sense of smell or the strength of the Indian odor that drew him, I don't know.

In this same region there was a freighter who had an educated crow. As his outfit was small, he did his own bull herding. For this he kept a trusty old pony that the crow was fond of. He also had another horse, a better traveler but not so gentle and trusty. At night he picketed his faster horse close at hand and Old Trusty farther from camp, on better grass. The crow stayed with Old Trusty, perched on his hips most of the time.

One night a horse thief came along and took Old Trusty. The crow went along, darting in and pecking the thief at every step. The fellow didn't dare shoot the bird for fear of waking the owner, and when the crow couldn't beat off the thief he flew back to the freighter's bed and scratched at his head until he woke up. Then, by flying toward Old Trusty's picket pin and back again, he finally made the freighter understand that something was wrong. When he went to see, and found the horse gone, he saddled the faster one and followed the crow, which would fly on ahead and then come back, but always heading off in the same direction. The freighter made good time, and about twenty-five miles from camp he came in sight of the thief. He then made a detour and got in front of Old Trusty and his rider, where he laid in wait. When they came along he threw down on him with his rifle and told him to put up his hands.

When the thief saw the crow and how happy it was to be with the old horse, he wanted to know if it really was an educated bird and if it had given him away. The freighter told him that was how it was, and then the fellow said the bird had pestered him all the time he was saddling the horse, and told how, about eight miles back, it had tried to hold him back by flying in his face. Then he admitted that he had finally taken a shot at the crow and was pretty sure he'd gotten a tail feather or two. Sure enough, when the freighter looked at the bird's tail, parts of two feathers were gone.

In 1882 I was sent down on the Running Water by the Grimes and Thornton Company, WG brand, as a rep.[2] I pulled in several days ahead of the start of the roundup, and so laid over at the Hunter, Evans, and Hunter ranch.[3] The wives of David Hunter and Si Funk were visiting at the ranch. The ladies were sisters and had come out from their homes in Kansas City and St. Louis to see what ranch life was like. They were mainly interested in wild and woolly cowboys, so their husbands had delegated Charley Nebo, king of that breed, to entertain them until the roundup started. Charley had been through the Seven Rivers war in New Mexico in 1877,[4] so was well

2. The rep (short for "representative") represents his ranch on the roundup, cutting out cattle belonging to his employer and throwing them back on (returning them to) home range.

3. R. D. Hunter had trailed cattle up from Texas to the Indian agencies in the late sixties. In 1877 he and his brother, David Hunter, along with A. G. Evans, built substantial log cabins and corrals on Deer Creek. He later combined with Evans in a livestock commission firm in Kansas City, and still later, with his brother David as a third partner, located the H3 Bar on the Niobrara at the mouth of Deer Creek. See Nellie Snyder Yost, *The Call of the Range: The Story of the Nebraska Stock Growers Association* (Denver: Sage Books, 1966), pp. 94, 97.

4. Mr. Lemmon is referring here to the Lincoln County, New Mexico, Seven Rivers War of 1877–1878. John Chisum had built up a huge cattle empire on the Pecos River; and when rustlers began to invade his range, Major L. G. Murphy, a former army officer who owned a hotel and a store in Lincoln and also a ranch next to Chisum's, and who was a known enemy of Chisum, was suspect. Murphy was also at odds with an English ranch owner in the area, John Tunstall, who had befriended Billy the Kid Bonney (already a killer) and had given him a job on his ranch. In February, 1878, the politically powerful Murphy sent the county sheriff and twenty armed deputies against Tunstall, killing him and most of his men. Billy the Kid was absent at the time of the attack, but on hearing of Tunstall's death vowed to kill every man who had had a hand in the murder. He is said to have killed nineteen men before he himself was gunned down by Pat Garrett on July 14, 1881. Following the fight in which Tunstall was killed, men on both sides—the Tunstall and Chisum outfits against Murphy's crew—were dry-gulched (ambushed by someone hiding in a dry gulch) and picked off one by one. See Paul I. Wellman, *Glory, God and Gold* (New York: Doubleday, 1954), pp. 368–374; and Dee Brown, *Trail Driving Days* (New York: Charles Scribner's Sons, 1952), pp. 161–167.

qualified for the job. He led off by telling the ladies of his experiences while trailing a herd to Europe. This struck Mrs. Hunter as a little odd, so she said, "But Charley, you would have to cross the Atlantic Ocean to get to Europe." But Charley came right back with "Oh, we didn't take that route at all. We went round by the ridge route."

Next he told how he one time helped gather a herd of two thousand buffalo, which they drove to Kansas City and sold out the same as cattle and reaped a rich profit. According to Charley, this is the way they handled that famous roundup: He said he had often noticed buffalo chewing the bones of both buffalo and cattle. He surmised they did it for the salt they got out of the bones, and so he got to thinking that after the bone pickers had gathered most of the bones off the prairie, the buffalo must be getting pretty hungry for salt. So he figured that by hauling out salt and scattering it, the buffalo could be tolled in. To carry out his scheme, he formed a company of about a dozen men, all to share alike in the profits if the plan worked. They loaded a couple of wagons with salt and started out, driving against the wind so the buffalo could smell the salt, while their outriders circled and herded them in toward the wagon.

They kept this up for eight days, with relays of wagons hauling salt. As this went on, the buffalo got tamer every day, and also somewhat stiff. All this time they held the animals off water, figuring that when they did let them go to water they would fill up and be so logy it would be easy to drive them any place they wanted to. But on the ninth day, just when they were ready for the big roundup, the whole crew took down with smallpox. Of course the buffalo went to water then, and sure enough, they were stiff and tame, but there wasn't a man able to handle them. And by the time the crew got over the smallpox the buffalo had recovered and gone wild again. So Nebo and his crew set out to do the job over. But this time it didn't work, because they only salted the buffalo for seven or eight days. They finally figured out it was the nine-day business that made the difference—that is, eight days on salt and the ninth day on water—for it seemed to work the same as it taking nine days after being exposed to smallpox for a man to break out with it. When they tried it that way again it worked fine, and they gathered their herd and headed for Kansas City, keeping a little salt out all the way to toll the buffalo along.

The company had bought salt from most every town along the way and, as they didn't have much money, charged most of it. After selling the herd for a good price they went on a week's spree. Then they began writing to the Patent Office in Washington to see if they could patent their nine-days idea so no one else could get in on their big discovery. And finally they went back over their trail, paid for the salt, and gathered another herd. By then, of course, they were out of money and had to charge the salt again. They were within about one hundred miles of Kansas City with their second herd when a courier came riding from the stockyards to tell them there'd be no market for their pickled buffalo, since all the users had found the meat so salty they couldn't eat it. By that time Nebo and his crew had run out of credit, too, so they just rode off and left their herd, which settled down in the pasture they were trailing through and wouldn't move until the salt oozed out of them.

After that the buffalo went wild again and started for their winter home in Texas. But the people in the neighborhood rose up and killed them all and sold the hides for enough to settle the damages, except for the salt. The salt creditors then sued and got judgments, which they filed and kept refiling. Because of that Nebo swore the ladies to secrecy, for, he said, those fellows seemed to think he was a part owner of the cattle on the Running Water and might try to collect from him. And that might cause a lot of trouble for the real owners, Hunter, Evans, and Hunter. Nebo also told the women that all during the Seven Rivers war he never touched a sprinkle of salt, as he wanted to be as vicious as the old-time Indians, who never touched salt either. As proof of the softening effect of salt, he said, just look at present-day Indians, the greatest salt eaters of all, who were now being led into willing subjugation by white men.

While in New Mexico, Nebo had been about to marry a promising Mexican girl, but some of John Chisum's Jinglebob peelers[5] had

5. Chisum's outfit was known as the Jinglebob because of their earmark, a split down the ear all the way to the calf's head, so the lower part of the ear hung down like a dangling earring, or "jinglebob." Peelers were the men who broke horses, although the term was sometimes used simply to designate cowboys.

gotten her away from him. After that, he said, he had lined up against the Jinglebob in the Seven Rivers War and tried to pick off all the Jinglebob men he could. Nebo had some bad shin creases, or scars, on his ankle; and when anybody asked about them he said that several times, when he was crawling up on Jinglebob peelers at night, rattlesnakes bit him on the shin. To take care of that, he just slashed out a strip of the bitten flesh and flashed gunpowder in the crease to kill the poison, and that was how he got the notches in his shin.

Furthermore, he told the ladies, he once tried crossing skunks with the little Texas musk hogs, hoping to produce an animal that would supply the Indians with musk to wear around their necks on a cord, such as they all wore to make such a terrible stench that they could eat putrid meat without smelling it. (Indians say they wear the musk bags to ward off sickness.) But dinner was called before Charley had a chance to tell how his experiment turned out, and the ladies never learned the outcome, for Charley had to leave then to go on the roundup.

Another well-known cowboy and cattleman of the Hunter and Evans outfit was Johnny Riggs. Johnny was born in Texas in 1834, but lost his parents when he was only eleven years old. He was then taken in by John Chisum, who taught him how to cowboy. By 1877 Chisum was running thousands of cattle over in New Mexico, where he headquartered his Jinglebob outfit. That same year Chisum sold twenty thousand head of mixed cattle to R. D. Hunter of Kansas City. Riggs helped take the cattle north to Hunter's new range on the Niobrara, at the mouth of Deer Creek, up in Nebraska. Charley Nebo and a one-eyed man, John Graham, also went north with the herds, and all three stayed on the Niobrara with the H3 Bar outfit.

When Sheridan County was organized in 1883, Riggs was appointed its first sheriff. At the first county election he was voted into the office, which he held until 1888. In '83, due to a drouth, a bad prairie fire, and incoming settlers, Hunter and Evans moved their big herds to Montana. Riggs, foreman of the H3 Bar by then, bought the ranch improvements and stayed on the Niobrara. That same year he married Anna Irwin, a sister to Billy and Bennett Irwin of Texas, popular top hands of Newman's N Bar on Antelope Creek. Jim Dahlman[6] was best man and the wedding was in Valentine.

The H3 Bar men, under their leader, One-eyed John Graham, were known as a tough outfit and not to be monkeyed with. Soon after coming to Nebraska, according to Edgar Beecher Bronson's *Reminiscences of a Ranchman*, Graham's outfit had a run-in with some other cowhands in Ogallala. The town marshal and several deputies took a hand, and when it was over two of the H3 Bar men were dead. After that Graham and his men came looking for trouble whenever they hit Ogallala.

The winter before Nebo was set to entertaining Mrs. Hunter and Mrs. Funk with his tall tales, a tragedy took place at the ranch. A nephew of the two ladies, a city-raised boy, had been staying there, and it seemed he now and then got into trouble with One-eyed John. There are different stories about the trouble and the killing that followed. One story I heard was that Graham was a bully who had it in for the boy. One day he missed his hoof-trimmer tools and accused the lad of taking them. He said he was going to kill him for it, but the boy drew first and shot the old man to death.

Another story had it that the boy, being a tenderfoot, was imposed on by the other toughs at the ranch, especially Graham. This went on until the day of February 4, 1881. A card game was going on in the house that day, and both One-eyed John and the boy were sitting in. Others in the room were John Riggs, Charley Nebo, and Wilk Whittaker, the foreman. Graham was bullying the boy as usual, and finally the lad rose up, gun in hand. Graham stood up too, his hand on his gun, but turned part way around where he stood, taking five bullets from the boy's gun in his body, and all without pulling his own gun. As the old man sagged, Riggs caught him in his arms and let him gently down to the floor. At the same time the boy, in a terrible passion, waved his gun and asked, "Any of you fellows want any of this?"

6. James Dahlman, born at Yorktown, Texas, in 1856, went up the Texas trail in 1877 to join a friend on the Newman brothers' N Bar ranch. He spent the rest of his life in Nebraska, serving as sheriff of Dawes County and as mayor of Chadron before going to Omaha, where he was mayor for more than twenty years. See Fred Carey, *Mayor Jim* (Omaha: Omaha Printing Co., 1930).

Then Whittaker stood up, his hand on his gun, and said, "Yes, I'll take some of it." But the tenderfoot, thinking better of his dare, ran out the door and headed for the stable, where he saddled one of the best horses on the ranch and left, never to be seen there again. Nothing was ever done about the killing, but some wondered why John Graham, an expert shot and forewarned besides, let himself be shot down by a city kid.

One explanation I heard was that a man and woman and their little girl were living in the house and Graham, who was very fond of the little girl, was afraid of hitting her, that in swinging himself around as he stood up, he was looking for her. By the time he was sure she was not in the line of fire it was too late. Whether this is true or not, I don't know, but I know I could've had the whole story from John Riggs himself, years ago, if I had been interested then.

Johnny Riggs buried the old man on the top of a bluff about eighty rods northwest of the ranch house and put a fence around the grave. At the head of the mound he set a stout wooden cross, and on it, outlined in brass-headed tacks, he wrote: JOHN GRAHAM DIED FEB. 4, 1881. Old John was buried on the bluff for a strange reason. Not long after the ranch was established, a tall pole was set in the ground on the bluff top, and on dark, stormy nights when any of the men were out, a lighted lantern was hung from its top to guide them home. The light had saved old John's life during a bad snowstorm only a year or so before he was killed. At that time the old cowboy had told his friend, Johnny Riggs, that if he died on the ranch he wanted to be buried at the foot of the pole.[7]

---

7. In 1965, Mrs. Ed Kerns of Rushville, Nebraska, Johnny Riggs's daughter, related the story as she had heard it from her father: The eastern boy had often provoked One-eyed John by borrowing his tools and not putting them back where he got them. On the day that he failed to return the hoof trimmers to Graham's saddlebag, the old man went to the bunkhouse, saw the lad hanging around near the door, and picked up a neckyoke that was leaning against the building. With the stout stick in his hand, he told the boy he'd brain him if he didn't put the trimmers back where they belonged, and that he'd better leave his things alone from now on.

The boy hurried away; and old John went into the cabin, where Riggs, Nebo, and Whittaker were playing cards, and lay down on his bunk to watch the game. Suddenly the boy appeared in the door, a six-shooter in his hand. Without warning he emptied it into John's head, then turned and ran. Johnny Riggs jumped up and turned to catch his friend, at the same time shouting to the others

Later on in the summer of '82 our outfit had two Texas horses stray off into the badlands near Harney Springs, where they went wild. We had tried a good many times to run them down and catch them, with no luck. Then an Indian on Wounded Knee Creek sent word he'd caught the pair and was holding them for a five-dollar reward. At the time I was on my way to the lower end of the range with a herd-camp crew of eight men. Our job was to begin pushing beef cattle west toward the herd camp, where we were to cut out our cattle and shove them north to our own range. We didn't take a roundup wagon along, as we could board at a line camp twelve miles east, where John Bovey [Beauvais] and Antoine Herman, mixed-bloods, were line riding.

John was of the Bovey family that kept the old Bovey Crossing station on the South Platte River. They ran the road ranch there for a good many years. Since it was a place where emigrants held up to get ready to make the crossing of the quicksandy stream, the ranch was a gold mine. I have heard Mother tell that when we stayed there overnight on our way east in '59, she saw Sioux squaws making men's clothing from three-dollar-a-yard broadcloth. The clothes were for their mixed-blood relatives, who later took part in the Custer massacre. Antoine Herman married the oldest daughter of Hank Clifford, a squaw man and early settler on the Medicine (near today's Stockville), down in Nebraska. I am positive that Antoine took part in the Custer massacre, too.

As our work took us into the Wounded Knee neighborhood anyway, I thought it was a good time to try to get my two horses back. So, starting early one morning, I went by the line camp, picked up Antoine for my interpreter, and went on some ten miles to get the horses from the Indian. We got the horses and made it back to the line camp a few minutes after the crew pulled in. The boys were all

to get the boy. But the lad had stationed nearby the fastest horse on the ranch, saddled and bridled, ready to go; and by the time the others had recovered from their stunned surprise and got outside, he was already out of gun range. He was never apprehended, and nothing was done about the murder.

More than half a century after the killing, the weathered headboard was found, on its face, on the bluff top where the lantern pole had once stood. Although nearly all the tacks were gone, the inscription was still legible. The headboard is now in the Rushville museum.

sitting around, waiting for supper, and Bovey was mad because Antoine had gone with me and left all the work for him to do. When we rode up he came out and lit in to cussing Herman, who jumped off his horse, jerked out his gun, and pulled off a few shots at him. Bovey broke and ran for the camp shack, but Herman was right after him, crowding him so close he couldn't take time to dodge through the door until the second time around the shack. That time he dived in and grabbed his rifle off the gun rack.

By then I figured I'd better take a hand and try to stop a killing, as I was, in a way, to blame. I jumped off my horse and ran in after Bovey, and was just in time to grab him and the rifle. At the same time I yelled at the others to disarm Herman. While all this was going on, my throw-back partner, Ed Grey, was about to bust his sides laughing. But he managed to help, and we soon settled Herman and Bovey down a little, though we had to keep a close watch on them for the rest of the trip; and afterward we had to take one of them away from the camp.

One of the horses we got back was a gray we called Glasgow. A little later he threw a Mexican, who had a new fifty-five-dollar saddle on him, and got away into the badlands again. About a year later I heard that a horse outfit trailing east with a bunch of horses to sell found him near Harney Springs with the saddle under his belly. They caught and sold him with the rest of their bunch, but kept the saddle, of course.

<h1 style="text-align:center">XI</h1>

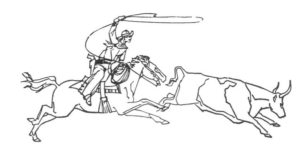

<h2 style="text-align:center">COWPUNCHING IN THE EIGHTIES</h2>

T HE NEXT YEAR, 1883, I was wagon boss for the WG under Hugh Adair, the general manager. Now Adair was all you could ask for as a cowman, but he couldn't handle or control men. And we had a bunch of men that year that needed a strong hand at the top. This came about because we had just consolidated four strong outfits that each had a couple of top hands. These fellows had filed on valuable claims where the ranch headquarters were located. As none of the claims were yet patented, they were in a mighty independent position, for their claims were needed by the WG owners, Grimes and Thornton, in the profitable handling of the outfit as a whole.

When Dave Clark, the office manager, saw that Adair couldn't manage these men, he came to me and asked if I would take them into my crew, one at a time, until I had them all. I already had a pair of the same kind in my outfit, so when I got the others I had eight. After shaping up my crew with those boys, only my horse wrangler and my cook, Isaac Miller, had not gotten their man or men. But man! what cowpunchers they were. I was then shipping from Valentine, Nebraska, and when I went to pen a bunch of beeves the other outfits and inspector Jim Dahlman just looked on in open-

[136]

mouthed admiration. One day Jim said to me, "If I had a crew like that I wouldn't mind going to South America." Going to South America was the big talk in the cattle country about then.

The leader of that bunch of cowboys was Bill Boggs, a Texan and the best cowboy I ever saw. Bill was transferred to me from the Moore and Allen L7 division. His town horse was Circle A Ben, a big bay of great speed and staying power. I won't try to tell of this bunch's high jinks in the towns, but will just say they were all fond of booze and painted dance hall women, and Valentine and Rapid City were then overflowing with both.

That same year my WG outfit delivered 4,750 steers to the Western Ranches Company. John Clay was manager of that outfit and Billie Moses was range manager. Delivery was made near where the Middle Creek stockyards now stand. On our return trips we always stopped overnight at Scoop Town (Sturgis) and took in the shows.

At that time Maude S and her tomboy dance were the big thing. Maude S was an octoroon, but her Negro blood didn't show. She had a perfect figure and could cut a pigeon wing in mid-air. She was just the best buck-and-wing or tomboy dancer I ever saw. She was finally asked to go to Chicago. From there she went to New York, and then to Europe, where, I've been told, she was applauded as the greatest in her line and was even called on to perform for royalty. When she was dancing at Scoop Town her audience was mostly cow punchers, bull whackers, mule skinners, miners, gamblers, and soldiers, both black and white. All appreciated her and showered down the tips in proportion to their earnings. The Hill brothers, gamblers of her color, followed her career and later told me that Maude S, even after her shows in Europe, said that her happiest days were spent in old Scoop Town.

I spent a part of that summer cutting trail herds on the Belle Fourche River in Dakota Territory. Most of the cattle in these herds had been shipped up to Orin Junction, the end of the railroad in Wyoming, and then trailed on north to the ranges, which were filling up fast with Texas cattle.

Texas had passed a law that any outfit driving a herd made up of several different brands had to use a registered road brand if it was taking the cattle out of the state. So it became the duty of brand inspectors to cut out and take over any cattle not wearing the outfit's road brand. This caused a lot of trouble. A good many times I had to cut big, fat steers out of these trail herds. The trail hands usually offered objections, as they had planned to butcher that same steer at their next camp. Quite a few unpleasant arguments arose over little matters like that. Brand inspectors had to be stationed at the Red River Crossing, at Wichita, Kansas, and then, as the trail moved farther west, at Doane's Crossing, Dodge City, and finally at Ogallala, where Dick Head was inspector for quite a while.

When stray steers, picked up from ranges the herds traveled through, got into the herds, they were sometimes mighty hard to cut out, and when you got them out they sometimes wouldn't stay out. When I was working trail herds, if a steer I had cut out kept joining up with the herd again, I would, after two or three times, rope and throw him and run sand in his eyes to blind him for a little while. Then I'd wait to see what he'd do. If he still went back in the herd or joined up with the next one that came along (as often happened the next day after I'd sanded his eyes), I would rope and throw him again and tie a knot in his tail. Then I'd wrap his knotted tail around one of his hind legs above the hock and run the split hoof on the other foot into the tail above the knot. I'd leave him like that until the trail herd had gone on, and sometimes for a couple of days longer, before I turned him loose. Fixed up like that, he could hobble along and graze but couldn't travel fast enough to keep up with a herd.

One instance of steers taking up with herds they didn't belong to came about in the spring of '81. A three-year-old steer from my outfit had strayed into the town of Rockerville, South Dakota, where he took up with the town herd of milk cows. He finally, after a fashion, took charge of the town, causing a fellow by the name of Pat Dillon to send me word that the steer had to be gotten out of town —or else he'd be made into mincemeat. So I fared forth to save the steer. After roping and putting a bosal, or halter, on him, I had Pat take his tail, and in a manner, twist him out of town about five miles. By then he was well halter broke, so a little farther on I turned him loose in Frank McMahon's herd on Spring Creek.

Another time, while cutting an agency issue of cattle, I came to the

White River and found it booming and full of ice. The ranch hands had been using an ice gorge about two hundred yards from the ranch house as a bridge. They told me it was safe and I rode onto it, but halfway across a cake of ice turned edgewise and my horse and I both went down. We didn't quite go clear under, since under-jam ice held us up enough that our heads were above water. The boys at the ranch saw me, and the horse struggling beside me, and ran down to toss me a rope. After they pulled me out they threw several ropes on my horse and pulled him out.

From a general description of a man who cuts trail herds and one who fills the job of stock inspector, it might seem that both had about the same job, but such is not the case. In those open-range days ranchmen always kept a sharp lookout for passing herds. One day, after cutting a trail herd on the Little Powder River in Montana Territory in 1889, I rode back to the home ranch (Scott and Hanks), at the mouth of the Little Powder. There I was told that another trail herd had passed down the Big Powder that same day, so I struck right out. I overtook the herd the next day about five miles below Powderville, on the Powder.

The crew was eating dinner when I rode into camp. When I told the foreman I was there to cut the herd, he asked me to wait until after dinner, when he'd put the herd on the trail again. We finished eating and rode out to relieve the four men on herd. They went to camp to dinner, but hadn't been gone long when one of them came walking back to tell the foreman that one of the boys in camp had killed the cook, then turned all the other horses loose and lit out for Canada on his own horse. The foreman turned to me and asked if I was a stock inspector. I told him I wasn't, that I was only cutting trail herds. If I had been an inspector I could have gone after the killer, but as it was I could not leave my job to follow him. I gave him the name of the inspector stationed at Powderville, Billy Caffee. The foreman rode over there and told Caffee of the killing. The inspector headed right out on the killer's trail, overtook him before he got to Canada, and brought him back to Miles City, Montana, where he stood trial and was sent to the pen.

A trail-herd cutter only had to work in the summer, when herds were on the move, but an inspector had to go any time he was called.

[139]

One winter in the Black Hills country, the South Dakota stock inspector sent to Wyoming for Joe Lefors [1] and another man. He wanted them to come over and help him run down and arrest some cattle thieves that were operating between the Belle Fourche and Cheyenne rivers. It was the dead of winter, and cold. By the time they were ready to go, a full-blown blizzard was raging, but the three of them started out on horseback, for no matter what the weather, the stock detective stayed on the job when needed. However, the blizzard was so fierce that the men got lost. They finally quit their horses and went on afoot until, played out and at the point of freezing to death, they stumbled onto a schoolhouse. Even then, because their hands were so numb, they almost didn't get a fire going so they could thaw out. As soon as the storm blew over, they found their horses at a ranch, where the poor beasts had taken shelter. Then they went on, caught up with the thieves, brought them in, and saw to it that they were sent to the pen.

It was Joe Lefors and his deputy inspectors who went into the Jackson Hole country on the Snake River and broke up some outlaw gangs that made that country their hiding place. Jackson Hole, in Lincoln County, Wyoming, just south of Yellowstone Park, got its name from Teton Jackson, the notorious outlaw who made the Hole his hideout. The Hole is completely surrounded by high mountains and can only be gotten into by a narrow road along a stream at one end. Teton Jackson had his ranch in there, and rustlers and other men of his kind would head for the Hole when law officers were after them. It shows you the kind of officers that were connected with the Stock Growers Association, when they'd go into such a dangerous place and clean it out.

When we began shipping from Valentine in 1883, the town stood at the western end of the tracks of the Fremont, Elkhorn and Missouri Valley Railroad, now part of the Northwestern. While I had already met some of the men I want to name here, it was in Valentine that I came to know them well. They were Jim Dahlman, Johnny Smith, Billy Carter, Lank and Johnny Keyes, Johnny Pierce, Tom

1. Joe Lefors, a Wyoming stock detective, later became a U.S. deputy marshal.

Allen, Jess Donaldson, Maut Eberly, and Archie Riordan. Some of these men are mentioned in almost any frontier history of this country. All were fairly well educated; all but Donaldson and Riordan were from Texas; and all had killed their men. I don't know of Riordan's killing but three men, so I concluded to have him tail the list.

Jim Dahlman was the leader of the bunch, but I didn't always know him as Dahlman. Down in Texas, along about 1875, he killed his brother-in-law for mistreating his wife, who was Jim's sister. He had warned the man he would kill him on sight, and he did, after giving him the first shot. Jim had then pulled out for the north under the name of Jim Murray, but when he wanted to get married in '83, he had to go back to Texas and get the indictment quashed so he could get married under his right name. I sold him many hundreds of dry cows when he ranched near Chadron, Nebraska, before he went down to Omaha to be the mayor there for twenty-one years.

I've already told how Billy Carter came to the Mabry outfit on the Niobrara after his long run from a lynching mob in Rawlins Springs. When the railroad got to Valentine, Billy went into a saloon and gambling house there and developed into one of the greatest and squarest saloon and gambling-house men of the West. When the railroad built on, he followed it, opening houses in Chadron, Hot Springs, and then Deadwood, all of them named The Bodega.

He got married while he lived in Valentine. A fellow named Hamlin, an Association inspector, married his wife's sister, but was abusive to her. One day Billy and his friend, Johnny Smith, rode out to meet Hamlin, who was riding in from the stockyards where he inspected cattle. Billy ordered him to get out of the country, but Hamlin drew his gun and began shooting, so Billy and Smith had to kill him. Smith took the blame and left the country, and Billy, though he stood trial, was acquitted. He was a fine fellow and I don't believe he ever pulled a really crooked deal in his life, for men of his nerve don't stoop to low tricks. I never heard what became of Johnny Smith.

Tom Allen went into business in Valentine, too, and was still there in the 1930's, but under his right name, which wasn't Tom Allen. He, too, had to get an indictment for something quashed so he could get married. I never knew what became of Lank and Johnny Keyes, or of Jess Donaldson. Jess was one of the first road ranch and station keepers on the South Platte River, near the old American Ranch that was run by John Morris, back in the late 1850's.

Early in the spring of 1886, Ed Grey and I set out with a string of horses for an Indian herd camp on the far bank of the White River, where we were to get in on an Indian roundup and cut and throw back any of our cattle that might be there. We knew we'd find the river swimming, so we stopped about five miles back, in a natural corral, and changed to our best swimming horses. When we got to the river we found it not only swimming, but full of slush ice as well. The herd camp was just across the river, so we took our bed pack off the pack horse (so the bedroll wouldn't soak up water and drown the horse) and took off all our outer clothes, even though it was plenty cold. Then we pushed our horse herd into the river and followed on our own mounts.

Our saddle horses were sweaty from prancing five miles behind the string of loose horses, and they chilled as soon as they hit the icy water. This made them go to plunging and trying to reach the bottom with their feet, and we had to get off. But the way they were tearing around in that deep water we couldn't even keep hold of their tails, and as soon as we let go of them they turned back for the bank we had just left. There was nothing for us to do but follow them. But when they reached the edge, they tried to climb out over a cut bank that was too high for them; and before we could get hold of them they turned again and followed after the loose horse herd, swimming back across the river. So we were climbing up the high bank on our side about the time the whole horse bunch was trailing out on the far bank where the Indians were waiting.

Ed and I took our pack rope off our bedroll and made ourselves a light raft by roping small logs together, and by the time we had it finished we were almost frozen stiff. Then Grey lay down on the raft and crooked his left arm over a limb that stuck up from a log, and I lay flat on my stomach in a crook in the logs, and we pushed off. We were about halfway across when Ed began squealing like a stuck pig. I thought he was just scared and paid no attention to him. When we were within forty feet of the bank, the herd camp boys tossed me a rope and drug our raft ashore. And they found that Grey had cramps and couldn't let go of the log his arm was hooked around. That was probably all that saved his life—otherwise he'd likely have rolled off the pitching raft—and they had to drag me off and roll me around a while to get my blood running so I could stand up again. After that, Ed said he'd stay all summer on that side of the river rather than swim it again, but I'd swum it so many times already that it was sort of a joke to me.

I remember that Ben Arnold had quite an experience with an icy river, too. I first met Ben on the general roundup on the North Platte River, northwest of Ogallala, in 1877. He was helping get together a stock of Captain Kaufman's range cattle to be moved to the Niobrara, about sixty miles west of the Missouri. In my first talk with him I learned that we had, in a way, been neighbors on the Ben Holladay stage line.

Born Ben Connor in Ohio in 1844, he had come west by way of Leavenworth, Kansas, to Kearney in 1861. His first marriage was to an Indian woman. They had a daughter, Marcella, in 1867. Then the Indian wife deserted Ben for a man of her own tribe. In 1877 Ben took unto himself a white wife, Florence Grandon. Florence, a brilliant woman, was a trained nurse and an undertaker, too, when necessary. She died in 1912, never knowing she had lived all her married life with a man going under a name not his own. And therein lies a story.

Ben had been a soldier, serving two enlistments, the first in the Civil War, the second as guide, scout, courier, and occasionally as cowboy and wood contractor around the forts, mostly between Fort Kearny, Fort McPherson, and Fort Sedgwick. At the end of the War between the States many Confederate soldiers were taken into the Northern army, though their defeat still rankled in their systems. One night near Fort McPherson, Ben overheard a bunch of the Confederates planning to mutiny and seize the fort, which they intended to use as a base for plundering. The leader was a man named Crawford.

[143]

So Ben Connor, to keep his sworn oath to support the Constitution of the United States, went to Phil Sheridan, the commander of the Department of the Platte, and told him what he'd heard. As a result, Crawford was arrested and lodged in the guardhouse. A short time later Ben was sent to deliver a message to a camp at the place where Fort Casper was later located. There he was told that Crawford had been turned loose and was right then in the same garrison, threatening to kill him on sight. Now Ben was still only a stripling of a boy, while Crawford, a desperate fellow, had already killed several men. So Ben decided to go elsewhere, and fast. At his first night's stop someone asked his name and he gave the first one that popped into his head—Arnold.

Ben's first work as a cowboy was delivering beeves to the Indian agencies. In the course of this work he often had to help swim herds across the Moreau River among floating ice cakes. Beeves issued the first of October were supposed to last until the first of the next July, but because of pilfering by the agents and other agency employees, or because of winter storm losses, they were usually gone by the first of March. In which case the contractors had to furnish more, no matter what the weather or other circumstances.

At one such time, Ben and the others were making a delivery at Fort Union during a spring thaw when the river ice unexpectedly broke up at night and the water rose. The crew was bedded down in two log cabins, sound asleep, and the roar of the breaking ice rousted them out in a hurry. The cabins were already surrounded by deep water and big ice chunks, so they grabbed a few cans of tomatoes and peaches and got up on the roofs. They had to stay there four days, with ice churning all around them, before boats came from Fort Union to take them off.

In 1872 Ben was sent out from Fort Fetterman with a scouting party. They stopped at a post hay camp, about twelve miles northeast of the fort, and there found the six-man crew dead and scalped. The work stock had been run off, so Ben and his men took the trail and overhauled the raiders. The Indians had the hay, the stock, and forty or fifty head of range horses belonging to the Janis brothers, but of course they abandoned all the loot and got away. When Ben was telling me this last story, he seemed to think the Indians had stolen the Janis horses, too, but I don't think so. The Janises were both married to Sioux women, and the oldest daughter of one of the brothers was married to one of Red Cloud's leading war chiefs, John Richaud.[2] Years later, both Nick[3] and Antoine Janis told me the Indians had never bothered their horses or cattle, so I believe those Indians Ben was telling about had just run onto that bunch of horses a long way from their home range, and were only heading them back toward where they belonged.

And I'd like to say here that, from what I knew of the ill feeling Confederate soldiers held for the North after the Civil War, I have no doubt but what Ben Arnold's warning to Sheridan, back there at Fort McPherson, saved the government millions of dollars. Yet when Ben was old, disabled, and in need and applied for a pension, it was denied him. He had no trouble proving his identity and his two enlistments in the army; but because of his desertion to save his life at the time he changed his name, his application was thrown out.

Ben, however, left many fine descendants. Marcella, his half-Indian daughter, was married three times. First to a white man, then to a mixed-blood, and then to a full-blood Indian. Her first husband's name was Hanley. They had a son, George, and a daughter, Helen. George married Gertie Duncan, a mixed-blood. Helen Hanley, one of the brightest girls ever in the schools at Lemmon, South Dakota, later went to Washington state and married well.

Marcella's second marriage was to a man named Ankle, a member of the Flyingby Indian family. Their son Henry gained the respect and admiration of the whites as well as the Sioux in World War I, where he earned more medals than any other mixed-blood. When he came home a council was called in his honor and he was elected war

---

2. James C. Olson writes in *Red Cloud and the Sioux Problem* (Lincoln: University of Nebraska Press, 1965), pp. 87–88, that John Richard, Jr., the mixed-blood son of the old Sioux trader, took refuge with Red Cloud's band after killing a corporal at Fort Fetterman in September, 1869. He adds that the reports that Richard tried to unite the northern tribes in warfare against the United States were probably not true.

3. Nick Janis, formerly an American Fur Company trader, had served as a government interpreter and scout and was with the Powder River Expedition of 1865. His wife was a Brulé Sioux. (Luther North, *Man of the Plains: Recollections of Luther North, 1856–1882* [Lincoln: University of Nebraska Press, 1961], p. 61 n.)

chief of the Sioux nation. But it was an empty honor, as there were no longer any warpaths to follow. Henry later married Ethel Many-goods, of the Sioux aristocracy. The five children born to Ben and Florence did well, too, growing up to be descendants to be proud of, men and women who did much to help develop the West.

After we moved up into Perkins County, one of my neighbors was Abe Jones. With his brother Dave, Abe located in Slim Buttes, over in Harding County, in 1886. Abe came from Yankton to Bismarck with General Custer's command in 1874, hoping to get his teams in with Custer's first expedition to the Black Hills. But the command used only government teams that trip, and hired no citizen teams. On his second trip to the Black Hills and on to the Little Big Horn, Custer used many citizen teams; and Dave went with the expedition, taking all the Jones teams, but Abe stayed in the Hills.

On Abe's first trip from Bismarck to Deadwood he traveled with a mixed train of immigrants and freighters, twenty-eight wagons altogether. Most of the freighters had trail wagons, too, but the immigrants had only single wagons. Some drove oxen, some mules, and some horses. Those with mules and horses objected to following the oxen, but before the round trip back to Bismarck was finished, many of the horses were dead by the side of the road and the oxen were coming in in the lead. The train had outriders in both the lead and the rear, and as they neared the Black Hills, where Indians were thick, they were ever on the alert. They made the trip all right, though, and back again, and pulled into Bismarck on the same morning that a boat came into Fort Lincoln, across the river, with the news of Custer's massacre.

When Dave and Abe first located in Slim Buttes, the only neighbors they had were Bill and Horace Stevenson, who came the same year. It was several years before they had any other neighbors, and they all had to get their mail at Macy, fifty miles away. At that time game was plentiful and there were fine springs and plenty of wood. All this attracted big encampments of Sioux, especially to a spot along the foothills north of the Jones ranch. Their many tents, lined up along the hills, made a never-to-be-forgotten sight. The Indians all seemed friendly, but Abe was never quite sure but what their savage nature might break out.

A white man by the name of Bill Quigley came back with Abe on one of his trips from the Hills. Bill had lived much of his life with the Indians and could speak their language well. While he was staying with Jones, an encampment of Indians moved in along the foothills. The two men went over to the camp, and Bill began visiting with the Indians in their own tongue. Then the Indians brought out a roll of paper that had all the important happenings of their tribal life recorded on it in pictures. They reckoned time by moons, and one part of the record told of the Crow Butte battle between the Sioux and the Crows. That battleground was about thirty miles west of the Jones ranch. The picture showed all the Crow braves scattered around dead on the ground, but the Sioux warriors were all standing, holding their guns and bows and arrows. That was stretching it quite a lot, even though the fight did end in a big victory for the Sioux.

The day they visited the camp, the Indians were planning a big feast for the next day. Abe and Bill were invited, and Bill said to Abe, "Now don't promise to come unless you mean it, because not keeping your promise is an insult to an Indian." They went on walking around the camp, and pretty soon they saw a big black dog hanging up. The dog had been dead so long it was about ready to fall apart, and Abe asked Bill if that was the dog the Indians were going to feed them. Bill said it was, and Abe told him, "Well, I sure couldn't eat that, or anything else here."

Bill told him if he came he'd have to eat it, and he couldn't just mince around with it, either. Abe said he couldn't do it, so Bill told him he'd have to tell the Indians he was leaving for the Black Hills the next morning, and then do it. So that was what he did. Long afterward, Abe said to me, "To this day I can't understand why old stale dog soup was considered a delicacy by an Indian when he had all kinds of fresh game around."

Along in the summer of '88 or '89 a young fellow named Woods, a brother-in-law to Carrol Smith, the Hot Springs banker, went with me to Wendover, Wyoming, to receive some beeves topped from Indian issue cattle of the A. P. Samples Company, which belonged to Senator Powers of Montana. His name could not appear on the company roll, as a senator could not approve contracts okayed by the government in his district, and Senator Powers' district covered the Dakotas, Wyoming, and Montana.

We took the stage at Lusk, Wyoming, and were due to reach Wendover late that evening, but there were some delays and it was getting dark when we hit the bluff of the North Platte River, a few miles out of Wendover. The graded roadway along the bluff was some two hundred feet above the river and so narrow there were only a few places wide enough for two rigs to pass. Among the passengers on the stage were two ladies and four men. All of us men carried six-shooters. We were traveling right along when we rounded a sharp bend in the road, right onto a big grizzly bear that reared up on his haunches square in our path. The horses squealed and sat back on their own haunches, at the same time spreading out fanwise all across the road and trembling like leaves. The women began to scream and cavort around in the stage, and all four of us men jumped out and pulled our guns.

The driver yelled at us not to shoot. We'd only wound the bear, he said, and then it would charge, in which case the team and the stage, with the screaming women inside, would all go over the cliff. I told him I could shoot an eye out of the bear at that distance, a scant thirty steps. The driver said likely I could, but the bear had two eyes and if wounded or mad he wouldn't even miss one of them. So I didn't get a chance to display my marksmanship and bravery before the ladies, but had to be satisfied with yelling at the bear and then laughing at the whole setup. For I wasn't afraid of that bear. The winter that I looked after that bunch of horses and mules in Chalk Bluffs, Wyoming, when I was thirteen years old, I had lived in a nest of them. A good many times I chased them out of my herd, where they laid in wait to slash at a horse's flanks to hamstring him. And out of that band of nearly a hundred horses I hadn't lost a single one in the five or six months I was there with them.

Well, our bear finally lumbered off up the mountain. But before we got back in the stage I heard one of the ladies say she believed those leather-pants-dressed cowboys were actually bloodthirsty and had enjoyed seeing them so frightened. I was wearing my chaps, all right, since I was getting out of the stage and onto a horse as soon as we pulled into Wendover.

XII

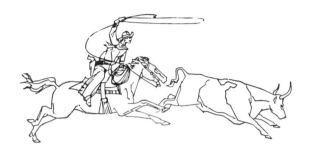

WOUNDED KNEE

IN THE MONTHS just before the Wounded Knee battle of 1890 the whole country was unsettled and uneasy. The whites were afraid of the Indians, who were coming in from the whole northwest; and the Indians were afraid of what the whites might be planning to do to them. The Home Guards had been organized and armed and patrols were out most of the time, checking on Indian movements.[1] I had been called to the Home Guard front several times, and most

---

1. In the autumn of 1890 many of the reservation Indians of northwestern Nebraska and southwestern South Dakota, demoralized by their desperate economic plight, joined the Ghost Dance movement, a religious movement which had originated among the Indians farther west and which preached the coming of a messiah to drive out the white man and restore the bison to the plains.

B. J. Petersen, an early resident of Rushville, wrote: "The 'Indian Scare,' as it was called, brought many interesting events in 1890 and 1891. . . . Each of the towns of Gordon, Rushville, and Hay Springs had organized a company of militia who were furnished arms and ammunition by the government. A captain among their number was chosen and they would get out every day for a little drill and target practice." (Quoted in Charley O'Kieffe, *Western Story: The Recollections of Charley O'Kieffe, 1884–1898* [Lincoln: University of Nebraska Press 1960], p. 216.)

of what I saw at such times convinced me that the Indians were only trying to get more liberal issues of rations, as their beef rations and other supplies had been cut to starvation size. For by this time there were hundreds of educated young men among the tribes, who knew the size and strength of the government troops and would advise against starting any kind of warfare.

So I didn't believe the Indians were hostile at all, and I thought if I could talk to some of my friends among them I could help bring about an understanding and quiet things down. One day I rode out alone on a very fast horse, in case I met some Indians I didn't know, and had reached a point four miles southeast of Major Wells' camp at the mouth of French Creek. From there I looked across Cedar Creek to the east and saw about a dozen Home Guards. I crossed over to them. One was a second lieutenant, another was M. H. Day, Lieutenant Governor, who had financed the arms and ammunition for the Guards. All of the party was busy watching Indians through field glasses.

For some time the Indians had been gathering on a wide flat between the Cheyenne and White rivers. The flat, some twelve miles southeast of the mouth of Battle Creek, is now known as Cuny Table. The place where I met the Guards was about eight miles from the flat, and through the glasses we could see the Indians breaking and training war horses, hundreds of them, and most of them stolen from nearby horse ranches. Then all at once flashes from signal looking glasses began striking us right in the eyes. Indian lookouts as far as three or four miles away were hitting us square in the eyes, as easy as you would swat a fly, and the flashes were coming from all around us.

This upset that little bunch of Home Guards so much that Day said we'd better head for the river and soldier protection. I tried to tell him that we were in a fine position to stand an attack, that we were well armed with long-range rifles and had plenty of ammunition, and that the Indians couldn't cut us off from the river anyway. So why not stay and see what the braves might try? But the Guards would have none of it, and we were soon on our way to the Cheyenne River and soldier protection. I met Day in Rapid City a few months later, and he said to me, before an audience, "We certainly showed them Indians on the Cheyenne River a thing or two, didn't we?" "Yes," I said, "we showed them how we could use our quirts."

Soldiers and troopers were thrown all around the Indian reservation in a loose cordon, with troop camps from ten to twenty miles apart. Wherever possible these camps were off the reservation, and the troops had strict orders to stay off, too, but the orders were often disobeyed by both the troopers and the Guards. One day Third Lieutenant Byron asked Major Wells for permission to reconnoiter with a dozen men. With Gus Haaser as guide, they went out toward the west end of Cuny Table. Byron wanted to see if he could get cannon within range of the Indian village, out there on the flat. On the way back they came onto a small band of Indians. Byron and his men intentionally cut the band off from their own village and killed them all. If this had been known at headquarters it would have been a court-martial case, so it was kept a secret.

Later on that fall I was down in Nebraska grain-feeding some steers that had been left on my hands after a season of peddling feeders we had bought in the Black Hills region and shipped to Hastings. I had left quite a lot of horses in a pasture on Lame Johnny Creek, and when I heard that Sitting Bull had been killed on December 15 I thought I'd better hurry back up there and see about them. When I got off the train at Buffalo Gap, one of the first men I met was Sam Sheffield. Our manager, Dave Clark, was in Florida that winter and Sam was, in a way, in charge. I asked him if he had moved their horses yet, and he said no, that he didn't intend to get scared until he was hurt. "After you're hurt is a poor time to get scared, when it comes to horses to handle your cattle," I told him.

I had been with the company on the Platte when the outfit was almost set afoot by Indians one time. They had had to go into Kansas City and buy clumsy American horses at the market there, so now I told Sam that if he didn't move the horses I would have to wire Dave. That brought him to life in a hurry, and he started right out to the ranch. But Dave, pretty sure there was going to be trouble, had left a letter with Eugene Holcomb, a neighbor, which was to be sent to the ranch whenever he thought it was unsafe for the horses

[151]

to be out there. Dave had even made arrangements with George Shingles for horse pasture on his Willow Creek ranch, so about twenty miles from the Shingles ranch Sam met the horses coming in.

I was also told, there in Buffalo Gap, that a day or two earlier seven of my old cowboys—Sam Bell, L. C. Peck, Gus Haaser, Alex Webb, Shorty West, Ike Miller, and F. M. Warren—had been set afoot by the Sioux. They were all staying at one of my old ranches and had spent the day scouting and rounding up all the horses they could find. In the evening, while they were in the cabin getting supper, some pussyfoot Indians stole up and got away with every-thing—horses, saddles, and all.

With Bill Lindsey and Ed Cole to help me, I went to the Lame Johnny pasture and got six or seven saddle horses. I had picked up a few saddles on the way, and with this outfit we headed for Bell's place at the mouth of French Creek. We pulled in at noon and found the company of cavalry from Fort Meade, under Major Wells, stationed there. Everybody seemed to be at dinner, and we were sure ready for ours. We jerked the bridles off our horses and turned them into the corral, where there was a big bunch of horses, including five, like ours, with saddles on.

We had barely got inside the ranch-house door when the Major came running from his camp, stuck his head in through the open kitchen window, and yelled at Sam to have everybody with saddled horses mount and ride for the Jack Daly ranch, four and a half miles below, where Indians were attacking the government hay haulers. A trooper had just come for help, he said, and he and his cavalry would follow as soon as they could saddle up. The eight of us that were saddled jumped on our horses and headed for the Table. But when we got there it was about over. It turned out that, unknown to the hay haulers, a troop of Home Guards under Eugene Aiken had been hid in the house and stable, behind trees, and under cut banks. One of the Guards, Neal Dennis, was stationed on a high place to the north with field glasses and a looking glass. He was to watch for Indians, and if he saw any to signal the hidden Guards with the looking glass.

The first of the three teams of hay haulers had just pulled into the hay corral when a shot from an Indian rifle, fired from a high point to the south, struck the ground between the leaders' heads. The dust flew and the horses sat back on their haunches. At the same time a big body of mounted Sioux braves dashed out of the timber south of the ranch—and that was when one of the dozen Home Guards went pell-mell for help. It was said afterward that Charlie Edgerton, one of the Guards, had spoiled a good fight by being in too much of a hurry. Charlie was hiding behind a big down cottonwood, some distance to the east of the others, where he had a plain view of the corral gate. He saw the lead Indian first, just as he was riding through the pasture gate next to the corner of the hay corral, and pulled off a shot. The gate was already down, and when the bullet struck the Indian his pony lunged ahead into the pasture and the Indian fell off in the gate. Two other mounted Indians scooped him up and rode for the shelter of the timber.

A few more shots were traded between the Guards and the Indians, who were heading for thicker timber near the Cheyenne River. Neal Dennis, the lookout man, said he saw at least two more Indians shot off their horses, but both were scooped up and carried away. A third Indian was shot out of the saddle, but his foot caught in the stirrup as he fell and the horse (probably a cowman's horse and not used to the Indian smell) ran downstream about two hundred yards, kicking the Indian's head every jump. When the running horse came to a gulch, he turned up it and got away, but Dennis said the Indian must have been dead long before that.

There had been several skirmishes at the Daly-Torkelson ranch during that spell of Indian trouble, and Frawley Sprague, Aiken's first lieutenant in the Guards, pulled the most daring stunts of all before the uprising was put down. But Frawley was a little on the loudmouthed order, and in my opinion his quiet brother, Vest, was the best frontiersman of the two. Their old father was a great hunter of the mountain regions. He was the one who first told me of the ibex that ranged in the badlands south of Battle Creek in South Dakota.

After the fight, Major Wells and his troops headed for the agency, and the boys who had lost their horses went along to identify and claim their stolen property. But the Wounded Knee battle came on before they got there, and they all stopped off at General Brooke's [2] camp at Wells' place on White River. All but Ike Miller, my old cook, that is. Ike wouldn't take the Indian trouble seriously, and said he was going on to the agency anyway. Wells and all his friends tried to stop him, but he went on alone.

It was only twenty-five miles, most of the way up White Clay Creek. About twelve miles above Wells' place was the Half Way camp, used by outfits moving issue herds to the agency. The camp was run by a squaw man, who was not at home when Ike got there. His Indian wife told Ike the No Water band was camped a few miles farther on and was dancing the ghost dance every night. She knew the Indians would not let him pass, and tried to get him to stay at the camp. When she saw that he meant to go on anyway, she managed to lock him up in a room. He promised her he wouldn't go any farther if she'd let him out, so she did, and he saddled up as quick as he could and lit out. He rode right into No Water's camp and they shot him down, breaking his back. He laid where he fell for three days, and finally died of thirst and exposure, it being December and very cold.

Now to go back a little. When the Flying V horses had been safely landed at Shingles' ranch, just after the middle of December, Lon Ayres and the cook, Red Johnson, were put to looking after them, herding them by day and corralling them at night. Most of the time the bunch grazed on range where there were some big boulders, some as large as cabins. One afternoon when Lon and Red went out to round up the horses they saw some Indians up among the boulders. The boys stayed out of rifle range and finally got most of their horses headed for home on the run. As the country was already all upset over what looked like an upcoming Indian uprising, their news of Indians in the rocks spread like wildfire.

The Indians moved on toward Alkali Creek and headed for the agency, but the next day a posse made up of three Culbertsons, two Julifs, and maybe some others crawled up on their camp and began cannonading it. When the battle ended only one old squaw was left

2. Brigadier General John R. Brooke, commander of the Department of the Platte.

alive. She reached the agency several days later, traveling the whole hundred miles without being seen. The boys who shot the Indians were tried for the killings, but it was proved that by then war had practically been declared between the Indians and our government. So even though that Few Tails band of Indians was out under a permit to hunt, and hadn't even heard of the Indian uprising, the boys were acquitted.

By then everybody was so uneasy that all settlers were ordered to go to the settlements for protection. But before the Jones brothers and their neighbors could move out, four companies of cavalry under Captain Howard came from Fort Yates and headquartered at the Jones' ranch in Harding County. The soldiers made good use of J. B. Hill, or Castle Rock, on the rim just south of the ranch buildings, for the rock served as a lookout and they could see the country for miles around with high-powered field glasses. The cavalry stayed all winter, protecting isolated settlers and turning back to the reservation any Indians who tried to leave.

The battle of Wounded Knee came off on December 29, and as near as I could find out, it happened this way: A rumor had reached officers' headquarters that a large band of Indians under Big Foot had left the Cheyenne agency to join the big camp on Cuny Table. Colonel Forsyth was then dispatched to head them off and bring them back to the agency. His troops cut them off somewhere along the lower Cheyenne River but did not try to disarm them. When Forsyth and his men, with the Indians, reached the Bartlett store on Wounded Knee, about twenty-five miles from the agency, Forsyth sent a courier on to the agency to find out if he was to disarm the Indians. Word came back to disarm them by all means. So a corporal went through the camp the next morning, telling the Indians to leave their arms in their tipis and come out into a hollow square formed by the soldiers. There they were to be searched for arms, while any weapons left in the tipis would be gathered up later.

The Indians came out as ordered. There were sixty or seventy warriors lined up in two rows, back to back, with their blankets drawn tight around them, because it had turned very cold in the night. When the soldiers started to search them old Big Foot stooped, picked up a handful of dirt, and threw it up in the air. That was the signal for every warrior to draw the gun hidden under his blanket and fire at the troops. With no time to aim, they did little damage to the soldiers, while the troop's fire simply mowed the Indians down. Next, the cannon were turned on the Indians and over two hundred were killed. Thirty-two soldiers died in the battle, most of them killed by their own cross fire. It was the deaths of so many soldiers that later called for an investigation by the War Department, not the slaughter of warriors, squaws and papooses.[3] I had known Big Foot well. Dave Butcher, foreman for Woods, White, and Woods, had employed him for several years to put up hay under contract and he had given the best of satisfaction.

After the battle I heard that one of our ranch boys had somehow been killed. However, the trouble had stopped all communication from the north and I couldn't get any more information about it, so I decided to ride down and see what had really happened. It was about thirty-five miles from Buffalo Gap to the battle field, and F. M. Stewart and a man named Smith went with me. We headed first for General Brooke's camp on White River, which was near the Indian beef camp. After we came to within seven to ten miles of the camp we could see roving bands of Indians and troopers going in all directions. It was hard to tell which was which, as the Indians nearly all wore government issue clothes. By using our field glasses we finally spotted an opening and dashed through, reaching the camp a little after suppertime.

We were at the herd-camp table, eating what was left of the herd boys' supper, when Bob Pew, the boss, came in. "Ed," he said, "I'm sure glad to see you. I have to have an issue of 420 beeves

~~~~~~~~~~~~~~~~~~~

3. Big Foot's fugitive band of 340 Indians, including 106 men, were coming in to the agency to surrender when they received news of the December 15 killing of Sitting Bull and fled in fright. They were intercepted by units of the Seventh Cavalry under the command of Colonel George A. Forsyth on Wounded Knee Creek about seventeen miles northeast of the Pine Ridge agency. Most of the Indians had been disarmed when a shot was fired, probably by a half-crazed warrior. The panic-stricken soldiers opened fire, killing 84 men and 62 women and children as they tried to flee; and many more died later of wounds and exposure. Thirty-one troopers were killed. See Herbert S. Schell, *History of South Dakota* (Lincoln: University of Nebraska Press, 1961), pp. 320–323; and James C. Olson, *Red·Cloud and the Sioux Problem* (Lincoln: University of Nebraska Press, 1965), pp. 320–330.

gathered tomorrow, but you know I'm no cowman. I don't know the location of the beeves, or how to gather 'em, but you know all about it and I want you to boss the job." Pew had often favored me and I couldn't very well refuse him, so I promised to take his crew, nearly all mixed-bloods and full-bloods of the first class, and do the job. But first I went to Major Wells' camp to ask for seventy-five cavalry-men as an escort, or support, to be stationed on three high places right amongst the cattle.

The Major had just agreed to supply the men when a courier rode in from General Brooke with a request that I pilot a delegation around the northwest corner of the reservation to the battle site at Wounded Knee. This delegation was made up of a Captain Baldwin and a *Harper's Weekly* artist, who was to sketch the battlefield at Wounded Knee. They were a part of the committee that was to look into Colonel Forsyth's handling of the battle and pass judgment on it.

At first I said no, that I had promised Bob Pew to gather the beef issue, but both Major Wells and Dr. Woods (of his force) told me I'd better go, as General Brooke could press me in if I didn't. The delegation was waiting and the Major advised me to go right away and not wait until the General served the press papers, so I went. Over at Brooke's headquarters I found him using his carbine as a walking stick, filling the barrel with dirt. If he ever shot it in that condition, he'd sure have an explosion on his hands.

Just before we started I was given an order for a change of teams at General Frank Wheaton's camp, four and a half miles west. Brooke's camp was on the north side of the river and the herd camp was opposite, on the south side. The hostile camp was about twelve miles away, and within it were about two thousand Indians, every one at fever heat. I started to take the north-side road, but Lieutenant Casey, who with another lieutenant from Wheaton's camp was visiting at Brooke's camp, spoke up and asked where I was going.

"To Wheaton's," I said.

"Oh, that isn't the way," he told me. "You should cross the river and go up the south side."

"Not me," I said. "Even if it is shorter, that road is all brush and gulches. This side is free of both."

He tried to press the matter, so I told him I'd go my way or not at all. Then Captain Baldwin spoke up and said, "Lemmon, you have been highly recommended as a pilot and put in charge by General Brooke. You are in full charge until I'm convinced you have made a mistake. So you go your way and we will follow Lieutenant Casey."

Besides Captain Baldwin and the *Harper's* man, I had in my party seven Cheyenne scouts, one of the Rowlands to act as interpreter, and the driver of the two-horse wagon that hauled the baggage and equipment. When we reached Wheaton's camp we found the officer party, still on horseback, waiting for us. Casey spoke right up. "If you had come my way you would have been here ten minutes ago," he said.

"But," said I, "I did not come your way." When he got sort of insulting, I said, "Of course you are soldiers and should know your business, but I was raised among those Indians and I think I know them. I think they've been starved into this hostile demonstration and I don't believe they're out for scalps. If they were they could've gotten all of yours as you came through those gulches and that brush."

Then Baldwin said, "Lemmon, your precaution meets with my approval. Now, I've already taken the liberty to order out a fresh team, so will you please hand me your order to turn over to the stableman?" We were soon on our way to Nick Janis's, at General Carr's [4] camp at the corner of the reservation, where we pulled in about midnight. There my mission ended.

Well, the very next morning Lieutenant Casey asked Wheaton for permission to take a scouting party of a dozen men over in the direction of the hostile camp. He set off and soon saw an Indian band of about the same size. He signaled for a powwow and met the leader in the middle, unarmed, as was the custom. But when they met, the Indian leader jumped to one side and the other Indians riddled Casey with their bullets. Lewis Peck told me later that a Mrs. Trimer, a full-blood Indian squaw at Wheaton's camp, had told

---

4. General Eugene A. Carr, commander of the Sixth Cavalry, which had been called out from Fort Wingate, New Mexico.

Casey the Indians would get him if they could, because they didn't like his bold, overbearing ways. Casey's killing ended the same way as the case where the whites killed the Indians over toward Alkali Creek. Though these Indians were charged with the Lieutenant's murder, it was shown that they were in a state of war with the whites, and they also went free.

From Carr's camp I went on to have a look at the Wounded Knee battleground. But all the dead had been buried by then and there wasn't much to see. I was told, though, how at the tail end of the battle the commander saw a wagonload of squaws and papooses making for a pass leading from Wounded Knee to the Porcupine Breaks. He trained a shell on it, and it all went up in smoke. Four days later, when the command was scouting the vicinity, they found a babe in the pass, one of those from the shelled wagon, unhurt but hungry and cold. She was a pretty child, well clothed and only a few months old. Colonel Colby,[5] of Beatrice, took her to his home, raised her, and gave her a good education. But eastern life was too tame for her wild blood, and at about the age of sixteen she joined Indian Pete's Wild West show at my town of Lemmon. When that didn't work out she picked one of August Back's sons for a skating rink partner for that season, and from there drifted back to the reservation, the G string, and the blanket.

Frank Huss, who was working for the Keystone Cattle Company that winter, told me later that his company, early in the winter, had taken a contract to furnish beef on the hoof to the Indians the following April. February and March, 1891, were extra-cold months, he said, with plenty of snow on the ground, 'and by time to make delivery of the issue the only fat cattle they had were three-year-old spayed heifers. The crew gathered the bunch and moved to the mouth of White Clay Creek, ready to take the beef on to the Pine Ridge agency. But the day they reached White Clay a message came from the Pine Ridge agent to hold the cattle there, as there were still two camps of hostile Sioux between them and the agency, making it unsafe to start up the creek. The outfit held the cattle there for two

---

5. L. W. Colby, later brigadier general and commander of the Nebraska National Guard.

weeks, herding them by day and bunching them and standing guard at night. During those two weeks, Frank said, they often saw Indians at a distance, riding along the ridges. But none came in, and they didn't entertain a single Indian at their camp, which was plenty unusual.

They finally got orders to come on into the agency, as the hostiles had finally broke camp. On the drive north they met a good many of the older Indians, many that they knew, and they were all a starved-looking bunch. A lot of them had run their few farming implements over the high, steep creek banks and had abandoned their wagons for the travois, believing they would be going back to their old way of living by the hunt. What horses they had were in very poor flesh, and there were many dead ones along the trail, starved to death by the deep snows of that February and March. And when the Keystone rounded up that spring, Frank said, they found a lot of their own horses, very poor and very tame, showing they had been ridden hard that winter, for the big hostile camp on Cuny Table had needed a lot of horses.

And when Dave Clark came home from Florida that spring after the battle, and was told by Woods, our Buffalo Gap merchant, of the stand I had taken with Sheffield about the horses, he came right down to thank me. Then he said, "I want you to take back your old place as general manager, and I'll retire from range work." Soon after that Dave was elected to the state legislature. Only a little later he died in Pierre.[6] I was general manager of the company as long as the old stockholders held their interest, after which I sold my interest to Sheffield in 1898. Sam held the management for five years and then closed out the company. But by then I was general manager of a much larger outfit, the L7, an outcrop of the old Flying V.

6. The prominent ranchman and legislator was only thirty-three years old at the time of his death.

XIII

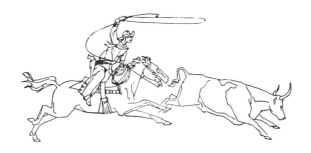

MANAGING THE FLYING V

I N APRIL, 1891, after I was put in as manager of the Flying V, I set out for Texas to buy cattle. This being my first trip to Texas and my first try at buying cattle on a big scale, I wanted to look the part of a big cattle buyer. It's not easy to suddenly transform a cowboy assistant boss into a wealthy-looking cattleman, but I did my best. I borrowed a gold watch and chain from our range boss, and a fine gold ring from a sympathetic and well-to-do friend.

I had never been any hand to deck myself out that way, but I wanted to be outfitted to keep dates and make schedules. That watch bothered me, though, and I was all the time dangling it with my fingers. This didn't attract much attention while I was traveling from Rapid City to Kansas City, and from there to Denver and on to Trinidad. But after I left Pueblo, where most of the passengers were cowmen and their families, I saw that my dallying with the watch chain was attracting their notice. So I took the T from my vest buttonhole and put the watch, chain and all, into my trousers watch pocket. But the chain was long and it kept slipping out, and my poking it back all the time made people notice me even more than when I was fumbling at my vest front.

At the Colorado Springs junction a lady with a sixteen-year-old daughter, fresh from the school at the Springs, boarded the train. Except for noticing that they seemed more refined than the general run of passengers, I didn't pay any attention to them. When we pulled into Trinidad, a few miles from the main line, the brakeman turned the seat backs so the passengers could face forward while the train was backing out to get on the main line to head for Texas. The lady and her daughter got off the train for lunch there, and when they got on again they were at a loss to know how to sit. One wanted to sit facing one way, and one the other. Then I began laughing at their predicament, and this in a manner was our introduction. We exchanged names and destinations, and, when we reached the main line, adjusted our seats so they faced each other, making a section.

The ladies were very friendly, and I found they had lately come from Texas, the most hospitable state in the Union, to the Neutral Strip in Oklahoma Territory which had lately been opened for settlement.[1] I was bound for Clayton, New Mexico, where I was to look at the Hill and North steers, thirty-five miles out on the Brazos, and the ladies would be getting off the train only two stations farther on.

Well, the girl was soon tucking my watch chain into my pocket for me, and when it kept slipping out she reached over and took it, watch and all, and strung it across her front. When the peanut vendor came along I treated, and in so doing hauled out my wallet. The girl laughed and reached over and took it, too, putting it in her handbag. Then her mother, Mrs. John Williams, said, "Mr. Lemmon, if you aren't careful Annie will have you in her handbag, too, along with your watch and wallet. She was raised among cowboys and cowmen and looks on them as brothers and fathers." Later on, Mrs. Williams said to the girl, "Now Annie, you watch Mr. Lemmon, and when you pick a husband you look for a man like him. You have a good education and there is no excuse for you to do as your sister did and marry a common cowboy." Then she said to me, "We don't even know if he married her under his right name, but we do know he doesn't even have a bed to call his own."

Before we got to Clayton, Mrs. Williams told me that they had

1. On April 29, 1889, a two-million-acre strip of land in Indian Territory that had been ceded by the Creeks and Seminoles was opened to settlement.

plenty of good saddle horses and there were plenty of steers for sale in their region, and that Annie knew the owners, and also every nook and corner of the country and would be only too willing to go with me to look at the steers. But I got off at Clayton as I had planned.

Al Sears, the Hill and North boss, met me at the train and we went to the Jim Crow Hotel for supper. As we got up from the table we heard shooting in the leading saloon. We went there at a lively clip to see what was going on. There were two dead men on the floor, and in the rear of the room a man was standing with both arms around a whiskey barrel, plugging two bullet holes on opposite sides of the barrel with his thumbs. A man beside the barrel was whittling wooden plugs as fast as he could.

The next morning Sears furnished me a good horse and we started for the line camp on the Brazos. As we rode I told him about the Williams woman and her daughter. When I came to the part about Annie's older sister marrying a common cowboy who didn't even have a bed of his own, and maybe was not even using his own name, Al began to laugh. The Williams, he told me, were fine people, and the worthless cowboy and probable outlaw was his own kid brother. Later that season, when Al came up the trail with a herd of Three 7 steers belonging to Henry Boice, I saw him again. Mrs. Williams and Annie, he told me, were still talking about the visit I had promised them. Much as I would have liked to, I never did get around to make that visit.

On the way home I stopped off at our Kansas City office to talk to Mr. Tomb, one of the owners. After a little he asked how his nephew, Frank Huss, was getting along. "Not very well," I told him. "A married man can't accumulate very fast on thirty-five or forty dollars a month."

The man we were talking about was a fellow I first met in 1885, when he came into my employ from our Platte River range, where he had been working for two years or so. I knew he was a nephew of Thomas B. Tomb, but thought nothing of it. Frank worked for me for about five years, and then Mr. Tomb suggested that I let him go, as he did not think it advisable to employ relatives. This came as a surprise to me, for there had never been a time since I had been with the company that there weren't relatives on the payroll. But I found Frank a job with the Keystone, which had range adjoining ours. While he was working there he married and began to accumulate a few cattle.

After I said what I did about a married man not getting ahead very fast on thirty-five or forty dollars a month, Mr. Tomb came right back by asking if Huss deserved any better. I told him yes, that by right and ability he should have the management of the Sheidley Cattle Company, the job I was filling. That dumbfounded him, and he then told me that reports coming in to Chicago from the men who went along with beef shipments had sounded like Frank was a soreeye to the outfit. That was the reason, he said, that he had suggested I shift him to another outfit. I told him that had been plain jealousy on the part of the shippers, just a fault of cowboys who have an inborn dislike for the boss's relatives.

Mr. Tomb then asked me to bring Frank to Kansas City when I came back a few weeks later on my way to Texas to receive and ship the steers I had bought. I did, and he arranged for Frank to go on with me so I could help him buy some choice steers, over three hundred head altogether. These matured into choice beef in two years time and almost doubled his money. From then on, with his uncle's help, he soon built up a stock of about two thousand head of cattle.

The next year, while riding a Santa Fe train from Wichita, Kansas, to Panhandle City, Texas, I first met Zach Mulhall. Zach was the local livestock agent on that division, and I was on my way to Texas to receive five thousand head of JA steers. At that time Zach had only a small ranch near Mulhall [Oklahoma Territory] and his job as livestock agent. That was before his fame as a stock and rodeo man. While he was away from home on his job his wife and two daughters ran the ranch. After about three years under that setup, Zach was offered the general livestock agency of a railroad out of St. Louis. He took this better job and moved to St. Louis, where he rented a big house in a select part of town. He took his daughters there with him, as it was part of his job to entertain the livestock men who shipped over his road.

Now the two girls, and especially Lucile, while running the ranch had turned out to be top hands in riding, roping, and handling cattle. They were also mighty good at singing, dancing, and playing the piano. Besides all that, they were small and pretty, with just enough Oklahoma tan to set them off. All of this made them just what their father needed for entertaining cattlemen from the big ranches and the open range. Naturally, a lot of singing and dancing went on at Zach's town house. As stock shippers seldom brought their wives or daughters along, there weren't enough ladies for square dances; so round dances, to the music of a phonograph, were the only kind they could have. And after the entertainment they had late dinners, with champagne but no drunkenness, for Zach was a stickler for gentlemanly behavior around his lovely daughters. Even so, some of the parties got pretty hilarious, and this seemed to bother the near neighbors, who were mostly retired businessmen and their wives.

One evening a committee of about a dozen of these men came over to Zach's house in a solid bunch and rang the doorbell. The leader told Zach he'd either have to quiet things down or move to quarters better suited to people of his kind. Zach asked to be excused a minute. He came back to the door with a six-shooter in each hand and cut loose near their toes, and then their heels, until the dust of their leaving hid them, so to speak. The next morning a couple of officers showed up with a warrant for Zach's arrest, and took him before a magistrate. Zach called his railroad's attorney, and when his man got there they entered a countersuit accusing the neighbors of approaching Zach's home in mob formation. So all parties, including the Mulhall girls, had to go to court.

The pretty girls took the stand and testified to their names and their former residence on the Oklahoma range, where they had learned to rope and ride and perform in local rodeos. Then they explained that they were well versified in piano music and singing and told how, with their father, they entertained cattlemen with a little music, singing, and dancing, and later with dinner and champagne, although they personally never touched a drop, or smoked cigarettes either.

The magistrate listened carefully to all this, and then asked if it would be too much trouble to have a piano brought in so they could play and sing a few of their pieces. Well, they had hardly started their music and singing before it was plain that they were charming the court and the complaining witnesses as well. The upshot was that the respectable witnesses asked to call the whole thing off. And they not only paid all the court costs and both lawyers, but asked if they might bring their wives and daughters to call. From then on, the Mulhall girls were taken into the best St. Louis society and often had their pictures in the papers.

Zach started a Wild West rodeo of his own, with Lucile as his star attraction as the lady roper and tie-down performer. From 1895 to 1900 she held the ladies' championship in this field. But Zach's show failed and he went back to his ranch, which his wife had managed all that time, even building it up a good deal. I've heard that Zach never drew on his ranch funds to finance his rodeo, not even to get his show or the family baggage out of hock. It was given to me straight that when the collapse came even Lucile couldn't get her trunk from her hotel room, so she put on all the silks she could under her outer garments, and had one of the male performers wear her choicest silk dress for underwear as they walked out. But Zach somehow settled all the show's outstanding obligations, since that was the code of the early-day cowman.

I well remember my first meeting with the Mulhall girls. It was at Wichita, where they had come with their father, who was overseeing the feeding of a long string of stock steers I was shipping through there. The yard management was out of hay, and Zach had to lease a pasture just outside the city limits. There the steers were grazed for two days for less than hay would have cost, and the girls helped with the herding and penning.

During those years when I was making a good many trips south to buy cattle, I ran into Tom Lawrence again. After selling out in Nebraska in '77 he had gone to New Mexico, where he and Dick Head stocked up a mighty big range. They had to go into debt to get started, and then a bad drouth hit that section of the country, a drouth so bad that water sold by the gallon and was almost as expensive as whiskey. That drouth broke Tom and Dick.

Dick then got a job as manager of the great Prairie Cattle Company[2] at, so I heard, twenty thousand dollars a year. Tom went to

2. The first big Scottish cattle ranch in the United States, the Prairie Cattle Company had ranges in Texas and New Mexico.

Omaha and into the commission business, but failed there, too. When I met him again in the south I was receiving[3] the LS cattle of Tascosa, Texas. The LS was owned by Julia Scott; her brother was the manager. He asked me to take an interest in the management, but I was satisfied where I was, so I told him I'd send him a good man. Tom Lawrence was the man.

While I was helping Tom get that job he told me this story: When he and Dick were running their own big spread they had a lot of line camps on the open range near Las Vegas. At one of them they stationed a young man and his wife. Then another young fellow who was working near the camp broke his leg. After the leg was set and splinted, its owner was left at the line camp to get well. The husband had to be gone a good deal, of course, and the young woman soon shifted her affections to the boy with the broken leg. As soon as Tom figured the fellow was able to travel he sent a team of gentle ponies and an old buckboard over to the camp for him to drive back to the home ranch.

About that same time word came that a big bunch of cattle had been seen drifting southeast toward the Bell ranch on the Canadian River. Water being so scarce on account of the drouth, the cattle had to be turned back as soon as possible. So the husband, with a pack outfit, took the trail; but the herd, finding no water, had turned back of its own accord, and the rider was gone only a couple of days. When he got back to the camp he found two notes on the kitchen table. One was from his wife, who wrote that she had no complaint against him, but she'd found she loved another more truly. The other, from the cowboy to Tom, explained that, as he had one hundred dollars in wages coming, he was taking the team and buckboard in settlement and leaving the country.

The couple thought they'd have plenty of time to get away; but on account of the cattle turning back, their plan didn't work. The husband, riding a fresh horse, caught up with them about the third

3. After purchasing a large herd of cattle, the manager or a trusted representative "received" the cattle at a designated point, that is, counted the herd to make sure the cattle were of the age and size contracted for in the purchase agreement.

day out. Without letting them see him, he made a circle around them and hid by the road up ahead. When they came along he stepped out and covered the cowboy with his gun. He hazed them to a shady spot in some timber, where he made his wife tie the man's hands. Then he tied her up, and next he killed and skinned a cow and brought the hide to where he'd left the tied-up couple. He told his wife and her lover that, since they seemed so fond of close companionship with one another, he was going to wrap them together in the green hide. It would shrink as their passions cooled, he said, and seal their embrace. And so he left them.

The man rode on back to the line camp, some sixty miles away. But on the second day he weakened enough to ask another line rider to go find the pair and cut them loose, but to tell the woman she was not ever to come back to him. The rider found the pair in a filthy condition and cut the stinking hide away. As soon as they were able to sit up and talk, the two of them turned loose and told one another how low-down the other was. When they had used up all the bad words they knew doing it, the line rider told them both to get going and keep going, and promised the man that if he was ever found in that country again he'd be hung without mercy.

The woman went to Las Vegas and into a dancehall, Tom told me, and he fired her husband. "He was too cool a proposition for me," he said, "for I believe he could've cut a man's throat and grinned while he was bleeding to death."

Tom did well as manager of the LS for a year and a half, and then he seemed to go to pieces. He gave up his job and went to Denver, and when I was there about a year later I heard someone holler "Ed." I looked back and saw Tom, but I hardly knew him. He had been a handsome man, but now he was a wreck, haggard and with a wild look in his eyes. He asked me for ten dollars and I slipped a bill to him, but I couldn't look at him while I did it. I knew if I did I'd slop over. I heard later that he went to his grave before he could be sent to the insane asylum, and for that I was thankful.

There was no better range cattleman than Tom had been when he was in his prime; and his partner, Dick Head, was the best steer classification man in the world. Dick was often hired to class herds for other men, usually at Ogallala, in the early trail days. His judgment of the age of a steer was practically infallible and was seldom disputed.

In the winter of '95 and '96 our company bought the Texas NUN outfit. About the first of March, I went to Memphis and bought two hundred Hereford bulls of O. H. (Bull) Nelson. The bulls were to be grained until the grass was fit for trailing them to the NUN ranch, two hundred miles away, where they were to be used. I then sent a fellow named Othe Arndt, one of our wagon bosses from the north, down to see to the feeding and to trail the bulls to the Texas ranch. That done, he was to come back to Dakota with the first shipment of cattle from Texas.

At the NUN he found that their trail outfit, like most of those used in Texas, was pretty poor when compared to what we used in the north. Arndt kept twitting the Texas boys about it, and he especially picked on their sourdough keg, which had a hinged cover with felt around the edges to make it dustproof and also airproof. Now and then gas would build up in the keg and blow the lid off with a loud pop. At such times the stench was usually worse than the noise.

Othe had joshed the boys so much about their outfit that it got to be kind of a ticklish proposition. Well, the first night on the trail from the NUN to Hereford, where the thirty-five hundred yearlings were to be loaded for shipment to Dakota, Othe and a hard-boiled Texan named Morgan were put on first guard together. All at once and for no reason that the boys knew of, the yearlings stampeded to the four winds. The boys had their hands full for about an hour, and when they met again after the herd was settled down, Morgan said, "Now what the hell do you suppose stampeded them yearlings?"

"Morgan, I'll be damned if I know, unless it was the lid blowed off that sourdough keg," Othe said.

Morgan wheeled his horse and rode away, hollering back, "You think you're damn smart, don't you?"

Later on we were shipping some NUNs out of Amarillo. I had gone to bed after a hard day's work. About midnight a messenger woke me up to tell me Morgan wanted me to come to the jail and get him out. When I got to the jail I found he'd only been smoking the town up a little, so I went his bail and the next morning paid his fine of forty dollars and costs.

Thrown in with the NUN ranch when we bought it was a fine pack of eight hounds, kept around for chasing wolves. The leader of the pack, Old Raney, was the biggest dog I ever saw. His tail hung straight down with never a twitch, which dog experts said was a sign of breeding and ability. Old Raney was a trailer, but he would also leap up from any elevation, such as an anthill or a prairie dog mound, sight the wolf, and then take a cutoff. And never once did he miss picking up the trail again. The big hound had been known to kill wolves unaided. He did it by grabbing the wolf by the throat, crouching, and then throwing it over his shoulder, snapping its neck. You can bet he was well known all over that plains country.

I'd like to say, though, that these were the only dogs ever kept on a ranch where I was manager. It seemed like dogs would always show up just as the lead of a bunch of cattle was about to come into the wings of a corral, and then of course away they'd all go. So no dogs on my cow ranches.

Later on that spring of 1896 I made my first cattle-buying trip to Arizona. I had made a pool contract[4] for five thousand steers to be delivered at Huachuca, and on the contract were two names I recognized, Big George and Little George.

Back in 1882 a man by the name of Hunter had transferred as boss from California to the Circle Bar O ranch on Hat Creek. He brought with him the two Georges, both mountain men. Reckless ropers and riders, they used seventy-foot rawhide riatas—and could handle every foot of those ropes. It was nothing unusual for them to rope deer, coyotes, wild cats, and mountain sheep. I had lost all track of them until I saw their names among the fourteen on that contract. And when I met the fourteen men in Arizona I found that all but two, Ed Roberts and his stepson, Ben Sneed, had killed their man or men. Big and Little George had gotten theirs too, for it seemed

***

4. A pool contract was one under which several sellers with small herds pooled their cattle to make up a herd of the size and kind the buyer wanted.

that that warm southern climate, along with the times, tended to make gun slingers of most men and the Georges had taken up the custom.

Uncle Billie Plaster, the leader of this bunch of killers, had once ridden with Quantrill's bushwhackers[5] but he was the finest man I ever did business with. He was seventy-one at the time and had served two terms as a sheriff in Texas. The Arizona boys told me he had lost all track of how many men he had killed. I know that twice in the fifteen days I worked with the pool outfit at Huachuca he came near adding more to his list. The only reason he didn't was because a spry brakeman dodged under the yard platform and hid, while the agent let old Billie slap his jaws good without putting up any fight. Old Billie's son Ben had already followed his dad's lead by killing five or six men. George Spindle was next with three, and Bake Thompson had two. Big and Little George had at least one each. W. C. Green, later first owner of the Diamond A of the Cheyenne agency, had killed his man, stood trial, and come clear. But he was thereafter afraid of his victim's friends, so he had hired Colonel Mossman as a bodyguard.[6]

I don't remember the names of the other men, but the whole bunch worked back and forth across the Mexican line, for they were all night hawks. It was impossible to keep their cattle from drifting across into Mexico, so they were allowed to go across on regular roundups and bring them back without paying any duty. These men also bought a good many cattle from small Mexican owners below the border. Such cattle were tallied with a short bar. While the tally bar brand on the bought cattle was still fresh, the men would slip over the border at night and gather more cattle. They would put the bar on these themselves, and at the next roundup south of the river

~~~~~~~~~~~~~~~~~~~~~~~~~

5. Quantrill's Raiders, a Confederate guerilla band under the leadership of William C. Quantrill, pillaged in Missouri and Kansas during the Civil War. Their most infamous attack was on Leavenworth, Kansas, in August, 1863.

6. Burton C. (Cap) Mossman had been range manager of the Hansford Land and Cattle Company, a Scottish firm that ran the Turkey Track on the Pecos River in New Mexico. He later obtained a lease on almost half a million acres of the Cheyenne River reservation in South Dakota. See Bob Lee and Dick Williams, *Last Grass Frontier: The South Dakota Stock Growers Heritage* (Sturgis, S.D.: Black Hills Publishers, 1964), p. 229.

would claim they had drifted back over, too, and none could dispute but what maybe they had. The duty on cattle brought over the border was two dollars a head. As yearlings could be bought in Mexico for three and a half or four dollars a head, they were making plenty of money smuggling them over.

This W. C. Green turned over to me only sixteen head of steers of the age and quality my contract called for. At that time he owned only about three hundred head of cattle, and was never able to gather over one-fourth of them in any one roundup of that mountain range country. After I settled with him for the steers he told me about his copper prospects over in Mexico. He seemed to think his chances to get rich in copper were first rate. But that fall when Ike Humphrey of Rapid City was receiving steers from the same pool, Green's hired man quit and Green had to borrow money from Ike to pay him off. In return he gave Ike an order on a Bisbee storekeeper, who acted as banker for the district. When Ike got there he found Green's funds extinct, and the order was turned down. Two years later Green came into his copper strike. He then settled with Ike in full, and with compound interest even. Not long after that Green was rated at forty million dollars, and everybody called him the copper king.

Then T. W. Lawson,[7] the fellow who uncovered the big life insurance graft that upset that business, got after the copper companies, too, causing such a slump in copper that Green lost twenty-eight of his millions. And for that he threatened to kill Lawson on sight. But Lawson, instead of waiting to run into Green, hunted him up and said, "Green, I was really after Rockefeller and H. H. Rogers. You just happened to get hurt in the landslide." After some more talk, Green put out his hand to shake with Lawson and they became good friends.

Years later Captain Mossman denied to me that he had ever been Green's bodyguard, but I know he and Green were together a lot, especially after Green made his fortune in copper, and that the two of them became Arizona cattle kings. The Captain told me that

7. T. W. Lawson, a stockbroker and speculator, was the author of an attack, published under the title *Frenzied Finance* (1904–1905), on stock market speculators and big insurance companies that was in part responsible for the insurance investigation of 1905.

Green later married the widow of Ed Roberts, one of the men in that 1896 cattle pool, and that he did a lot of good with his money—like buying a fine furnished home for a widow in Pierre and setting aside enough money to run it as long as she lived. The widow had once nursed him through a bad sick spell.

I never met Green but that one time, there in Huachuca, but in an hour's talk he sure told me a lot of history. He spoke Spanish as well as he spoke English, which paved the way for making his fortune in copper in Mexico. I never met Lawson, but I saw the man who was mixed up with him in that Star Route mail scandal a few years earlier. The man was ex-Senator Stephen W. Dorsey, who, with others, was charged with the million-dollar swindle. Bob Ingersoll, the famous atheist, had been chief counsel for the Senator and had secured his acquittal.

Well, I had gone to Springer, New Mexico, in 1895 to meet and cut a Waddingham Bell–branded herd of steers that was to be loaded at Clayton. At Springer I hired a saddle horse and a guide to ride out five miles with me to the mesa where the roads forked. I had been directed to go by way of the Ingersoll and Dorsey ranches, and from the mesa top the guide pointed out the road, which I could see, cutting over a high ridge thirty miles away. It led into a valley, he said, that would lead me to the Ingersoll ranch.

Late in the afternoon I came to the ranch. The house there had twenty-five or more rooms, including a poolroom, and had water piped all over. The mansion had cost about forty thousand dollars, I was told, and had been a present from Dorsey, in addition to his fee to Ingersoll for winning the case for him. (A Denver banker had told me that just after Dorsey won that case he walked into his bank and deposited a United States government check for three million dollars.) The place was used only a few times a year as a resort for big blowouts, and there was nobody there but a caretaker. Dorsey's ranch, which was even fancier, was used as headquarters for a medium-sized bunch of cattle.

It was a couple of years later that I saw Dorsey himself, in Demming, New Mexico. He was being cussed out by a furious bartender for passing a Mexican dime on him in payment for a drink or a cigar and then running for a departing train. The barkeep told me it was the second time Dorsey had caught him that way. I was told then that he was on his last legs financially.

Now to get back to that Arizona pool outfit. Where we rounded up and cut that herd there was a wide, open flat that was free of malpies,[8] which was unusual in that section of hard-to-find roundup grounds. But when I picked that flat for our roundup, Ed Roberts made quite an objection because, he said, it was his hay ground. Now there wasn't a spear of any kind of grass anywhere, just clusters of roots about every four feet where the wind had whipped the sand away. I asked him when he had ever cut hay there, and he said about twelve years ago, that it was a lot better than any other hay and there was more of it. But I insisted on using the flat and he finally gave in.

After receiving that batch of five thousand head, I contracted for another five thousand for fall delivery. Bird Rose of our outfit was to receive them. When Bird came back he told me he had taken delivery near that same flat, and that it was lined with choice haystacks. But I never heard whether Ed had to wait another twelve years before getting another hay crop or not.

While I was receiving and loading those cattle I roomed for a while with an old adventuress and huntress by the name of Smith. Every morning she was out at daylight shooting wild pigeons. She'd bring in as many as fifty or sixty at a time and ship them to the Harvey Hotels at Santa Fe for a good price.

This old huntress had wall and floor trophies of her kills of almost every wild animal on the continent. I remember bear, panther, wildcat, lynx, couger, lobo wolf, coyote, badger, skunk, fox, groundhog, coon, beaver, otter, and mink. And when I left Huachuca she was lying on the windward side of a hole I had run a wildcat into. She had a lunch along and was going to stay until she got him, even if it took two days and nights, she said. She was about forty-five years old and brown as a berry but active as a cat, and what she didn't know about guns wasn't worth knowing. Her home was only about eighteen miles from the Mexican line, and I asked her if she

8. Malpais (literally, "bad country"), terrain formed of sharp-edged decomposed lava, very hard on the feet of cattle and horses.

wasn't sometimes afraid of the rough fellows that plied back and forth across the border. But she only laughed and said those fellows were more afraid of her than she was of them.

On one of my trips to Arizona, Bird Rose and I were there to receive the Sansamon cattle. The boss of that outfit was a man named Duncan. His wife was there on the ranch, but she was a lot younger than he was, maybe only seventeen or eighteen, and very pretty. She didn't look weather-beaten like most ranch women and girls, and seemed rather childish and full of pep. Duncan, though, was all for the ranch and the cattle.

While they were gathering the cattle for us a horse fell with one of the boys and broke his leg. The break wasn't bad enough to put him in the hospital at Bisbee or Demming, so they splinted him up and took him to the ranch house, where the young wife looked after him. After a few days, though he was well enough to go to a hotel, he stayed on at the ranch. Finally, on one of his trips to the ranch, Duncan saw that all wasn't as it should be between the two. But when he called them to account the wife lit out for her folks' home in the town of Benson. The cowboy left the ranch, too, and shortly afterward began calling on Mrs. Duncan. This caused talk in the little town, and the girl's father told the cowboy he'd have to stop it, as the girl was still the Sansamon boss's wife. But the cowboy told the old man he'd visit her when and where he pleased.

This argument happened in front of a saloon where Bird and I could take it all in from the porch of our hotel. The cowboy was wearing his six-shooter, but the girl's father was unarmed. So the old man hurried home and got his double-barreled shotgun. He came back with it in the crook of his left arm. The cowboy was waiting just inside the saloon, and when the old gent came up he raised his six-shooter and let go with a shot. The older man, expecting such a move, dodged to one side and then let drive with both barrels of his own gun. That double charge of .36-caliber buckshot just about cut the boy in two. The old man went right over to the constable and gave himself up. But within an hour he was cleared, as he deserved to be.

Just a year later I was back there again, buying and receiving more cattle and stopping at the same hotel. I was sitting on the porch that evening when I saw a pretty girl of eighteen or twenty playing with some children in a back yard. She was about the prettiest girl I ever saw, and, naturally, I asked the hotel man who she was. "Why, that's Mrs. Duncan of the Sansamon," he said. "You saw her boy friend killed here just a year ago." Then he asked me if I'd like to meet her. But I said no, thanks. She was too cool a proposition for my warm nature.

During those years when I was shipping thousands of cattle from Arizona, I had Frank Smith's name put on one of the return contracts so I could ship him out to Arizona. I had picked Frank up at George Shingles' Willow Creek ranch, seven miles east of Newell, South Dakota, and had kept him on as a horse wrangler for about two years, or until 1897.

Frank was what I'd call a harmonica fiend, because it seemed he couldn't live without tooting on his little music box. Since he had a lot of time to himself on his wrangler job, he put a good deal of it into his playing, and so got to be a master on the harmonica. And many an evening he entertained the boys with choice music. But after a while we could see he was, in a manner, blowing his lungs away, so much so that Shingles, who was somewhat his guardian, took him to a doctor. The doc told him he'd have to go to a drier climate and quit tooting on his harmonica, or he'd soon blow himself under the sod.

So I sent him to Arizona, but when he got off the passenger train the town marshal stepped up, looked him up and down, and said, "Young fellow, if you think you're going to stop here and cash in your chips and be buried by our city, you are mistaken. We've had that worked on us too often, and now we make it a policy to carry all such remains as yours will soon be to the top of yon knoll. We just brace them upright and in a few months they mummify. We've found a good market in museums for all we can get, and we make a tidy profit. So if you don't want to wind up as such, I'd advise you to head right back where you came from. I see some stock cars loading out at the yards, so you just mosey down there and see if you can't get aboard as helper to the shipper."

Frank did, as the shipper was Bird Rose, loading out our cattle. "I'd rather die in our country than live here," the lad told Bird, "so please let me ride this train to Belle Fourche." Bird told him to hop on, and when he was home again he told Bird and me what the marshal had said to him. So I sent him out to Shingles' ranch, where he died within three months. He was buried there, together with his beloved harmonica, in the Vale Cemetery in Butte County.

Along about 1898 one of my partners and I went out to Clifton, Arizona, to pass on the Double Circle cattle, which we bought and shipped to our Nebraska range. From the Santa Fe main line to Clifton, a copper-mining town, we rode a narrow-gauge railroad combination coach that called for close association with our neighbor passengers. One of these was a flashy hash slinger, and my partner soon got on a pretty familiar footing with her. I couldn't very well pass her up either, so everybody in the short-seated compartment was soon in an uproar over the jesting, which at times got pretty raw. After a while I happened to look behind me, and there I saw a high-class Spanish lady and her daughter, a pretty lass of about eighteen. They were such nice-looking ladies that I was ashamed to have them see me cutting up with a biscuit shooter.

Our engine was a wood burner, and when we stopped at a pile of mesquite roots by the track to take on fuel, my partner and Black Marie, the hasher, got off the train to stretch their legs. I then introduced myself to the Spanish lady and started to apologize to her, but she stopped me, saying that while traveling one couldn't shut up like a jackknife. She then introduced me to her daughter, Eulalia Escarity, and I recognized the Escarity name as one of the finest families of Mexico. This branch of the family had a ranch a few miles out of Clifton, and the Señora had been down in Mexico to get her daughter and bring her home from school.

As the train pulled into Clifton, my partner asked me to keep cases on Black Marie while he rushed to the telegraph office to send some telegrams. He said he wanted to take her for a ride if he could beat her steady friend to it. But when we got off the train the first thing I saw was a fancy barouche behind four Spanish mules, with a stove-pipe-hatted driver perched on the high front seat.

The lady introduced the young Spanish gentleman who got out of the carriage as her son, and the whole family insisted I make their ranch my headquarters while in their country. The Señora said she wanted her daughter to get to know gringo cattlemen better, as she had met few of them so far. The daughter told me she had some splendid riding horses and would be glad to share them and show me over their entire holdings. But I knew there would be a peon following on our heels wherever we went, as such is their custom, so I didn't get enthused over the invitation. I was never much for company when entertaining a pretty girl. But with all this I forgot to watch Black Marie, and of course got chewed out by my partner when he got back and found her gone.

All this time I was still buying cattle in Texas, too, and on my 1894 trip Frank Huss went with me to buy another 325 head for himself. I was receiving the JA cattle that trip and we were sitting on the veranda of the Attebery Hotel in Clarendon in the evening. Suddenly we heard a couple of shots diagonally across the street to the southwest. We ran over to see what was going on and found a big negro face up on the sidewalk and kicking his last. We were told that a few minutes before, he and the marshal, Green, had had words and the negro had said he'd heel himself and be right back. Of course, Green was looking for him; and as the negro turned the corner and threw up his shotgun, Green poured two bullets into him before he could bat an eye.

Playing the towns of Amarillo, Clarendon, Memphis, and Panhandle City at that time were the Bell brothers, gamblers, but about the pleasantest boys I ever met. There was also the stock inspector, Bean Grissom, who was a prince. Green, the marshal, was a gunman of the first magnitude and, so I always thought, unprincipled and too ready to show his authority. The Bell boys resented this, too, and one evening shortly after Green killed the negro, two of the Bell boys, Bean Grissom, and the marshal were in the leading Clarendon saloon when a personal row started. When the smoke cleared there were three dead men on the floor—Green, Grissom, and one of the Bell boys. Nearly the entire community was glad for the riddance of the marshal, but many mourned for Grissom and Bell.

A few years after we bought the NUN, a settlement wave set in on our Texas range, since our leased land was subject to homestead entry. Most of the land, though, was being taken up by what we called "bonus men." These fellows took up choice pieces and wind-mill sites, and when we bought them out, as we had to do to get them off the land, they just moved on to some other big pasture and filed on another piece. This was illegal, of course, but hard to prove, and so we had a good many lawsuits going for a while.

There was a lawyer in Lubbock who made a specialty of en-couraging and defending these bonus men, and one day he was found dead in our pasture. He had been shot twice with a .30-30 from a distance of three or four hundred yards, and the ejected shells were found behind a low cut bank. Our man, Morgan, usually carried a .30-30 on his saddle, so he was indicted for the murder. But before they could arrest him he went north to our Standing Rock pasture and laid up in one of our isolated line camps on Rock Creek. Morgan bunked with our line rider, Eugene Allen, for about four months, and by then the Texas affair had cooled off and he could go south again—I hardly think back to the NUN—but any-way he was never tried for the killing.

Years later old Bill McGregor told me that he was living on Cedar Creek the winter Morgan stayed at our line camp. Allen, he said, had put Morgan to watching for beef butcherers, and one day when he (McGregor) went down to the creek and pulled a beef hide out of the water, Morgan came up and shoved a cocked revolver under his arm. "He came near killing me," the old man said, "before I could get him to look at the brand and see that the hide was mine." McGregor said he had had the hide soaking so he could take the hair off it and use the leather to cover an armchair he had made.

[179]

XIV

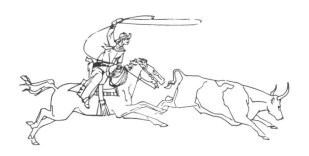

RUSTLERS AND RANGE DETECTIVES

B Y 1891 CATTLEMEN'S losses to rustlers in western South Dakota were terrific. This was mostly due to the thriving market for beef in the Black Hills mining-construction camps. So that year eight of us ranchers met in Buffalo Gap to decide what action to take against the thieves. We organized a protective association at that meeting, but didn't have enough power to take any real action. We met again the next year in Rapid City, and that time we had quite a crowd. We ended up with forty charter members. James Wood of Rapid City was our first president, Lon Godard was vice president and Frank Stewart secretary-treasurer. The first board of directors was made up of Ed Stenger, Ike Humphrey, Charles Hamm, James Cox, Ed Barthold, William Borst, C. K. Howard, Sam Moses, and myself.[1]

1. According to Bob Lee and Dick Williams, *Last Grass Frontier : The South Dakota Stock Growers Heritage* (Sturgis, S.D.: Black Hills Publishers, 1964), pp. 189–192, a temporary Western South Dakota Stock Growers Association was organized in Rapid City in February, 1892. Wood was elected president,

To finance the work of the association we voted to assess ourselves two cents on cattle and one cent on horses. We were very liberal in listing our herds for this assessment, too, a lot more so than when the tax assessor came around. But rustling was so bad that we later had to raise the assessment to three cents. Sam Moses was hired as association detective at $125 a month and expenses while on duty. He was also to receive $750 for each conviction secured. Before two years had gone by he had obtained thirteen convictions, and rustling losses had gone down quite a lot.

Sam, a six-foot, three-inch Texan, first came up the trail in '78 with a herd that was sold at Julesburg. The next year he came north with another herd, crossed both Platte rivers, and scattered the cattle in the Black Hills country. As association detective he was so good that five prisoners, out on bail, raised one thousand dollars as a reward for the man who would kill him before they came to trial. But Moses heard of the offer, cooped the five again, and upped their bail. The badmen then got cold feet and pled guilty.[2] Sam was later made a special agent—his job to run down Frank Smith, a killer who had ambushed a deputy U.S. marshal. On horseback Moses trailed Smith down through Colorado, across Texas into Mexico, and back into Texas. Three and a half months after he started, he took his man prisoner in the wilds of Indian Territory. Smith went to trial but was acquitted.

To help things along, the Berry-Boice Cattle Company on the Little Missouri, the Riverside Cattle Company of Mandan, and my own outfit, the Sheidley Cattle Company, made daily patrols over the ice of the Missouri River from Mandan to Pierre each winter, and so pretty well stopped cattle thefts on that front for some years. Also, the Wyoming Livestock Association, older and larger than

~~~~~~~~~~~~~~~~~~~~~~~~~~

Charles Hamm vice president, and Frank Stewart secretary. In April a permanent association was formed, with H. A. (Lon) Godard as president. Various sources give the differing figures for the number of men present at the April organizational meeting.

2. While the authors of *Last Grass Frontier* agree that Sam Moses was a competent association detective, they make no mention of this incident or of any agreement by the association to pay him $750 for each conviction. They state that he was hired December 1, 1892, at a salary of $125 per month.

ours, helped in checking at terminal markets, since most of our big west river outfits belonged to the Wyoming Association, too.

During the early years of our organization, James Craig of Western Ranches, Ltd., F. M. Stewart, and myself made up the arbitration committee which directed the movements of all detectives and inspectors. By the recommendation of Craig, we hired Joe Elliott as another of our detectives. Joe, along with some fifty cowmen and hired gunmen had, only a short time before, been acquitted of outlawry over in Wyoming. This had come about as a result of the Johnson County War of '91 and '92 in that state.[3]

Joe had been the detective the Wyoming cattlemen sent out to spy on Jack Flagg's Hole-in-the-Wall gang of cattle rustlers and home-steaders. He had spotted and named at least thirty-two men, two of them Nick Ray and Nate Champion, who were killed by the cattle-man force in a log cabin in 1892. The affair had ended with the cattlemen being rescued from Flagg's men at the old TA ranch. Under arrest, they were taken to Fort McKinney by Colonel Van Horn and some U.S. cavalry troops. The case was fought through the courts until it broke Johnson County, and in the end the ranch-men and their aids, including Elliott, were dismissed. But Elliott's

---

3. The Johnson County War of 1892 was an attempt on the part of the Wyoming Stock Growers Association to use vigilante methods in bringing about an end to cattle rustling. Alarmed at their losses to rustlers, the association brought in twenty-five Texas gunmen, who, along with slightly more than that number of ranchers, armed themselves and secretly entered Johnson County, thought to be stronghold of the rustlers, in early April. Although accounts vary as to their intentions, they apparently planned to take over Buffalo, the county seat, lynch some of the rustlers on their list, and give the others twenty-four hours to leave the state. However, through miscalculation the invaders wasted a full day in a gun battle with (and finally killed) two rustlers, giving the Buffalo residents time to get wind of the scheme. Led by sheriff Red Angus, a force of some two hundred Buffalo men laid a countersiege to the ranch to which the invaders had retreated. Meanwhile, Acting Governor Amos Barber, having received word of the events, requested President Harrison to intervene with federal troops, which were dispatched from Fort McKinney, near Buffalo. Because of gross ineptitude on both sides, fatalities in the affair totaled only four —two Texans in addition to the two assassinated rustlers. Although forty-three invaders were arrested, their cases were never brought to trial. The invasion, however, gained national notoriety and poisoned Wyoming politics for many years. See T. A. Larson, *History of Wyoming* (Lincoln: University of Nebraska Press, 1965), pp. 268–284. A fuller treatment is Helena Huntington Smith, *The War on Powder River* (Lincoln: University of Nebraska Press, 1967).

part in the trouble had made him a marked man as far as the Hole-in-the-Wall outfit was concerned.

During the "war" Craig was working for John Clay of the Western Ranches and the Swan Land and Cattle Company of Buffalo, Wyoming. While the Invaders, as the cattleman force was called, were holed up at the TA ranch under attack by Flagg's bunch, a man from the TA had slipped away and high-tailed it to Craig's headquarters with an order for grub and ammunition. Craig had loaded out a four-horse load of supplies for the TA, but the load had been captured by the Johnson County sheriff, Red Angus, and his men, who fought on the side of Flagg and his outfit.

So Craig, knowing Elliott's sympathy was with the ranchmen, proposed him for the detective job, and the association hired him. Before long Craig asked him to go into the Bear Lodge Mountains to look into some range-cattle beef butchering. As a cover-up, Elliott was to buy cattle near Sundance for Craig. Joe held back a little at first, not caring to get so close to the men who had sworn to get him, but in the end he went. He purchased and delivered two small bunches of cattle, then went back a third time—and disappeared. For years afterward Craig and Mike Shonsey[4] looked for his dry-gulched remains. They even put a Pinkerton detective on the case, but no one could find hide nor hair of Joe Elliott.

Another man who helped us catch rustlers was Ed Blakely. Ed first came to our section of South Dakota from the Spade outfit in Wyoming. For a while he busted broncs for the Bar T ranch. Later he set up a place of his own in Fall River County and was elected sheriff in 1889. After that he teamed up with Sam Moses, our detective, and made him his deputy. Then they set out after Spokane (Bill) Augher. Spokane specialized in furnishing beef, from other men's herds, to the railroad construction camps.

One day, near Cascade, they watched through their field glasses as Spokane and a boy helper, driving a wagon and leading a saddle horse, rounded up a little bunch of cattle and shot a cow with a six-shooter. The shot stampeded the bunch, but Spokane jumped on the horse, rounded the cattle up again, and tried to shoot a steer. After

---

4. Shonsey was foreman of the Western Union Beef Company of Wyoming.

shooting the poor critter three times without downing him, he roped him and finished the job at close range. As soon as the pair started skinning their beef, the officers, with Sam in the lead, came down on them. The rustlers had just rolled the cow onto her back when Sam ordered them to throw up their hands. The boy shot his sky-high; but Spokane, who had dropped his six-shooter beside a water bucket over by the wagon after shooting the steer, jumped for the gun, grabbed it, and dropped down behind the cow. He began shooting, but Sam and Blakely kept on coming, shooting through the cow with a Winchester and a Sharps.

Finally Spokane, who didn't have anything but the six-shooter, raised up and surrendered. He stood there with his hands hanging down and blood streaming from both of them, and said, "This is the first time I've gone out on a job like this without my Winchester. If I'd had it, I'd of made it hot for you."

"And you'd of gotten killed," Sam told him, "for we wouldn't of charged a Winchester."

Spokane was sentenced to two and a half years in the pen, but got out six or eight months short of that on good behavior. (While in the pen he patented a pair of stirrups and a bridle bit, and I bought some of each from him after he got out.) But they still had a charge against him, that of resisting an officer. So he was arrested again and given ninety days in jail on that count. During both terms in the lockup he made big threats against Sam for putting him there. But when he got out he went to Montana, established his ability as a cowman, and then applied for an inspector's job at a shipping point there. Now Spokane was a likable fellow and had many good friends among cowmen. I was one of them, and Judge William Gardner was another, as shown by the short sentence he gave him. So when Augher applied for the inspector's job, Judge Gardner recommended him and he was hired, and then was bushwacked by an outlaw while doing his work.

Ed Blakely had had a shooting scrape with Kid Rich in an Oelrichs saloon, but this was a purely personal quarrel and they both did their shooting from behind whiskey barrels, so the only damage done was to the barrels. The loss was something like fifty gallons of whiskey that leaked from the bullet holes.

A few years later Rich killed my night hawk, a fellow named Johnson. Kid was sent to the pen for only two and a half years, as Johnson was a rounder and the law didn't consider him much of a loss. The day after Rich got home from the pen I hired him for my night hawk, but he later got into a little cattle-stealing trouble and became one of Sam Moses' short-time convicts. Like Spokane, he threatened to kill Sam on sight when he got out of the pen. But Sam, not waiting for an accidental meeting with Kid, hunted him up and said, "Rich, I am established here and this county is not big enough to hold us both, so I will shoot on sight, too." At that, Kid, in something of a hurry, moved onto the Cheyenne reservation, where he married a sister of Narcisse Narcelle. Narcisse didn't care for that marriage at all, and some years later Rich was bushwacked on his way home one dark night. No one was ever arrested for the killing.

While serving as our stock detective and as deputy sheriff under Blakely, Sam Moses was stepped up to sheriff. This happened when his brother-in-law, Lon Godard, resigned from the sheriff's office to take over the general management of the Z Bell Cattle Company, with headquarters on Slate Creek and a stock of twelve thousand head of cattle.

Before Lon's resignation, and while several of Sam Moses' arrests were on trial for butchering a Bar T spayed heifer, I happened into the Fall River County courtroom. I was at once sworn in as an expert on cattle and brands, and sheriff Godard then took me outside to examine the hide of the animal in question. I looked at it and said, "Aren't the defendants under indictment for butchering a Bar T heifer?"

He said, "Why, yes, of course." And I said, "Well, this happens to be a steer hide."

I pointed out the evidence, and he threw up his hands and surrendered. Then he said, "Say, Ed, you haven't seen our new jail vaults yet, so let me show 'em to you." I had been a county commissioner of Fall River County a little while before that, so I went right along with him. We walked into one of the new vaults and I was looking around, when he slipped out and slammed the door shut on me. "Ed," he apologized, "this is pretty raw, but we don't want your

[185]

expert evidence now. The case is about over anyway, so you'll be turned loose pretty quick."

But right at the end of the trial the defense came up with a bill of sale for the steer that hide came off of, so the prisoners were, of course, released. I was turned out, too, and that was the only time I was ever locked in a jail cell, though I can't truthfully say I should not have been on a few other occasions.

The mystery of the hide was never solved. Through glasses, Sam Moses had watched those fellows shoot down and butcher a black Bar T spayed heifer, which he had planted there on purpose. While they were loading the carcass in their wagon, Sam had lit out for Hot Springs and a couple of deputies. The three of them had then met the butchers on the road to Hot Springs (where they had planned to sell the beef) and arrested them, beef, hide, and all. The only way I can figure it out is that, as they crossed the Cheyenne before they were arrested, they had raised a steer hide they had soaking under the ice and substituted it for the heifer hide.

Around 1900 Jack Sully, a squaw man of the Rosebud reservation, was the prince of cattle thieves of all that region. Ed Blakely arrested him once, but he was not convicted. Consequently he kept on with his nefarious business until about 1908. He was arrested a good many times before and after Blakely tried it, but was always turned loose, clearing himself by alibis until the last time, when he got out by breaking jail. The jail break happened during the first year of life of my town of Lemmon, which was *the* rough and ready town of Dakota at the time. It was said that Sully was on his way to Lemmon, where others of his ilk hung out, and once there he would be shielded by his friends.

A son of the well-known Scotty Philip[5] was deputized to take his trail. Though young Philip had long known Sully, he had no liking for him and his kind. His father, a long-time friend of mine, had advised him to come to me and get the low-down on his man as soon

5. James (Scotty) Philip, an Englishman, went to the Black Hills in 1876. After working as a cowboy, a teamster, and an army scout, he became a prominent ranchman, owning a large cattle and buffalo ranch near Fort Pierre. He married into the Sioux tribe. Along with Ed Lemmon, he was one of South Dakota's first honorees in the National Cowboy Hall of Fame in Oklahoma City.

as he reached my town. Sully had two friends, Aut Black and Ed Delahan, who were beholden to me because of a speculation deal on lots in my town. So I went to them for information about Sully, but they both told me he hadn't passed through Lemmon, wasn't in the town or anywhere nearby.

Now Delahan had, only a few years before, been under indictment for killing a man in Pierre, and Scotty Philip had done him a favor then. So, on second thought, he decided he owed Scotty something and turned around and gave young Philip some valuable pointers. It seemed that some relatives of Scotty's Indian wife had shadowed Sully to his home, and this piece of information caused the young man to go back to Pierre and organize a posse, which rode to the outlaw's place and surrounded it.

No old cowman such as Sully was wants a second taste of jail, so he chose to try to run. He slipped out to his stable, saddled his fastest horse, and headed him down a draw that led away from his ranch. But he had the bad luck to run square into the men who were holding the posse's horses. He swung to the off side of his horse's neck and tried to dodge the bullets, but the men shot him down. Sully, who had specialized in thoroughbred horses, died as he had lived—astride a splendid horse.

Of all the men mentioned by name in this chapter, every one except the night hawk, Johnson, were, so to speak, the salt of the earth. Moses and Godard were among the best; but Blakely, though a law officer, was a man I never really admired, even if I was chairman of the committee that hired him. Of them all, Kid Rich was probably the friendliest.

The general roundup of the spring of 1898 was working up the North Moreau River when I sent John Anderson to lead a circle into the east end of the Short Pine Hills, a scope of country around the head of the North Moreau that included Bill Fugate's ranch. Fugate came back with Anderson from that drive, and I hurried over to shake hands with him, as I hadn't seen him since the end of the roundup of the year before.

A VVV man named Bill Carson was repping with our wagon that spring. Carson had worked on Fugate's ranch the winter before, while the owner was visiting in the East. So now Fugate shook hands with me, then pointed to Carson, who was in the roundup cutting VVV cattle right in front of where we stood. "Lemmon," he said, "when Carson comes out of that roundup I want to have a talk with you and him." I told him I had to ride over to another roundup bunch to give some orders, but by the time I got back Carson should be through here. When I got back, Carson was just riding out. He rode over and stopped on the north edge of a bunch of about forty idle men. I rode up to him, then called to Fugate to come on over, that if he was ready for a confab, we were.

Fugate's rep, Trig Brinson, came out of the bunch and both rode over to Carson and me. I didn't know what was coming, but Brinson did, which was why he came along. Fugate rode up to Carson and said, "Did you, while working for me last winter, know of me killing any beef but my own, or have any reason to believe I had done so?"

Carson said, "No."

"Then what are you telling such lies for?" Fugate asked him.

Carson denied that he had told anything like that. Fugate called him a damn liar and every other kind of a bad name he could think of. Then he said, "You've been telling that I butchered stolen beef and peddled it to the Macy road ranch and other places."

When Carson still denied it, Fugate jumped off his bronc and tossed the reins to Brinson, who had been waiting for some such move. Then he tried to run around me to get to Carson, still calling him every vile name in his well-stocked string. While I was trying to keep my horse between the two of them, Carson got his six-shooter out and cocked and aimed it across my horse's neck at Fugate's forehead.

"All right," he said, "I did suspicion you were killing beef that wasn't yours. Before you left on your visit you pointed to a little stack of hay that you said was extra good and you wanted it saved for spring work. I couldn't see any difference in that stack and the others, so after you left I dug into it and found a CY hide."

At that Fugate just naturally boiled over. He tried harder than ever to get at Carson, even with that cocked gun covering him, but I kept my horse between them. When he saw he couldn't get his hands on Carson that way, he got back on his horse, but kept on getting madder and madder. Then he jumped off again and tried it once more on foot. The third time he tried it Carson got his gun right on Fugate's forehead. I reached out and pushed it away.

"For gosh sake, Carson," I said, "that gun might go off."

He said it certainly would if Fugate crowded him any closer, so then I got my horse out from between them. Then Carson said that if Fugate was so determined to settle this, just let him get his gun and they'd take care of it once and for all. I said, "Oh, you make me tired. If Fugate had a gun you'd break out of here fast."

"Just let him get a gun and see," he said.

I saw then that, steady as his aim and nerves were, I'd spoken too soon. I finally got them separated, though, and when the morning work was finished we started for camp. I asked Fugate to eat with us and he did, but you can bet I kept a weather eye on both of them. We were rounding up Fugate's range that afternoon, and I asked him if he'd lead the circle. He said he would if I'd furnish him a good circle horse, which I did. As the scattering of circlers began, I called for eighteen men to follow him. Carson was the first to ride out. I called him back and said, "Carson, you ride with me this afternoon." He said he wanted to go with Fugate and see if he got a gun.

"When he comes back I'll ask him if he got a gun," I told him, "and he'll tell me the truth."

So Carson rode with me, and there were no more hostile actions that day. And when Fugate came in from the circle I asked him if he'd gotten a gun. "No, I didn't dare. If I had I'd of killed a skunk," he said. Until the roundup ended a few days later, Carson took my orders as usual, but after that he would never speak to me. When we met I'd always say "Hello, Carson," but he wouldn't say a word.

A few months after the showdown on the roundup, Carson and Fugate met in a saloon in Belle Fourche. Fugate was unarmed and Carson got the drop on him, and again Fugate called him every name in the book. Not long afterward the matter came up in the Spearfish clubroom. Besides myself, the Driskills, Tony Day, and Tom Mathews—all old Texas longhorns—were there.

At first Tony said I was a good one to uphold a butcherer of stolen beef, and I came right back by saying I didn't believe Fugate had butchered any stolen beef, but even if he had I didn't think Carson should report it when he was working for him at the time. Tony stood his ground, though, until one of the Driskills chipped in and said, "Why, Tony, you were born and raised right here among us, and I believe you've always been a good Sunday school boy and never ate any but your own beef." This somewhat cooled Tony.

A couple of months later I met Tony again. Fugate had been on his range, repping for himself, he told me, and then he went on, "Ed, I apologize for my stand against Fugate in the clubroom. Since I got to know him and heard his story of the hide business, I'm of the same opinion as you. He's a straight shooter, and too wise to keep the hide of a stolen critter in his own haystack."

But Jimmie Craig, range manager of the VVV after 1884, had a different view. He heard of the trouble soon after it started and in a manner took Carson's part. And that was the only difference of opinion Jimmie and I ever had in twenty years of close association. Craig, F. M. Stewart, and I made up a subcommittee of the South Dakota Cattlemen's Association (with myself as chairman), and it was natural for Craig to take Carson's part, as he had recommended him for the job of stock detective for our association. So I never could convince him that if Carson did find a CY hide in Fugate's haystack, he was wrong in reporting it.

But Craig finally did admit that my code was likely the one used in the early days, since my experience dated back at least fifteen years earlier than his, to the time when no one butchered his own beef. He even admitted there was a possibility someone had put that hide in Bill's haystack to get him in bad, for Bill had just moved in from Johnson County, Wyoming, where he had been accused of sympathizing with the Hole-in-the-Wall men.

XV

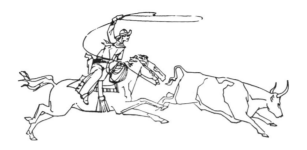

THE COWBOY'S BEST FRIEND

IN THE SUMMER of 1893, while the World's Fair was going on in Chicago, some western horsemen got the idea of putting on a spectacular called an Endurance Race. These fellows wanted to prove to the rest of the world that the western horse was the best to be had, for both speed and staying qualities. Since it was just one thousand miles from Chadron, Nebraska, to Chicago, they decided to run the race between those two points. The time allowed for the race was thirteen days, which meant traveling an average of seventy-seven miles a day. The United States had never staged a race of this kind, but France had. The record there was fifty miles a day.

Each man in the race was to start with two horses, riding one and leading one. He was to register himself and the horses at stated places along the route, and he had to come into Chicago riding one of the horses he started with. A great deal of money was bet on this race, and six men made the trip all the way through, with not a horse killed or badly hurt. The big race turned out to be more of a success than its promoters ever dreamed of, but even so, it was not all on the square, for there are tricks to all trades.

John Berry, a civil engineer for the Northwestern Railroad, entered the race, registered himself and his horses according to the rules, then, just before train time, hurried to the depot, expressed his horses, and boarded the train himself, riding the first one hundred miles. The fault was Buffalo Bill's. His Wild West show was playing in Chicago, that summer of the big fair, and he had offered a fine silver-mounted saddle to the first racer to ride up to the door of his tent.

Another of the riders was Abe Jones's nephew, George Jones, or Stub, as he was called. George was a small man, weighing about a 135 pounds, and he rode a light stock saddle. He was hardened to the saddle and knew how to ride to save himself and his horse. Abe picked and furnished the two horses George rode. One, George Stanwood, was by Louis Stanwood, sire of Maude S (the great Standard-bred trotter) and out of a little western-bred mare. A clean-cut gelding, George Stanwood weighed about 950 pounds, and Abe was confident he could make it through to the finish.

To ride seventy-five miles in one day is not out of the ordinary. Many men have done it. But to average that many miles for thirteen days in a row would test men and horses to the limit. The rider would not be mounting a fresh horse every relay and then riding without regard for the horse, as he'd do if he knew he'd have a fresh mount at each stop. No, these men would have to save their horses' strength all they could.

Then, too, a rider with a fresh mount under him can stand a long ride much better than he can on a jaded horse. And if the road was rocky he'd have to let the horse pick his way, lest he sprain his leg or be lamed by a rock bruise. If the road led through hilly country with steep slopes he'd not dare ride at high speed either uphill or down, but would have to take advantage of every chance to make time when the temperature and the lay of the ground would let him. But a real horseman understands his horse, and it is almost un-believable how a good horse will respond to such a rider.

The money cost of this race was high, too, since each man who made an entry had to send a pilot ahead of his rider every day, in case the rider got off course or had other trouble. The pilot drove a team and buggy, and a fresh team and driver relayed each day. Even so, many of the pilot horses were left dead by the road. Also, a groom traveled by train and stopped at the appointed stations to await his rider and the horses. When they came in, the groom took care of the rider by having a bed ready for him in the barn, and then took the horses, rubbing them down and giving them every care.

Abe Jones's groom was Bill Smart, considered one of the best in the United States for conditioning horses in a race of this kind. At Hazel Green, Iowa, Smart put Stub Jones to bed and was taking care of the horse, George Stanwood. Then he had to leave the stall to go to a drugstore to get something he needed for the horse. He had noticed a man wrapped in a blanket on the barn floor, probably a drunk sleeping off a spree, but there was no one else around and all looked well when he left. When he came back the drunk was sneaking out of the stall; but Smart couldn't see that he had bothered anything, so he thought he'd just been taking a good look at one of the famous Chadron-to-Chicago race horses. But the horse had gone only twenty miles on the next lap of the race when he crumpled in the road.

From the start of the race hundreds of curious people had tried to follow the riders, some in buggies, some on horseback, and some on bicycles. They were always dropping out along the way, with new ones springing up to take their places, and all of them cheering wildly as the racers passed. The day George Stanwood went down, one of the followers happened to be a veterinarian on a bicycle. He examined the horse and said he had been poisoned.

The vet worked hard to counteract the poison, which had been injected into the horse with a hypodermic needle. They knew this by the "buttons" that came out around the place where the needle went in. George Stanwood lost twelve hours because of the poison, but the next day he made 103 miles, and the day after that 104, and so came into Chicago next after Berry's horse. The other four riders were close behind. Berry won the saddle for being the first into Chicago, but was barred from the purse because he had not ridden his horse all the way. So the purse was divided among those who did ride to the finish. The Jones horse was judged the fastest and was awarded the biggest amount.[1]

~~~~~~~~~~~~~~~~

1. There are many varying accounts of the race. A booklet published by the Blaine Motor Hotel of Chadron states that Jim Dahlman, sheriff of Dawes

This race made more of a stir in the country than the World's Fair itself. It was something new and its effect was far-reaching, for it had proved the high value of the western horse. Before the race no western horses had been shipped across the Atlantic. Afterward both France and England wanted these horses, and this country did a big business in light cavalry horses, with South Dakota the leading state in furnishing such mounts.

I have noticed that most writers of today seem to think that the wild horses of the northern plains originated from a few mares and stallions lost by Cortez and De Soto. I don't believe this, mostly because horses are not migratory. When I was in Mexico in 1900 I asked a lot of questions about horses lost by Cortez. And I learned that, in fifty years time, those horses had increased to about two thousand head, but they covered a region not over one hundred miles square, which proves they were not migratory.

County, fired the starting gun and that Frank Hartzell, a local cowboy, won the race. J. R. Johnson, in *Representative Nebraskans* (Lincoln: Johnsen Publishing Co., 1954), p. 62, gives the number of entries as nine riders with seventeen horses, and the distance as fourteen hundred miles, which five riders covered in less than fourteen days, John Berry coming in first.

John Carson writes in *Doc Middleton, The Unwickedest Outlaw* (Santa Fe, N. Mex.: Press of the Territorian, 1967), that Jim Dahlman persuaded his friend Doc Middleton to "lend himself to the stunt." Ten riders signed up for the race, which carried a one-thousand-dollar purse contributed by Chadron merchants. In addition, Buffalo Bill offered five hundred dollars, and a silver-mounted saddle was also to go to the winner. June 19 was the starting date, and the nine riders (apparently one who had signed up did not start) included Doc Middleton, Joe Gillespie, Davy Douglas, George Jones, Rattlesnake Jim Stephens, Joe Campbell, Charlie Smith, Emmet Albright, and John Berry. Five of them finished the race. The rules stated only that "the first nose across the line wins"; however, because he shipped his horse part way John Berry won only the saddle, and the fifteen-hundred-dollar purse was not awarded. Joe Gillespie won a Colt .44 revolver, and Doc Middleton was awarded a velvet saddle blanket lettered "Chadron to Chicago."

The Nebraska State Historical Society's file on the Chadron to Chicago Horse Race, a collection of contemporary newspaper stories, lists, in addition to the nine entrants named by Carson, a man by the name of Crawford. According to these accounts, Berry rode up to Buffalo Bill's show tent in Chicago in thirteen days and sixteen hours, arriving at nine-thirty on the morning of June 27. Because Berry had helped lay out the route, however, he was considered by the other riders to have had an advantage, and his participation was challenged. Nevertheless, he is reported to have won the entire fifteen hundred dollars. Gillespie is listed coming in second, and Smith third. It is also stated here that Emmet Albright shipped his horses part way, and that J. O. Hartzell fired the starting gun.

When my father crossed the plains in 1847 he didn't see a single wild horse. Twenty-eight years later, in 1875, I was out with a buffalo-hunting crew on the Republican and its three tributaries, the Black Wolf, the Arickaree, and the Frenchman, and we saw only two small bands. But by 1879 the country was swarming with them, mostly in bands of about seventy head, each under a leader stallion. So, for myself, I am convinced that the wild horses of the plains sprang mostly from mares lost from emigrants, Union Pacific construction crews, and frontier expeditions. Another reason I believe this is because, at an early date, the Indians were not well mounted. And in all my time in the West I never saw or heard of a wild-horse Indian crew. No, the Indians mostly got their horses from the whites.[2]

It seems to me that all wildlife depends more on the sense of smell than on sight or hearing, but when the animal is asleep this sense is dulled, or scarcely active at all. It has been my experience that wild horses have the keenest sense of smell of any hoofed animal. Anyway, I was never able to slip up on them, even when they seemed to be asleep. In fact, I believe the leader stallion—and there was always one to each band of the usual size of fifty to seventy—slept with one eye and one ear open.

I have several times roped single stallions from a wild herd, but they were always on the run and I could only come up with them by riding a faster horse or by timing my approach to a time when they were full of grass and water. And really wild stallions were vicious. Once, on a cold, windy day, I came up with a wild horse band about thirty-five miles northeast of Sidney. A twelve-hundred-pound black stallion was standing guard on a high hill, and I decided to try a throw at him with my 7-16 Manila saddle rope. I made a dash in between him and his band and tossed my loop. When he tried to pass me, I swung in beside him and put my horse in motion to relieve the strain when the rope tightened on his windpipe. But before the

---

2. It is generally believed now that the Indians first got horses from Spanish ranches and missions in the Southwest during the latter half of the seventeenth century. Comanches were the first tribe known to have horses, but other tribes soon obtained them through trade, capture, and theft. See Walker D. Wyman, *The Wild Horse of the West* (Lincoln: University of Nebraska Press, 1962).

loop had hardly closed on the stallion's neck he came at me like a charging bull, squealing in rage, his teeth bared. My horse dodged him a couple of times, and then the stallion hit the end of the rope with force enough to snap it like a pipestem. And I was sure relieved, because he would have tangled us up good if he'd stayed in my rope much longer.

I have a son in Hollywood now [1936] who, some twenty years ago, followed the wild-horse business. He roped a wild stallion in a box canyon in Colorado once, and it nearly ate him up before his partner could shoot it down. Five years later he still had silver tubes in his sides to carry off the pus from those wounds, and even today he hasn't fully gotten over the stallion's chewing on him.

Several months after I roped the stallion that broke my rope, a bunch of Iliff cowpunchers relayed that same band and finally caught all the horses—about twenty-three, I believe. In the bunch there was a little Spanish mule wearing brands that showed he had come up the Texas trail. In the same bunch was a hobbled saddle horse that I had caught from the band a few months earlier. I had put the hobbles on him but he'd gotten away from me anyway, and the boys said he and the little mule had kept up with the band to the finish. The Iliff boys got several ropes on the big black stallion and tried to tame him down, but he fought them to his death.

In the Stinking Water region of Nebraska, south of Ogallala, I have seen thousands of wild horses. When stirred up, as many as five to seven hundred head would gather in one herd. But when let alone they soon broke up into the little bands again, each made up of about as many as one stallion could control. During mating season we often found scrub stallions that had been whipped out of the regular bands. These would gather in small sympathetic bunches that were sometimes a nuisance to us. This happened when they took up with our saddle horse remuda. And then, though they couldn't hold their own in a wild band, they could sure fight and chouse our saddle horses around. Sometimes they kept us all busy chasing them off.

I would like to say here that I've known a lot of good horses in my time: circle horses, roping horses, long-distance horses, night horses, swimming horses, and the top horse of all, the cutting horse. I've already told about that great horse, the Bosler Blue, probably the greatest cutting horse that ever lived, but there were other mighty good ones. A top cutting horse can guess which way a cow is going; that is, he knows what she is going to do before she does it. When you hear a cowboy say of his horse, "He can turn on a dime," it means he is bragging about his cutting horse. And I found that it takes less time to train a cutting horse than to educate a good cutting man. To do the cutting business, and do it right, there has to be complete cooperation between the horse and rider; and I've seen top cutting horses fail in their work when ridden by a man that didn't know his job.

I always had one or two bread-and-sugar-eating horses in my outfit, horses I could call to me from as far away as they could hear me. In camp they'd follow me around like dogs. And the best roping horse I ever rode, old Pink, weighed only 850 pounds, but a 1,300-pound steer couldn't jostle him with a side run.

And wild horses were even spookier than wild Texas cattle. I used to crawl up on the wildest of Texas calves when they were asleep and scratch their sides and bellies. They seemed to like it a lot—until they began to wake up and get a smell of me. Then they'd take off like a shot. Yes, in my estimation, wild horses are a lot wilder and keener than wild cattle.

XVI

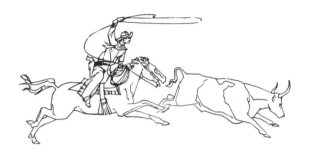

HONEYMOONING

ROSELLA BOE and I were married in 1899. We went to Chihuahua, Mexico, on our wedding trip, and her sisters, Olivia and Lenora, went with us. The hotel where we stayed was run by a full-blood Spanish gentleman who took great pains to show us the city and all its horrors, as well as its pleasures.

First we went to a brewery, three stories high, with vats twenty feet across and ten feet high. When we got to the third story they were bound we all had to sample the beer. Their sample glasses were about the size of our smallest table drinking glasses at home. I only had two, and didn't drink more than two-thirds of either of them, but just the same they had to help me down the stairs. The other five in our party seemed to make it on their own and to carry their beer without showing it.

Then we visited a quilt factory and watched them stitch quilts. The worker guided a long, adjustable arm along a chalk-mark design and could run off a quilt in about twenty minutes. Of course we had to buy a quilt, for twenty-five dollars, but the customs officer passed it through without duty, and Rosella was mighty proud of it.

Next we went to a slaughterhouse where they had nothing but

bulls to butcher. The bulls came through a chute in a solid line and the killer stood at the side of the chute, near the outer door, with an eight-pound hammer that had a three-inch knob on one end. He struck only one blow apiece as the bulls passed, and fully one-third of them rushed on by, barely stunned. The live bulls were soon among the hanging quarters of beef, hooking them down and chasing the butchers and the sight-seers. One chased Lenora clear out a back door. A butcher flashed the door open for her, then climbed some wall pegs to save himself. Maybe they were doing their work in that manner for the benefit of us sight-seers, but it was terrible the way those bulls hooked the beef quarters down into the dirt on those filthy floors.

Another great sight was the cock fights, which lasted all one afternoon. Hundreds of dollars were bet, a lot of it by ragged kids you wouldn't think had a dollar to their names. But they'd dig into their pockets and pull out a handful of Mexican money and challenge a boy with a fighting cock. The challenger, if his offer was taken by the other one, put his money in the hands of the accepter. There were no stake holders, but if lost, the money was given up at once, for the judges were official and their decision stood without question.

A swordlike metal spur about two and a half inches long was bound to one leg of each cock, and the fight seldom lasted more than one stroke, as the throat of one would be slit by the metal spur of the other. Often the throats of both cocks would be pierced at the same time, and then the dead birds would have to be pulled apart. In that case, the fight was judged a draw, but under no other circumstances did I see a draw.

And then came the bullfights, with about seven bulls killed, but not a single Mexican, which is what I was really looking for after seeing the first poor old horse killed. The horse was blindfolded and they had a leather apron across his breast to hide the hole the bull's horn made. The rider's right leg was covered with a hinged case of sheet iron which he always kept toward the bull. The matador's finishing touch was well performed and skillful. He kept a red-sided cloak on his left arm, and when the bull dropped his head to hook the cloak he plunged the two-foot, eight-inch sword into his neck, piercing his heart. If the matador made an extra-good plunge he

could pull the sword out without a drop of blood on it, and then the
ring would be showered with silver money. Those bullfights were
the most exciting performances I ever saw.

Next we went to see the gambling games. The hotelkeeper went
with us and went in first to ask the proprietor to keep order while
we were there. So a policeman was detailed to follow us around.
There were a lot of games, but the roulette wheel had the biggest
stack of money. On that table there was a circle of twenty-dollar gold
pieces about eighteen inches across, drawing to a peak about two
feet high and finished off with five-dollar gold pieces. I should judge
there was about twenty-five thousand dollars in that pile.

Three couples of us went in: the hotelkeeper and Lenora, the
hotel's chief clerk and Olivia, and Rosella and I. We were walking in
that order when we came out, and as we walked on back toward the
hotel we passed the palace headquarters where there were some big
porch pillars. Suddenly the hotelkeeper's wife jumped out from
behind a pillar and lunged at Lenora with a dagger in her hand. Her
husband must have seen her in time, because he caught her and took
her back to the hotel, where he locked her in her room with a guard
for the balance of our stay, which was about three more days.

The next year my wife and I took a trip to Mobita, Texas, a town
that had no railroad and less than forty houses. We were there about
a week, waiting for a herd of 4,300 steers to be delivered at Canadian.
And while we were there I heard news of an old acquaintance,
Panhandle Pete. Panhandle Pete was said to have killed more buffalo
then even Buffalo Bill, but his killing time extended over more years.
It was also said that he had sold more rotgut whiskey and served
more dirty meals to hungry wayfarers than any man of his day. And,
with the possible exception of Jack Marrow, had traded more guns
and ammunition to the Indians for rich cargoes of buffalo hides,
furs, and pelts. These he had freighted by ox team to the railroad to
be sold on the Kansas City market. He also traded beads, knives,
hatchets, cheap jewelry, and calico for heavy work horses and mules
the Indians had stolen from the whites.

In about 1875, Pete took unto himself a wife, Miss Malinda
Thomas, an educated mixed-blood squaw, and his reign among the
Indians was then supreme. Malinda was a rather nice-looking girl,

and very entertaining in a way. She was also a bum cook and did not add much to the road ranch bill of fare. But Pete, with his wife's able seductions, kept on gaining in wealth until all Malinda had to do was entertain.

After a while Pete was sending whole bull-train loads of hides, pelts, furs, and tallow to market. Malinda often went along with the trains to Kansas City, where she took flyers in parading in her silks and satins and chartering boxes in the playhouses. On such occasions she would fill the boxes with Pete's patrons and serve them all kinds of luxuries at his expense. Pete, of course, did not go along, as none could rob the Indians to their complete satisfaction as well as he could.

Mobita was said, at one time, to be the wickedest town in the country except for Yellow House Canyon in what is now Lubbock County, Texas. It had absolutely no government, while Mobita was supposed to have a little. A big gambling house there was built of adobe, and the Indians called it the Yellow House, which was how the place got its name. The gambling, said to be financed by a bandit leader, was mostly patronized by Mexicans, and killings were so commonplace that they were scoffed at.

By the time my wife and I were there in 1900 things had tamed down and Panhandle Pete had long since gone broke. He had retrograded to a real squaw man and was living with his wife's people on the reservation. Malinda's father, however, was a chief, and Pete was an honored guest in his home, where he was served dog stew and left to loaf in the sun.

Malinda still entertained, but cowmen now, who came to the reservation to solicit grazing leases from the chief. She was interpreter and adviser for these deals, and it was said the old chief spent the "sweetening money" on fast horses and big council feeds. Pete had his place at these feeds, but being a business failure himself was not allowed a seat in the council lodge. He still had his six-gun and rifle nerves, though, and not long before my visit to Mobita had added another notch to his gun handle—for a Mexican bootlegger who had trespassed on his range.

The Yellow House was only a few miles from the northeast corner of our NUN cattle pasture in Lubbock, Donley, and Scoby

[Crosby?] counties of Texas, and I had often seen the remains of the notorious old place. A strange story was told me there about two young brothers who had taken up with the outlaws of that region. The boys had been born and raised in that country, and when the law came in and the place began to tame down the brothers didn't want to leave. Instead, they holed up on an island in a salt lake in what later became our pasture.

The lake was about a mile and a half across and the island was near its center. It was covered with scrub timber and had a shallow approach across the lake from the west side. The boys crossed that three-hundred-yard-wide stretch of water on two planks, which they relayed as pontoons. They built themselves a log cabin in the timber and lived there for quite a while. The authorities tried to get at them, but they were both crack shots and kept the approach clear. They also dug themselves a shallow well on the island, which gave them a big advantage, as there was no other usable water within forty miles. For this reason they were never captured, as posses could not hang around long without water for themselves and their horses.

I was never on the island, but John Ivy, our ranch manager, had been there several times and had seen the old stronghold close up. I could see the tumble-down old cabin from the far bank, though, and we had to put down forty wells with windmills, and build thirty-two earthen tanks to take care of the seventeen thousand cattle we ran there. For our NUN pasture was made up of 360,000 acres and, except for that salty lake, there wasn't a drop of surface water on it.

XVII

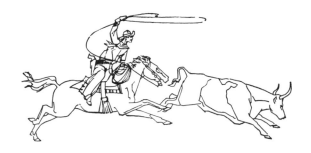

BUSINESS AND PLEASURE

IN 1900 THE National Livestock Association held its convention in Fort Worth, Texas, and we made up quite a party from our district and went down on the train. We had the secretary-treasurer of our Western South Dakota Association, Frank Stewart, and his wife; and Tripp, an agent for a patent branding iron, and his wife; and M. C. (Milt) Connors, who squired Bessie Burton, an opera singer from Spearfish. We took her along as the singing entertainment for our delegation. Then there was Ike Humphrey, banker, cattleman, and board member, who was with Bell Scott of Omaha. Bell had just won a trip anywhere in the United States from the Omaha *Bee* and the *World Herald* in a newspaper contest. She had decided to go with us to the convention, and then on to San Antonio and Galveston. The odd men in the bunch were Tony Day, Scotty Philip, and myself.

Scotty was the big buffalo rancher of Pierre. He had come up from Texas in '75, took unto himself a mixed-blood Indian wife, and raised quite a family of boys and girls. One of his sons was a member of our state legislature. Scotty was the Buffalo Bill type, a good mixer, much admired by the ladies, and always the leader of any group he was a part of.

All the men in our party except Tripp were delegates to the convention, with free admission to all shows, balls, and carnivals in the city during the meetings. Mrs. Stewart was in charge of entertainment for our crowd, and she made it a point to see that the ladies were passed around to the men escorts, as men outnumbered the ladies two to one. In this manner Scotty soon became well acquainted with the ladies and was very much a favorite with them all. This was mortifying to Tony Day and myself, who were rather on the scrub order. In the evenings after the public entertainment was over, a crowd usually gathered in the parlor of the Worth Hotel, where we all put up, to hear Bessie Burton sing, since she had a wonderful voice, and we'd all have a fine time.

Scotty spent quite a lot of time in the shops, looking for curios to take home to his wife and daughters he said. One evening he brought in a flashy bracelet and showed it to the hotel parlor crowd. Bessie especially admired it, and Scotty said, "Well, I'll just make you a present of it." Then he said it had a puzzle clasp that no one but himself understood and he would have to put it on her. But in so doing he put his arms around her and took quite a while at it. It seemed to us scrubs that he, in a manner, held her tighter than he needed to, just to fasten a bracelet.

The next evening he came to the parlor with a fine necklace. It had a puzzle clasp, too, and Bell Scott almost went into hysterics over it. Scotty gave it to her, of course, and again managed to put his arms around the lady while fastening it on her neck. And again we scrubs had to look on from the side line.

He came in with a pair of long, shiny filigree lace stockings the next evening and handed them to Mrs. Stewart. She held them up and her eyes were shining with admiration. But when Scotty started toward her she said, "Now, Scotty, I admire your taste in hose, but if you intend to put them on for me I'll have to decline your present."

Scotty never batted an eye. "The treats are on me," he said. "Just name the place and order the best grub they've got. And if you will see that this story doesn't get back to Pierre, you can order the finest silk dress on the market and I'll pay for it." Yes, Scotty was game, all right. At one time he owned a thousand buffalo and had a boat on the Missouri River named after him.

Cattle buyers from just about all over the world were there at that convention, and a lot of them stayed at the Worth. On the opening day of the meetings the hotel waiters, all union Negroes, struck. Hardwick, the manager, then brought in a full staff of nonunion men, or scabs, also all Negroes. The dining room was on the second floor, and a sixteen-foot-wide hallway led from it to the elevator. When we all sat down at the table for our noon meal that day, I had a Cuban stock cattle buyer named Pierce on my right and John Shy, of the John Clay Company, on my left, all facing the hallway and the elevator.

Suddenly one of the striking waiters jumped off the elevator and came running down the hall toward the dining room. He had a six-shooter in his hand and looked like he meant business of some kind. He was within twenty feet of our table when a scab waiter met him with a razor in his hand. The gunman began shooting and the razor man began slashing. My table mates started to get up and stampede out of the line of fire, but I grabbed one in each hand and yelled, "Sit down or you'll catch some lead." For I could see by the elevation of the gunman's arm that the bullets were going just over our heads. But there was no holding Shy and Pierce, or anybody else at the table for that matter, and they were all soon bunched in the ends of the dining room.

The gunman had fired off about three shots when the scab head waiter simply tore into that pair. Grabbing the razor man first, he whirled him backward about twenty feet and the razor went flying through the air. Then he grabbed the gunman, disarmed him in a second, and waltzed him to the elevator, where they met a policeman someone had called in. After that show of nerve, no one can ever convince me that Negroes don't have plenty of it. But when I twitted Shy, an old friend, about his lack of nerve he came right back at me by saying I was too scared to move out of the way.

[205]

Two years later (1902) my outfit leased 865,429 acres of range on the Standing Rock reservation. I had this big tract fenced with 270 miles of three-wire fence, making it the biggest fenced pasture in the world at that time. I had had dealings with the Standing Rock people ever since Colonel [James] McLaughlin came to the agency in 1881. He had taken unto himself a well-educated mixed-blood woman from the Pipestone reservation east of the river, and had developed into a fine, competent agent. After ten years as agent he had come to know Indians and their ways so well that he was made a special agent, or inspector, and sent to Pine Ridge in 1891 to sit in on a case where three thousand range cattle had been impounded for trespassing on the reservation. Including myself, there were forty-two of us cowmen as defendants in that case.

At this hearing I clinched my friendship with the Colonel by furnishing him information that helped him with the case, and, strictly on my statements, the verdict came back from Washington in the cattlemen's favor. The government ruled that so large an industry as ours, which bordered on the reservation, could not be jeopardized by Indians swinging off the reservation at night and drifting livestock onto their land so as to collect trespass and gathering fees. Therefore, said Washington, if the Indians wanted to protect their grass they would have to fence their lands. This they did. But the fences lasted only two or three years, due mostly to their own mixed-bloods, who were too lazy either to hunt gates or to reset staples after pulling them out to make "let downs" so they could cross their horses over the fence.

On my own fencing crew that spring I had a young mixed-blood, a son of Buckskin Harrison. Buckskin had associated with Indians since Hudson's Bay times and had married three squaws. He later had a white wife who, in the 1930's, still lived in McIntosh, South Dakota. The Harrison boy who worked for me was a tall, handsome lad of about nineteen. He had earlier gotten into some kind of trouble on the reservation and was wanted at Fort Yates to explain it. Two Indian police were sent out to bring him in, and the day they came the cook wagon happened to be camped quite a ways out from the fence work.

Hugh Johnson, a post and wire hauler, was in camp when the

police rode up and asked for Harrison. Hugh slipped away, jumped on a saddled horse belonging to our wolfer, Matt Classen, and took a roundabout way to the fence line. He cached the horse in a thicket some two hundred yards from the end of the fence and hotfooted it over to the crew, where he told Harrison the police were after him and that there was a saddled horse over there in the brush. Harrison streaked up the draw, got the horse, and left for far away parts.

Of course Johnson was still there when the police rode up a little later. They recognized him as one of the men they'd seen at the cook wagon and figured out the rest. So they arrested him as an accomplice and took him to the agent, who was judge, jury, and executioner for all Indian business. But as Harrison's offense had been a tribal matter of little importance to the agent, he paroled Johnson to me when I showed up at the agency a bit later.

As for Harrison, since he wasn't sure what kind of a sentence the tribal court would dole out to him, he kept riding. He was the kind that has to live in the open, and he wasn't taking any chances. He never came back to his homeland, nor did he return the horse and saddle, or pay for them, but Matt didn't mind. He was glad the boy got away, for such is the code of the West. We heard later, though, that Harrison didn't stop until he got to the Crows in Montana, where he took up with a Crow family that had just lost a son of about his age and appearance. The family adopted him, so the story went, and had him put on the ration and annuity list. They had a new agent on that reservation, and to him all Indians, like Negroes or Chinese, still looked alike, and they could get away with their scheme.

We shipped in a lot of cattle to run in that Standing Rock pasture, and one time, about the third year after we fenced it, I contracted for seventeen hundred two-year-old Oregon and Nevada steers. They were to be shipped to Dickinson, unloaded there, and driven to the pasture by a crew made up of the boss, Roger Boe; the cook, Ed Comstock; the night hawk, Tom Fly; the wrangler, Rusty Gilmore; and cowhands Ed Armstrong, Bill Claymore, Tommy Traversie, Albert Antelope, Jess Dalton, and Clyde and Frank Glover. Most of these boys were pretty strongly seasoned with Sioux blood.

[207]

Well, when the crew got into Dickinson they found there'd been a delay in receiving the cattle at the west end of the line, which meant they'd just have to wait there until the shipment came in. In earlier days, when the Marquis de Mores, Teddy Roosevelt, the Huide-kopers, and the 777 outfits had in a manner made Dickinson their main beef-shipping headquarters, Dickinson had been a wide-open cattle town. But all that had long passed away.

So when Ed Comstock drove his four-horse team, old Tom, Jerry, Widy, and Schneider, down main street, his four reins in one hand and his four-horse buckskin whip in the other, the whole town, including the mayor, turned out to see him and the crew. Right away the town turned the keys to the whole place over to them, and all they asked was that they not run down any ladies or children, or shoot out any plate-glass windows. And it wasn't long until Connie Huffman spied old Ed and came running out to fall into his arms and promise the whole outfit her undivided attention and a whale of a good time.

Connie had been the leading painted girl in Deadwood in the early days when Henry Weare, George Jackson, Bill Brady, Jack Tolbert, Ump Hood, Charles Connely, M. C. Connors, Tom Mathers, Billie Thatcher, Cap Willard, and Billie Moses were the leading sports of the region. She had been a straight shooter in her day, for she wouldn't permit any rolling of customers knocked out by too much redeye in her emporium. Neither would she let them be locked up in the sobering-up guardhouse. Instead, she bedded them down in her house until they were sober enough to straddle a horse and head for the ranch or roundup where they belonged. The boys had appreciated Connie's consideration so much that they had taken up a five-hundred-dollar collection and had a Chinaman dressmaker fix her up a silk dress with all the stock brands of that section embroidered on it. The biggest brand of all was Henry Weare's Cross Anchor, about five inches high and right in the middle of the back of the waist. They gave it to her with a fitting ceremony, and Connie wore it only when that particular crowd was in town.

When the cattle-business center moved from Deadwood to Spearfish and Belle Fourche, Connie's admirers sort of lost track of her; and anyway she was growing older and new girls had come in to take her place. She happened to be living in Dickinson when our L7 bunch came to town that summer of 1905. And when she saw Ed, one of her old friends of the Deadwood days, she rejuvenated in a hurry and gave the whole outfit a hearty welcome. Right away she put on the silk dress, which had been packed away for ten years or more. And every afternoon Ed would hitch up the four horses to the wagon and get Connie up beside him on the high seat in her silk embroidered dress, and they'd parade through the streets with the L7 boys lined up on each side of the wagon.

On the day before the steers finally came in, the boys put on a real celebration. That day Ed wore Connie's silk dress and Connie, in her own best straight silks, perched beside him on the seat. Then, with the cowboys riding on both sides of the wagon, they went down main street on the high run, smoking up the town. Everybody in the place came out to watch that last fine big fling. Each of the boys probably had about seventy-five dollars in his pocket when the crew hit town, and the boss, Roger Boe, had more. But all of it was soon gone, and when their money ran out the boys charged their drinks at all the saloons. Because the delay on the cattle shipment had stretched out to about two weeks, the bills that were finally mailed to me added up to almost $450. The only thing I could do was prorate it among them and take it out of their wages.

Some twenty-five years after the parade Connie and the L7 boys put on, Frank Glover and I were talking about it and Frank said that, including the grub bill, he figured the boys left about $1,900 in Dickinson that trip. In telling about that last grand day in later years, Ed always declared he had that wagon going at a twenty-mile-an-hour clip. But I know better, because those were the biggest teams I ever saw on a mess wagon. Each horse weighed over fourteen hundred pounds, and I know they could hardly strike even an eight-mile-an-hour gait. But we never argued with Ed about his fast teams. Poor little Ed died in Brisbane, North Dakota, where he ended up running a little cream station in his last years.

XVIII

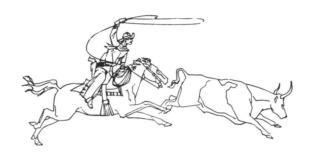

EARLY CATTLEMEN

T O THE BEST of my knowledge, the first range cattle in the Little Missouri region were brought in by the Deffenbach brothers—Dan, John, Rassey, Ed, and Levi—in 1878.[1] Joel Collins had brought in 600 cows two years earlier, but those were for slaughter. Lank Forbes came next, with about 800 mixed cattle that he turned loose in August near the stage·crossing on the Cheyenne River. A good many herds came in '79, brought in by the Driskill brothers—Tobe, Bud, Dell, and Jess—and by the Dickeys, Val and John; M. C. Connors; and maybe the Hashknife, with Ump Hood as manager.

William Bradford Grimes, on the Cheyenne River, threw in with Lank Forbes with about 5,000 head, mostly steers, and W. F. Phillips as range manager. Soon after came Major Smith and his manager, Bruce Sebastion, to set up the Capital B on the Little Missouri. About the same time came Hilan Hulan, Maurice Apple, Godkin, and A. Giles, all near Belle Fourche.

1. According to Bob Lee and Dick Williams, *Last Grass Frontier: The South Dakota Stock Growers Heritage* (Sturgis, S.D.: Black Hills Publishers, 1964), pp. 47, 48, John and Erasmus Deffenbach took a beef herd from Colorado into the Spearfish Valley in 1876 and settled there.

In 1880 cattle and owners came in by leaps and bounds: D. H. Clark and Company, Flying V brand, with myself as assistant foreman; Stearns and Patterson, John Higgins, foreman, the Quarter Circle Acorn their brand. Haft and Jacobey, Bill Blair, foreman; Frease and Gregory, Bow and Arrow brand; Morris Brothers; Pete Duhammel; Eli Lonzeman; the Gould brothers, Hank and Lee; and Bill Young: all these came in from Colorado.

The next season, 1881, nearly all the old Black Hills freighters went into the cattle business. Among them were Morris Kelliher; John Hart; Mike Quinn; Alf Hart; Jack Daly; Nels Torkelson; Tim Brickley; Stevenson and Sons; Holcomb and Sons, Eugene, Bud, and Fred; Tingley, on Alkali Creek; and Billie Adams, who bought out Frease and Gregory's Bow and Arrow.

The Weares, Henry and P. B., stocked up on the Belle Fourche River, east of Hulett, mostly with what we termed Minnesota dogies,[2] but also with at least one herd of Texas cattle. These were received from M. C. Connors at the Cheyenne crossing on the stage line from Sidney. It was there that Henry Weare had an unpleasantry with Connors over the classification of two-year-old steers. Weare was a much younger man, and Connors declared he would not be dictated to by a whiskerless tenderfoot. Henry then pulled his gun and shoved it under M. C.'s right arm. But P. B. rushed up, grabbed the gun with both hands, and said, "Henry, you damn fool. If you kill him it will spoil this whole deal." I well recall that M. C. never batted an eye, but went right on with the classification.[3]

At that time Weare was, after a fashion, the leader of the cowboys of that region, seconded by Jack Talbert, George Jackson, Bill Brady, Ump Hood, Lee Cresswell, Charles Connely, Ves Merritt, Jess Borland, Jim Dahlman, Manuel Coy, Bud Baird, and old Josh Jones.

The next summer twelve-year-old Alex Duhammel punched the drags[4] of a herd all the way from Colorado; and the King Cattle

2. Mixed cattle, mostly dairy and scrub stock.

3. A note inserted by Ed Lemmon describes M. C. Connors as "the greatest roulette and faro gambler I ever knew. He and his wife went down on the *Titanic*, as one was bringing the remains of the other back to the United States from a tour abroad. I am not certain which one was the corpse."

4. The slower, weaker animals of the trail herd. Since the drags brought up

Company put two herds on the Belle Fourche near the mouth of Alkali Creek, with Jack Talbert as manager. Later came J. W. Buster of the Hashknife, with Bill Lefors and Quint Hunter. All except Buster were expert gunmen. Other well-known cowboys of that time and region were Billie Moses, the great roper, Sam Moses, Cheyenne Bill Taylor, Jim and Arch Crawford, Hank Lovett, Johnny Owens, Webb Arnett, Al Powell, Charles and Ed Graham, Bill Hudspeth, and Sam Griffith. These all centered, in a manner, in Custer.

Then there was Sam Bell, no slouch with a six-shooter, who got his remount education on Missouri mules in the early seventies. Sam came up the trail in '79 with the W. B. Grimes outfit. George Moore was another of the early comers. He trailed L7 cattle up from the Indian Territory that same year and ranged them with the Shiner Brothers' herds on the Cheyenne, east of the Grimes' stock, under the management of Nat Haines. Jack Depolster and Lum Bagwell also came in '79. Lum followed Ross Willson as manager of the K6 on Grand River, an outfit owned by Dorr, Clark, and Plumb. Clark was a brother-in-law of Henry Weare.

I had my first look at the territory that is now Perkins County in 1881, on my way home from Fort Yates, where I had delivered over seven hundred head of beef cattle, the first the Sitting Bull Indians got for their exclusive use. When we came up onto the tableland now known as Delaney Flats it was simply swarming with buffalo. The reason there were so many was that the country was then an Indian reservation and hide hunters were not allowed inside it. We didn't bother the buffalo either, except to rope a couple, earmark them, and play with them a little while. Later that fall Colonel James McLaughlin came out there with the Sitting Bull Indians and killed 5,000 buffalo, the last big killing of buffalo in the United States. The killing ground covered about two townships and was mostly in what is now Perkins County, but also partly in Adams County, North Dakota.

The first cattle in Perkins County were brought in by Clark and

---

the rear of the herd, punching them was the dirtiest, most unpleasant job in the outfit, and was usually given to the newest or youngest member of the crew.

Plumb of the E6 brand. A herd of 7,000 head, mostly steers, with a sprinkling of cows to help keep the steers on the home range. They were brought up from Texas and located on the Grand River in 1882. The second herd was brought in by Robinson, the father of Mrs. Lou Kirkland. This was a small herd of about 175 head. The third herd, brought in by Giles and located near White Butte on the North Grand, wore the OG brand.

In 1892 the Cresswell Cattle Company bought out the E6 and right away added many thousands of cattle to the range. By 1900 they had the largest stock of cattle in the north, about 70,000 head. In 1901 Ben Garland bought the OG and brought in 7,000 more steers from Texas and the Indian Territory. But only about two-thirds of this herd ranged in present Perkins County. The rest were over in Harding County, west of us.

In 1883 we (the Sheidley Cattle Company) put about 10,000 stock cattle bearing the Flying V brand on the Moreau River. We kept adding to this herd and by 1889 had 25,000 head of mixed cattle. By then we had several subsidiary outfits, mostly with the same owners but different names. The first of these was the D. H. Clark and Company. The second was Sheidley, Lake, Tomb, and Lemmon; the third was Lake, Tomb and Company. Two years later the Lake, Tomb Company owned about 67,000 cattle in all. Some of the cattle were in Texas and some in Montana, about ninety miles northwest of Miles City.

In 1891 L. K. Wilson came to Perkins County and settled on the Moreau River about fourteen miles below Bixby. He had about 800 head of cattle. Joe Green came about the same time, with a like number of cattle from the Little Missouri, and located three miles below the mouth of Rabbit Creek. The Wells horse outfit brought in 700 head of horses in 1899 and 1900 and settled at the mouth of Rabbit Creek. In 1902 Henry Duncan moved from the Cannonball to Rabbit, just below Usta, with about 160 head of cattle. Soon afterward "Shock" Hall, A. W. Drew, Ed Barthold, Henry Pilger, Ernest Smith, and A. D. Reder moved to Antelope and Rabbit creeks. These men jointly owned about 3,000 cattle, which I took to range, the owners furnishing the necessary men to look after them.

[213]

In 1893 Sam Williams settled on the Moreau River, near Joe Green, with about 500 cattle. At about the same time the Anderson brothers, John and Bill, came in on the mouth of Deep Creek. The next year the Witchers, Ed Moran, Adburn Clapp, and Alex (Scotty) Milne came. In 1900 Miles and his son-in-law, T. B. Veal, came in. The last six had from 75 to 400 head of cattle apiece. Charles Hall and Charles Settle came about 1900. Alex Rail, a trifle ahead of them, had located on Thunder Butte Creek about five miles below Veal. By this time there were nearly one hundred thousand head of cattle in what is now Perkins County, but we (the Sheidley outfit) were the largest owners within the county, as most of the Cresswell cattle ranged in other counties and states.

As far as I know, Mrs. Crawford was the first white woman to make her permanent home in Perkins County. She came to Bixby on June 10, 1891. Mrs. Wilson came a little later that same year, and both of them stayed for the rest of their lives. Mrs. Henry Duncan came in 1892.

Families who came early to this wilderness country mostly had a hard time of it. One of the earliest to come into the Black Hills region before the country to the north was settled was the Davis family. T. G. Davis and his son Will first came to Deadwood in May, 1877. They picked a location on the Redwater, then went down to Sidney in December. They left their teams, one pair of horses and one pair of mules, and their covered wagons there and went back to Mondamin, Iowa, for the rest of the family. They came back to Sidney by train, picked up their teams and wagons, and headed north. At Spring Creek, about fourteen miles south of present Rapid City, a three-day snowstorm caught them. When it was over, snow three feet deep covered the valley, but the ridges were bare. By meandering on the ridges they were able to make a few miles a day, and so reached the Redwater a week later, sometime in March, 1878.

They first took to gardening, under irrigation, and their main crops were watermelons and yellow danker onions. Both were valuable crops in those days, especially the onions, which they peddled to miners to ward off or cure scurvy. This dreaded disease was brought on in the winter mining camps by inactivity and eating too much sowbelly. Onions were even better than potatoes as a cure for that, and brought a high price at such times, even as much as a dollar a bushel.

The Davises became well acquainted with the Deffenbachs, who stopped at their place on their drives up from Texas with cattle. On one of their drives John Deffenbach was killed by Indians on the upper Belle Fourche.[5] Russ Wilson, the Deffenbach foreman, was with him when he was killed, and a man by the name of Tom Smith came back by the Davis place right afterward, riding the horse John was riding when he was killed. Russ was Ben Wilson's brother. He was fresh from Missouri when Ben and Hervey picked him up in Texas in 1874. After giving him some pointers on cowpunching, they had recommended him to a trail-driving crew. He made good there, and was soon a boss for Walker and Johnson, near Cheyenne. The Deffenbachs then hired him from Walker and Johnson to help them make their cattle drives through the Indian country on the way to the Black Hills. At that time he was also a captain in the Wyoming Rangers, helping to put down Indian depredations. Russ was later a boss for Clark and Plumb, where he stayed until the outfit was turned over to John Clay, whose range manager was Billie Moses.

I have a diamond willow cane that was given to me by Frank Glover. Frank, an old cowboy friend of mine, carved fifty brands on the cane, all brands of outfits I knew well or was connected with. The stick measures three feet from end to end, and the brands, instead of being cut into the wood, stand out in relief, the willow being cut away from around them. Along with the brands there is my name and Frank's, then a carved dogie wearing my L7 brand, and crawling around the brands are two big rattlesnakes, one with seven rattles, the other with nine. The fifty brands represent about half a million cattle and 4,000 horses. Many more brands and

5. According to Lee and Williams in *Last Grass Frontier*, p. 48, John Deffenbach was killed by the Sioux while trailing a beef herd to the Hills from Wyoming in 1877.

thousands more cattle were on this range in those years, for it was all open country, subject to the working of the roundups that operated over the territory each summer and covered western North and South Dakotas and eastern Montana and Wyoming.

The number of cattle given as represented by each brand indicates the number that outfit had on the range at a given time and which was maintained from one year to another. As each outfit shipped cattle to market it replaced about the same number by shipping in more or by branding calves. The range given here for each brand means where each outfit had its home ranch, or where it "turned loose." Thus the E6 was on Grand River in Harding County. It later belonged to the Turkey Track, the biggest cow outfit on the range, carrying over 60,000 head on its books, and maybe on the range, too.

The Turkey Track home ranch was a small two-room log house and a fair-sized horse corral. If the assessor had ever got around to them, he wouldn't have assessed the value of their improvements at more than two hundred dollars, or about the price of three good steers. But there each year 60,000 cattle were turned loose. Of course they didn't stay put, nor were they meant to. In a few months after the roundup was over you could find more Turkey Tracks at most any point in western South Dakota than at the home ranch in Harding County. Nor did these cattle all drift southeast, for some of them would be gathered in Wyoming and Montana, come spring. And by the same token the Turkey Track home range pastured many cattle of other brands for most of the year.

Here below are the brands Frank carved on my diamond willow cane:

AA, John and Bill Anderson's brand. It marked 1,000 head of cattle ranging in east Perkins County from Grand River to Rabbit Creek. John Anderson, the second sheriff of Perkins County, was an expert at reading brands. When John said, "The herd is clean," nobody else ever rode in.

BXB. This brand, owned by the Vermont Cattle Company, marked 12,000 cattle that ran on the Moreau River. The post office of Bixby was named for their brand.

The Can't Savvy, or No Savvy, brand was owned by Charles Dumont, who ranged cattle in the southern Black Hills.

CATTLE BRANDS AND RANGES *(legend overleaf)*

LEGEND

AA	
BXB	
Y	Can't Savvy
⊙	Circle Dot
◎	Circle O
⌐Γ	Reversed L7
NUN	
RR	
S	Cross S
⊖	Mill Iron
CY	
G⊰	C Lazy Y
Ⱥ	Diamond M
DP	
E6	
⼋	Turkey Track
∨	Flying V
4L	4HL Connected
G—	G Bar
JA	
ℬ	JB Connected
JℍL	JHL Connected
JX	
✠	Maltese Cross
MC	
M̲D̲	MD Bar
N O	NO
NSS	
O̲	O Bar
♀	O Cross
OHO	
P̲E̲	PE Bar

P̲K̲	PK Bar
℞	Reversed RR Connected
✕✕	Square and Compass
TX	
V+	V Cross
Ս5	U5
V̲	V Bar
VVV	Three Vs
ⵁ	YO
W	YW Connected
YT	
ⵣ	ZT Connected
ZZZ	Three Zs
DZ	DZ Connected
OG	
—L	Bar L
B—	B Bar
O-O	Circle Bar O
Ⱥ	Diamond A
=	Two Bar
Z∩	Z Bell
—T	Bar T
777	Three Sevens
⳹	Cross Anchor
B	Capital B
♡	Heart
C	
76	
WG	
H̲3̲	H3 Bar
N̲	N Bar

Circle Dot O, owner James Lemmon, ran 150 head of cattle on the Moreau River.

Circle O, a brand owned by Lake, Tomb, and Lemmon, who ran 4,000 head under that mark on the Moreau River.

Cross S and the Mill Iron, both owned by the Franklin Cattle Company, branded 40,000 cattle ranging from the Powder River to Box Elder Creek in Montana.

CY and C Lazy C, brands owned by Robert Carey, were used on 20,000 cattle ranging on the Little Missouri in Wyoming and Montana.

Diamond M, owned by Carl Mossman, who ran 35,000 head of cattle.

DP, Dan Powell's brand, marked cattle running on Four-mile Creek.

E6 and the Turkey Track, both belonging to the big Cresswell Cattle Company. Cattle under those brands ranged all over Harding and Perkins counties. The main street of Bison long showed the imprint of the hooves of those old Longhorns belonging to that outfit, the biggest in the country.

Flying V, the Sheidley Cattle Company, whose range stretched from Rabbit Creek to the Belle Fourche and from Slim Buttes to the Moreau River, where ranged some 30,000 head of cattle under that brand.

4HL Connected, a brand belonging to L. Hill, who ranged 500 cattle on Four-mile on the gumbo.

G Bar, owned by the Glover and Sosh outfit, was the brand of a horse ranch that ran several hundred head of horses on the Belle Fourche.

JA, the brand owned by Mrs. J. A. Adair, who ran 10,000 cattle on the Belle Fourche.

JB Connected. Abe Jones ranged 3,000 head of Percheron horses over all of Perkins County under that brand.

JHL Connected, owned by Bill Holst, who ranged cattle on Four-mile on the gumbo.

JX. Walt Willard ran 1,000 cattle under this brand on the Upper Moreau in the Slim Buttes region.

L7 [the Reversed L7] was owned by Lake, Tomb, and Lemmon. The firm ran 33,000 cattle on the Moreau River under this brand.

Maltese Cross. One of the most famous brands in the country, it was used by Teddy Roosevelt between 1880 and 1887, when he ran 6,000 head of cattle on the Little Missouri in southern North Dakota. Roosevelt pitched right in and did the regular work of a cowboy on the range, riding circle in the daytime and standing his two-hour hitch on night guard. He took orders from the wagon boss, the same as any other waddy. In those days he often drove from his headquarters ranch at Medora to Deadwood in a buckboard. On the way he'd stop off with Mrs. Sallie Catron, near Camp Crook, where she cooked many a good meal for the man who was one day to be President of the United States. I believe I sold, for Roosevelt's account with the OX outfit, the last range cow he ever owned. She wore the Maltese Cross brand and was a bunch quitter. She always ranged in the Slim Buttes country, and no one had ever been able to hold her under herd long enough to get her back to Roosevelt's home range near Medora. I finally sold her to Zeechler Brothers, Deadwood butchers.

MC, a brand owned by Mort Connor, marked 25,000 cattle on the Little Missouri in Wyoming and Montana.

MD Bar. Martin Driskill was the owner, running 1,000 cattle on the Belle Fourche.

NO. The NO brand, owned by L. C. Peck, marked 1,000 head of horses on the reservation line south of Lemmon.

NSS was a brand belonging to Narcisse Narcelle, who ranged 5,000 cattle on the Lower Moreau.

NUN, a brand owned by Lake, Tomb, and Lemmon, was worn by 22,000 cattle ranging from Thunder Butte Creek to the Belle Fourche River.

(O), Rosella Lemmon's brand, was used on 150 head of cattle on the Moreau River.

O Bar, a brand owned by Hunter and Bergman, who ran 2,000 cattle on a range in the southern Black Hills.

O Cross, the Woods, White, and Woods brand, marking 35,000 head of cattle ranging along Sulphur Creek and the Elms on the gumbo.

OHO, a brand worn by 10,000 cattle owned by Eugene Holcomb. His range was in the Cedar Canyon and Frozen Man Creek country.

PE Bar, owned by Arthur Edwards, who ranged 600 cattle along Willow Creek.

Pitchfork, the brand of George Glover, was used on four hundred cattle on the Belle Fourche.

PK Bar, brand of Paul Kinsler, another rancher on Willow Creek.

RR, another Lake, Tomb, and Lemmon brand, worn by 20,000 head of cattle on the Moreau River, Frozen Man, Sulphur, and Camp creeks.

Reversed RR Connected, a brand owned by Peter Hafner, who used it on 200 head of cattle on the North Moreau.

Square and Compass, a brand owned by Alphie Johnson, a rancher on the Cheyenne and Belle Fourche rivers, where he ran 1,000 head of cattle.

TX. Ben Garland owned this brand and ranged 7,000 head under it on the North and South Grand Rivers. His first cattle, a few over 3,000 head, came up from Texas in the summer of 1890. The herd left Texas April 15 and was turned loose at the forks of the Grand in Perkins County on July 19, making an even one hundred days on the thousand-mile trail. Charley Ross, a long-time resident of the county, had charge of that drive.

Turkey Track—see page 217.

U5, a brand marking 600 cattle on the Lower Cheyenne. Jim Cox was the owner.

V Bar. H. C. Wilson owner. Five hundred cattle under this brand ranged the Elms on the gumbo.

V Cross, a brand marking 6,000 cattle owned by C. K. Howard, whose range was on White River.

VVV or Three Vs, owned by John Clay of Clay, Robinson and Company of Chicago. This outfit used range on the Chugwater and the headwaters of the Belle Fourche for its 15,000 cattle.

YO, John Glover's brand, used on 500 head of cattle ranging on the Belle Fourche.

YW Connected. Whitlock's brand. He ran 500 head of cattle on Pumpkin Creek in Montana.

YT, a brand belonging to Hunter and Bergman, used on 15,000 cattle ranging in northeastern Wyoming.

ZT Connected. W. I. Walker's brand on the lower Belle Fourche. One thousand cattle.

ZZZ, the brand owned by Bill Jones on Rabbit Creek. Bill ran 1,000 cattle.

Dan Zimmerman ranged 7,000 head of cattle on the lower Moreau River in the firesteel and Flint Rock country.

XIX

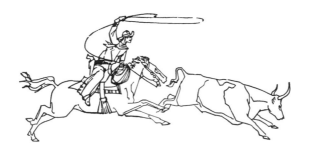

THE COWBOY'S LIFE

OLD-TIME OPEN-RANGE spring roundups lasted about fifty days, and it was "get there" from start to finish, with no time for nice toilets. So clean underwear, and especially socks, were at a premium. The clean socks were important because boots make sweaty feet, which bother a rider because he bears so much weight on them in the stirrups. When a man rolled out of bed at a quarter to three in the morning and didn't get back to the wagon until between seven and nine at night, he didn't feel much like hunting a mud puddle and washing out a pair of socks—not when he still had to slice a two-hour hunk of night guard out of the little piece of night-time he had left for sleeping. So all hands usually started the roundup season with several changes of socks, but along about the last two weeks they would all be used up. About then it got to be a custom for the boys to keep their eyes peeled for a newcomer into camp who might happen to have a fresh supply.

I remember one time when I joined the roundup on Bad River in '96. While looking for something in my war bag I foolishly pulled out half a dozen pairs of new socks. Now it was quite a joke in the whole outfit that I never carried a bed, but just crawled in with whoever I found sleeping alone. This time it happened to be the cook, Frank Cannon. As was to be expected, when I came into camp that evening I found half a dozen pairs of dirty socks piled at the head of Frank's bed. I had to scrape the socks over the cliff before I could go to sleep, and without looking in my war bag I knew how they came to be there.

Later on I was passing Grindstone Station, where they kept some goods for sale, and bought myself another pair of socks. At camp I turned them over to Frank to keep in our bed until I pulled out at the end of the roundup, when I intended to wear them home. On the morning of the day I was to leave, for a joke I said to Frank, "I guess you better cut out my bedding from yours, as I expect to pull out after dinner and I don't want to be delayed." Of course I had no bedding, and only a very light war bag, including that pair of socks.

But after I left camp Frank got the war bag out of his bedroll and hung it over the edge of the wagon box, and then hung the new socks on the off end of his dish towel line, which was strung from the mess box to the wagon-box bow. The first man to ride into camp asked the cook who the socks belonged to. He told him they were my share of the bedroll I had ordered him to cut so I could leave right after dinner. Of course the cowboy took them and hung his dirty socks in their place. When I came to camp I smelled a rat. In fact it smelled worse, and I had to ride home in dirty socks after all. But first I pulled out my daybook and charged seven pairs of socks to each man in the Frank Cannon crew, since I didn't know but what one man had gotten them all.

It was the custom to render a statement at the end of each month, and I was told that when my statement came in the mail, the boss, Ves Sprague, showed it to the boys and they all threw their hats in the air and yelled until they were hoarse. If the boys wanted to go to a dance or to see their best girls, and were shy a clean shirt, it was nothing unusual for them to go through my war bag and take one, or as many as could be found. They didn't consider it stealing, but the same didn't go for anything else a man owned, except maybe a necktie or a handkerchief. And in the case of the seven pairs of socks charged to each man, I scratched them all off before the checks were made out.

Petty thievery was almost unknown among old-time cowboys. I once slept with one Arthur Morris, of the John Clay outfit. At breakfast one morning he showed a roll of three hundred dollars in bills and said, "Ed, I guess this must be yours. I just now found it in my bed when I went to roll it." Another time, when I was roping calves on Dirt Lodge Creek in 1904, the pull of the rope across my right hip dislodged a roll of several hundred dollars I had in my pocket. One of the boys, Charles Edson, I believe, picked it up and handed it to me. Either one of them could've kept the money and I wouldn't have known where I lost it. In fact, during my fifty-three years of cowpunching I never knew of but two petty thieves among cowboys. One was a Shiner Brothers man in 1881, and the other was a man in my own outfit in '95 or '96. When I say "petty thieves," I mean men who would pilfer money or small articles from the other boys. But man! how some of them would go after a maverick.

I once had a sub-boss, Ves Merritt, who kept his day-book accounts by following a charge of the same kind of an article as the one before it with the word "ditto." About the only things that were carried along in the wagon and issued to the men by the sub-bosses were Climax and Durham tobacco, cartridges, and cigarette papers. One of the men, Bill Boggs, always had a long string of charges, especially cartridges, for he smoked up every town or road ranch he struck. But Bill had almost no education, and when he was handed his first Merritt account for approval he found it something like this:

1 box cartridges	$1.00
Ditto	$1.00
Climax	.50
Ditto	.50
Durham	.60
Ditto	.60

The list was about a foot long, and Bill sure exploded. "I got those cartridges and the Climax and Durham, all right," he yelled, "but I never got a single damn ditto. Why, I never used any o' that in my life and I positively won't pay for it."

It was told on Bill that when he started back to Texas by train in the fall of '84 and the conductor started to pull out his ticket punch to take care of his ticket, Bill whipped out his Colt's .45 and stuck it in the conductor's ribs and said, "Not much, you don't get no drop on me." I won't vouch for that story, but I know that I paid an eighty-dollar damage bill at the hog ranch [1] in Valentine, where he smashed the bar mirror and fixtures about a month before he left for Texas. And at that I paid nothing for the shock he gave the proprietor, Charles Strickland, and the girls he chased from the place before he took full possession. But with all that, Bill was the second-best cowboy I ever knew, Bird Rose being the best.

Bill was never known to carry tobacco, but about once a month he'd have the wagon boss issue him about $3.50 worth of tobacco. Then he'd toss it around through the crew and not keep a single plug or sack for himself. Twenty minutes later he'd be begging the "makings" from the boys. The last I heard of Bill, he and a friend were riding out of Glendive, Montana, with a marshal and some deputies shooting at them.

I think it must've been born in cowboys to like a good joke. Like the time, late in the fall of 1902, when Bird Rose of the L7 and his outfit were coming back from shipping out the last beeves at Evarts. They were riding empty-handed, with no work to do, so anything in the way of excitement was grabbed up in a hurry. The first day out from Evarts they nooned at the Dry Buttes reservoir. They camped on the west side, only a few rods above the dam, which was faced with big, dry, hollow cottonwood logs to keep the splash from eating off the front of the dam.

While they were unhitching and getting dinner they saw a tramp looking at the logs. It turned out he was looking them over with the idea of making one of them his bed ground for the night. Rose invited him over for dinner, and while the tramp was eating he asked where the outfit was headed. They told him Seim,[2] and he said that was where he was going and he'd like to go along. Bird told him he could.

Before they moved on to the Little Moreau for their night camp,

---

1. This term was used for saloons and houses of ill repute that were operated outside the city limits of early-day towns.
2. A town that went out of existence when the railroad came through and Lemmon was established.

they loaded one of the breakwater logs and took it along for a night visiting fire. As the dam was fully settled by then, the logs were no longer needed there. After supper the crew lined up on both sides of the fire log, visiting and resting. Then Tom Cornett and Jim Davis got an idea. They slipped out of sight of the fellows at the fire and took the bullets out of their six-shooters and tamped some yellow rosin soap chunks in instead. When they came back to the fire they sat down so as to have the tramp between them.

Pretty quick they started to quarrel, and then to call each other some vile names. At that stage they both exploded at once, each of them saying no one could call him names like that and live. And so declaring, they pulled their guns and cut loose at one another, but all the time aiming at the tramp. The poor fellow bolted east toward the reservoir, and when he reached its west bank, two hundred yards from the dam and the hollow logs, he dived in, swam to the logs, and crawled into one.

It so happened that another returning beef outfit had camped for the night on the east side of the reservoir. When those boys heard the splash and saw the ripple made by the swimming tramp, they followed to where it ended at the breakwater logs. They got some lanterns from the wagon and went back to see what was going on. The wet tramp had left a plain track over the dry white logs, right to the one he had crawled into. Of course they drug him out, though he was begging them to let him stay hid, for gosh sakes, from those bloodthirsty cowboys who had shot him all to pieces and were still on his trail.

The tramp said he had dived into the water, which was rimmed with wafer ice, to cover his blood-spattered trail and throw them off his track. He also swore he'd been shot in at least ten places and was bleeding to death. The boys pulled down his trousers to see where he'd been shot, but all they found were plenty of black and blue spots, made by the hard-tamped rosin soap. When they finally made him understand a joke had been played on him, he declared he'd have no more of the West, or cowboys, but was heading straight off for the East and his old home of peace, if not plenty.

Back in 1877, Billie Irvine, later state treasurer of Wyoming, was branding a big herd of trail cattle in the Walrath pens near Big

Springs. In those days everyone carried six-shooters, and a lot of men carried Winchester saddle guns, too. One such rifleman was in the crew, and one day at dinner one of the boys got to joshing him about carrying the rifle, as he figured he couldn't hit a flock of barns with it. This went on until the joker offered to bet the rifleman $2.50 he couldn't hit his hat at fifty yards. The rifleman took him up, and the money was put up and the distance stepped off.

The joker had just bought a fine John B. Stetson hat in Ogallala, the kind you could drop down anyplace and still have the wrinkles come right out of it, especially if it was wet. Now nothing had been said about how the hat was to be set up, so the joker cut a slim switch and wrapped his hat around it and tied it with a cord. This made the target not over three and a half inches across, and about eighteen inches high after the switch was stuck in the ground. The Winchester man looked on unconcernedly, and when the joker got out of the way he put his rifle to his shoulder and let go. The hat and peg flew about twenty feet. When the joker took his hat off the switch and took a good look at it, he found ten or twelve holes in it, and he'd lost the $2.50 besides.

And then there was the tale of the Blocker Dude of Texas. This affair was told to me by Joe Green, a fellow who was raised near San Antonio but later came to Lemmon and became a well-to-do sheepman.

Back in the seventies, when many Texans were busy roping and dragging wild Texas steers out of the brush for trail herds, a lot of men became expert with the rope and hogging string. This led up to contests of skill in rope and tie-down ability. From about 1873 to 1879, John Blocker, a big San Antonio rancher, had won all the big prizes in the San Antonio rodeos. He had won so many prizes of fine saddles that his office was decorated all over with them. Another big rodeo was coming up, and he had cleared a space on the wall just back of his desk for the saddle he expected to win there. This saddle would be the finest one yet, for rodeos were getting bigger and more popular all the time.

Now some months before this an invalid college boy from San Antonio, a young man threatened with TB, was brought to Blocker by his mother. The lady had begged John to take her son to the ranch and keep him until he got well. He could keep the ranch books, she said, and would not need to be thrown into the company of the rough, tough cowboys, nor be expected to become a cowboy himself. She also suggested that Blocker pay him regular cowboy wages so he would feel independent, and if he didn't earn the wage she would be glad to make up the difference, just so her son didn't find out about it.

Blocker took the boy out to the ranch in his buckboard, along with a load of trunks, valises, and baseball and polo outfits. The kid had a flock of suits in the trunks, and ties of as many colors as were ever in Joseph's coat, and for a long time he changed his clothes several times a day. Since he lived in the ranch house and was not asked to do any work, he was soon known as the Blocker Dude.

It didn't take the Dude long to find out that the name wasn't exactly a compliment, at which time he set out to change the men's opinion of himself. As soon as the crew would leave on cow hunts, as roundups were then called, he'd begin practicing riding and roping. First he roped the hitching posts, then the ranch pigs and barnyard calves. It was soon plain that he was doing right well with his rope and hogging string. Pretty soon, if the crew happened to be working near the ranch, the boys would let him ride out with them, but never so far but what he could come home to his feather bed (furnished by his mother) at night.

During the first weeks of his practicing he did not neglect his body care and many changes of suits, but as he gained in cow ability he began to leave off his nightly baths and to let a few days go by between changes of clothes. At that period in ranching, cooties, always a problem in warm climates, were not looked on as a disgrace, but rather as a necessity. They kept a man in an ambitious attitude, scratching, where such warm weather otherwise tended to make him lazy. So it was noticed after a while that the Dude seemed to be courting their multiplication instead of trying to get rid of them. All this time his refined old mother had been making visits to the ranch to see how her son was doing, but after he began, so to speak, to go to the wild she stopped asking him to visit her in San Antonio. Finally, as his liking for life in the raw grew, she gave up trying to recivilize him, though it was plain by this time that his health was of the best.

After he had gone on this way for a little over a year and had gotten to be the best rider, roper, and tie-down man on the Blocker crew, the Dude took the ranch books under his arm and asked Blocker to please accept his resignation as bookkeeper and give him a string of cow ponies. "Now boy," Blocker said, "don't get mad if I refuse, because you know your mother warned me to guard your health."

So the Dude cast the books at Blocker's feet and said, "If you will not take me on as a full-fledged cowhand I will be compelled to seek other pastures."

Of course Blocker had to dole him out a string, which he used to the full satisfaction of the crew and the surrounding country. And it was about this time that the rodeo John had felt so sure of winning came up. Now the more he had seen of the Dude's skill, the more he worried about filling that space on the wall back of his desk with the fine trophy saddle, as everybody in the country was urging the Dude to enter the contest.

At the rodeo, when the names of the contestants were called out, it could be seen that John was nervous, but he had first try and made the best catch and tie-down of his life. Then the Dude made his try. His loop sailed through the air for a perfect catch, but when the steer met the strain, the honda parted and the loop end bounced right back into his right hand, which seemed stretched out on purpose to catch it. It was plain that he could've made a second loop and still have beat Blocker's time, but he just laughed and rode back to the starting place.

It later leaked out that Blocker had paid him a handsome sum for stranding his honda. But anyway the fine saddle filled the space cleared for it on old John's office wall. Of course the name of Blocker Dude forever after stayed with the college boy. But now that he was one of Blocker's best cow-hunt bosses, he cleaned up and threw away his dirty clothes, cooties and all, and his aged mother then took him to her bosom again.

Now there has been a lot of argument as to who bossed the biggest roundup ever held. I have read that Lum (or C. C.) Slaughter of the

Texas Panhandle claims to have thrown together twenty-five thousand cattle on the southern plains. That's a lot of cattle, but Lawhorn claims that the Kildeer Mountain roundup of North Dakota was the biggest, only he does not give the number of cattle rounded up. Then comes Ed Spaugh of Manville, Wyoming, claiming through Frazier Hunt to have in a manner bossed Wyoming roundups of nearly two hundred thousand head. Ed, though, was directly concerned with only three of these roundups—the Hat Creek, the Running Water, and the Upper Cheyenne—while to command the whole two hundred thousand head he'd have had to cover fifteen roundups numbering from one to fifteen.

Be that as it may, in 1897 I bossed the Peno Flat cleanup on a wide tableland at the head of Bad River. Four distinct roundups came together there, along with a swing I made with one of my wagons through the south brakes of the Cheyenne River, bringing in three thousand northern cattle. This, in a way, made five roundups, with fifteen wagons and crews. There were about three thousand cattle to each wagon, making some forty-five thousand head altogether out there on Peno Flat. In the whole outfit there were nearly three hundred men, about sixty of them reps. At the Pierre roundup meeting, George Jackson had been appointed boss of this cleanup. I had learned most of my technical cow knowledge from George, but he had not handled anywhere near such big batches of cattle for some years, while I had, so he insisted that I boss this cleanup.

The flat was wide and level, so I separated the big bunch into herds of about five hundred head each and put them in a big circle on the flat. I ordered all movements to be made to the left, so there wouldn't be any head-on collisions when moving cuts. Then I took my stand on a high place where I could see and straighten out any mistakes, of which there were few. So the big roundup went off to the satisfaction of all, even the sixty reps, who had to have a close look at every one of those forty-five thousand critters. By working five herds a day, three in the forenoon and two in the afternoon, we finished the job in three days. And I defy anybody to prove a greater number of cattle on one roundup ground than we had on Peno Flat in the spring of '97.

[229]

Back in 1881 I also had a part in the biggest northern movement of open-range cattle ever made. There had been a heavy drift of cattle from as far north as the South Platte River, between Julesburg and Brush in Colorado—a drift that didn't halt until it came against the Canadian River of Colorado and Oklahoma, the central point being on the range of the Canadian Cattle Company of Texas, with Hank Cresswell as manager. There were some twenty-two wagons stretched across this long front of about 110 miles, and the assembly was made on May 10, when calves were dropping by the thousands. So the owners and bosses got together and decided how best to save the calves and at the same time move the cattle back home. They came up with a plan to start the wagons, two in a place and about ten miles apart, and all move forward at the same time.

Hank Cresswell, who was appointed boss, took the middle station and had couriers riding back and forth daily from each end of the line to report on weather conditions, since on a front that long there could be starts at some places but not in others and it was important that all the wagons move at once. They rounded up the front every third day, cutting back cattle belonging behind and branding calves. As the roundup moved north, the front narrowed due to settlement on the east and west ends. On the first day's forward movement some big steers were seen, but owing to the homing instinct of the big fellows, after we stirred them up we didn't catch sight of them again until the finish on the South Platte River, near present Iliff.

This was probably the largest body of cattle ever moved, anywhere in the world, but seldom were there more than five or six thousand cattle on the roundup ground at one time. Altogether, I would estimate that over three hundred thousand head were handled on that drive. Later that year of 1897, after the big roundup was over, I went to Chicago with some shipments. While there I was visiting with Harry Landers, the Montana cattle inspector, and happened to speak of a man named Crawford, a Billings saloonkeeper. Landers then asked me if I knew who Crawford really was. I said no, that he'd been introduced to me as Crawford.

"Well," he said, "he is really Matt Coats, the fellow that killed Jackson down on the Platte in '77, near where we first met when you were cutting our Newman herds the next year."

"But as it happened, he didn't kill Jackson," I told him.

"Why of course he did," he said.

The beginning of that story went back a long time and a long way —to Texas in about 1875. Three boys who had been schoolmates together had come up the trail from Texas to Ogallala that year. One was Matt Coats, one was Jackson, and I've forgotten the name of the other one. Coats and Jackson were sports, but the third one, who never gambled or drank, and saved his money, had quite a roll.

At that time cowboys going back to Texas from trail drives traveled with only a pack outfit. Matt wanted to stay in Ogallala a couple of days longer, so the other two took the trail with the pack horse. The agreement was that Matt was to catch them at Buffalo Station, down on the Kansas Pacific. He could do that easily enough, as he was riding a fine horse and wouldn't be carrying any pack.

But after Matt crossed the Republican there seemed to be only one man in the outfit he was trailing, and that one, from the reports he got in the towns he passed through, was Jackson. Matt began to suspect foul play, so he turned around and took the back trail. He must have found what he was looking for. But Jackson got suspicious, too, when Matt didn't show up at Buffalo Station when he was supposed to. For he knew that Coats came of a killer clan, being a cousin of Luke Short and Marion Cook. So Jackson speeded up and reached Texas well ahead of Coats, and then fled Texas, too.

Matt held to his trail, though, and followed Jackson into the North Platte River country some two years later, where he was working for Tusler Brothers, south of the river. Matt took a job with Bruce Powers, who was getting a herd ready to start for the Black Hills. A few days later two riders came down the south side of the river and separated. One went straight on and one crossed over to Powers' camp on the north side, where one of the boys asked him who the other rider was. "That's Jackson, of the Tusler outfit," the man said. Matt then stepped up and asked him what this Jackson looked like, and a few other questions besides. As soon as he was sure he'd spotted his man he crossed the river and caught up with him. Riding right up to him, Matt told him he was going to kill him and why. Then he whipped out his gun and shot him square in the right cheek. Jackson fell, and Matt sent two more bullets into his groin.

Matt rode on up to the nearby Camp Clarke bridge and told the fellows there he had killed Jackson for the murder of his school chum, and that they'd better go get his remains and bury them. Then he rode back to his herd and went on north to the Black Hills. Some of the Camp Clarke men went after Jackson's body, but found him still breathing and sent him on down to Sidney to the hospital, where he recovered.

Along in December of that winter, when I was staying on the Rush Creek ranch forty miles northeast of Sidney, Jackson came to the ranch and stayed overnight with George Green and me. The two groin wounds had healed in good shape, but the cheek wound was almost as raw as the day it was made. He kept it bandaged, but there was drippage from it all the time. Green asked him what he intended to do, and he said he had no idea. "Matt will follow me up and kill me, so it won't do me any good to dodge him," he told us, and after that I heard no more of him.

We started our Big Dry ranching deal in Montana in 1896 and were branding in Billings that summer when I was introduced to the man called Crawford. Well, after I convinced Landers that Jackson, so far as I knew, was still alive, he said, "Matt sure never knew that, and if he finds out he'll likely take his trail again." But before either of us had a chance to tell him, Matt headed up a crew that stole fifteen hundred head of cattle off the Crow reservation and was caught and sent to the pen.

It was no wonder that I hadn't recognized him in the saloon, for when I first knew him he was a slim, well-built cowpuncher, and when I saw him in Billings nearly twenty years later, he weighed over two hundred pounds and looked like a fat Jew. He owned three nice brick buildings in Billings then, but soon afterward met with hard luck and tried to get back on top by rustling the Indian cattle. After he got out of the pen I heard no more of him.

XX

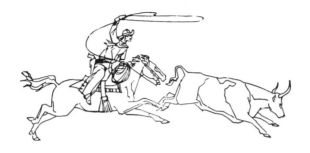

SHEEPMEN

T HERE WERE a good many differences between sheepmen and cattlemen in the early days of the open range. Many bloody wars were fought between the two over the use of the public domain, where, actually, both sheep and cattle were trespassers. These troubles were not nearly as noticeable in the Dakotas as they were farther west and south, where most of the fights took place. I can recall only one instance of bloodshed in my state, and that was in the Fall River country in the early nineties, where one of our old Texas cowboys, Ben Harrison, killed a sheepherder. Ben was tried and acquitted.

A common-law practice over most range territory held that possession of range was granted to the first man putting herds, either sheep or cattle, on the land. But sheep had to be moved at least twice a year, three times in a mountain region, so they could not stay the year around in one area as cattle could.

In the early days it was thought that cattle would not graze or water well after sheep had been on the range or had used the water, so cattlemen usually did all they could to keep the woolly blatters out of a territory. Of later years this belief was proved to be a mistake, for it was found that sheep can use a range and its water, and then, if there have been rains to wash away the sheep smell and make fresh grass spring up, cattle will not mind using the same range. In fact, if sheep graze off the first grass cover, which is often coarse, the new grass is usually better. I learned that from Jess Driskill many years ago when he, on account of the country settling up, had to put his season's beef crop under herd, and often on ground that had been used by wandering sheep bands. He found the results very good, he told me.

As for my personal opinion, I will state that as manager of the Sheidley Cattle Company I never openly put a straw in the path of sheep, because the way we looked at it, we were all trespassers and one had as good a right to the range as the other. As evidence, just ask Billy Marty of the Sheep Creek country of Harding County. Together with Hines and Curington, he moved in with sheep in the middle nineties, and during my cattle days we were all good friends and neighbors. Now that we are all in the sheep business we are still good friends.

Paul C. Murphy, another sheepman, trailed a band of six thousand yearling ewes from Big Timber, Montana, to his range near Rapid City in 1897. He and Bob Boyd, onetime sheriff of Pennington County, had bought the ewes and were trailing them south over the route that was watered by reservoirs built by the Northwestern Railroad through their Belle Fourche shipping territory. All animals—cattle, horses, sheep, or for that matter billy goats and hydraulic rams—were free to use these watering places.

Besides Murphy and Boyd, there were two sheep tenders and a cook with that band of sheep. The cook drove a single team to the sheep wagon, and the rest of the outfit traveled on foot. They left the Little Missouri one morning and made a dry camp that night, planning to make the Valley Creek reservoir by noon the next day. But when they got up the next morning their hobbled team was gone.

They couldn't move until they found their horses, so they scattered on foot to hunt for them. Murphy had walked several miles and was about done in when he saw an old YT cow hazer riding toward him. When they came together the cowman wanted to know what he was doing on foot in that forsaken country. When Murphy told him, the cowman advised him to wait a bit. Since Murphy had bought the team with the sheep in Montana, the cowman said, the horses had naturally taken the back trail to their old home. But his outfit, he said, was coming south on that same trail with a beef herd and would likely pick up the team and bring it along, it being the range custom to pick up and backtrack wandering horses.

Sure enough, the herd soon hove in sight, with one of the cowboys leading the team and the hobbles hanging from the horses' necks. The cowboy said they'd met the team heading north, with one hobble end dragging on the horse that seemed to be the leader. The other, still hobbled, was coming along the best he could. The herd boss then asked if, as a favor to them for returning the horses, they would please hold their sheep back a trifle from the reservoir until they could water the beef. Their herd would stampede sure, he said, if it came onto a band of six hundred blatting sheep. Of course Murphy said they would, because they had no choice, as the beeves were out-traveling the sheep, and anyway the team was not yet hitched to their wagon.

It was several days, Murphy told me, before he and Boyd tumbled to the fact that their team had been unhobbled and led away by the cowboy on purpose to hold their sheep off the water until the beeves got there. The cowmen had done this because, if the sheep watered first, the beeves wouldn't drink there for a while; and this would've caused a bad shrink to the fat herd, which was to be shipped right out of Belle Fourche for the Chicago market.

And while we are on the subject of sheep, I well remember Mandy, the sheep girl. Mandy came into the Buffalo Gap country with her parents, her brother, and a band of sheep in the eighties. The old folks rode in the covered wagon, while she and her brother boosted the sheep along. She was a good-looking girl of about sixteen, and at that time, except in the towns, there was only one other girl in the country for miles in any direction. So Mandy was appreciated by all the young bucks in that part of South Dakota.

One of our men, Levi Peck, discovered her first, about ten miles to the south of our camp. It was not a very busy season of the year, so he did not share his discovery but, at the rate of less than ten miles a day, was her faithful guide and helper for about three days.

As I couldn't quote Shakespeare and Byron to her like he could, I couldn't cut him to the drags [demote him]. But my position in boss rank being a little higher than his, I finally managed to have him put to work, leaving the field to me. As I was much better acquainted with the trail, my services were appreciated, and I helped the family as far as French Creek, about thirty miles on north.

Of course a lot of other cowboys had gotten a running view of Mandy by then, but as there was no need for more than one pilot at a time, they could hardly be of any use. For months afterward the sheep girl was often spoken of, and you'd hardly hear talk of any other girl. I guess it was her winning way and "go get 'em" smile.

Mandy had a lot of relatives in Rapid City and I kept my eye out for her there, but another sight of her was several years in coming. Then I moved to Rapid, and there one of my nearest neighbors was Mandy. She had married a lawyer with a good practice and had two children. She often visited our house and, though married, was as gay as at sixteen, and I often had the pleasure of treating her to ice cream, soda water, and maybe wine on the q.t.

One day at a carnival in Sturgis I ran onto her and one of her lady friends, a girl no more bashful than Mandy. I treated them both several times, and then Mandy said it was her treat. We were standing on the edge of the dance pavilion and she was carrying her hand purse in her sock. To get it, she hoisted her skirt about half as high as they wear them now, and the shock tilted me backward off the platform. Mandy came to my rescue, and when she promised not to do it again I forgave her.

Mandy and her husband, Fred, sometimes had little spats, mostly about her boldness. But one day when I was on my way to Deadwood on business she saw me in the coach and came and sat beside me. I could see she had been crying, and when I asked the reason she said she and Fred had had the worst quarrel they'd ever had and she was leaving him for good. I tried to persuade her to change her mind but it didn't do any good. Finally I asked if she had any money. She showed me eighty cents.

I didn't want to be seen giving her money, so when the train went into a tunnel near Deadwood I slipped her a five-dollar bill. Then I made her promise to go to the Bullock Hotel and stay there until I could see her again that evening, as I had too much to do to keep on her trail during the day. When we got off the train at the depot I spied one of our Rapid City preachers. There was a train back to Rapid right away, so I got hold of him, told him Mandy's intention, and asked him to go right to Fred and tell him the whole story. He was to tell him he must drop everything and come to his wife's rescue as fast as he could.

Well, Fred got there in time and took Mandy home. I didn't see him that day, but a few days later he came to give me back my money and thank me. In fact I thought he would never stop thanking me. He said there wasn't another man on earth who could've saved Mandy that day, the mood she was in, for he said she had sworn by me from the time I first met her with the sheep band. Soon after that they left for the Klondike, where Fred became a prominent lawyer and Mandy a contented housewife.

XXI

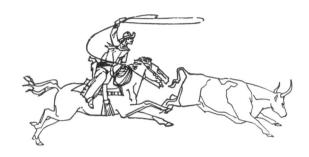

MY CAREER AS A COWMAN

I HAD GONE into the cattle business on my own in a gradual manner, starting in the fall of 1878 by buying a remnant of 16 Texas yearlings from Jim Burns of Tiffin, Ohio, for $180. I added 15 head to my herd by purchase and otherwise, then ranged the whole bunch on Rush Creek, forty miles northeast of Sidney. I sold the lot to George Green for $400 in February, 1879. My second purchase was 50 yearling steers in July, 1880, for $450. I lost half of that bunch by winterkill, but sold the rest to Dave Clark in April, 1882, for $880, range delivery. That August I bought 85 mixed steers, twos and threes, for about $1,200, and disposed of most of them by peddling them to butchers during the building of the Fremont, Elkhorn and Missouri Valley Railroad, making about $700 on the lot.

In 1884, I bought 200 steers at a cost of $2,600. A hundred head were yearlings, and I lost half of them to winterkill but still netted $4,000 on the rest on a strong market. In 1885, I bought 225 mixed Shorthorns for $5,625 and peddled them out the same season for $6,750. During the seasons of '86, '87, and '88, though I bought no cattle, I had a few cows I had traded for. Those years I loaned my money out at 2 per cent per month. Through '89 and '90 I traded in all kinds of cattle, 2,000 head in all, bought in the Black Hills and mostly peddled out to feeders southwest of Fremont, Nebraska, at a profit of about $5 a head.

In 1891, I went into the Sheidley Cattle Company with a 15 per cent interest in 3,500 Texas steers, twos and threes, and this 15 per cent interest in our concern I carried until I sold out of the company in 1906. In 1892 our company bought 6,000 two-year-old steers, most of them from the famous JA brand,[1] for our South Dakota range. The next year we bought 7,000 more of the JA steers, and another 8,000 in 1894. That same year I bought three hundred shares of the Sheidley Cattle Company stock.

In '95 we bought 15,000 steers—ones, twos, and threes—in Mexico, New Mexico, Arizona, and Utah for our own ranges, besides 7,000 head that we cornfed near Hastings at a fair profit. The next year we bought our usual stock of mixed steers, and then bought the NUN cattle, 17,000 head (with 4,000 calves thrown in), together with 54,000 acres of school land which we didn't want but had to take to get the cattle. We then leased another 306,000 acres, making a 360,000-acre pasture, and bought 4,000 cows for the NUN pasture to replace the steers we shipped from there to our northern ranges in Dakota and Montana.

I sold my Sheidley Company stock to Sam Sheffield at a good profit in 1897, and took as part payment 700 steers, then turned those to the company at a fair profit, too. The next year we bought our usual 15,000 mixed steers, along with a few heifers that we spayed. We also shipped six thousand NUN yearlings north, and that was also the year I bought the 300 Hereford bulls from Bull Nelson for our Texas ranch. In 1899, in addition to the 15,000 purchased steers, we shipped 6,500 NUN yearlings north. You can see how our calf crop from the original 4,000 cows, bought in 1895, was increasing.

Our operation went along at the above rate until 1902, when we bought 17,000 steers and also shipped our usual 6,500 yearlings north, putting them into the Standing Rock reservation pasture. That year, too, we brought 1,400 head of young stuff down from our

---

1. The JA steers were from the Palo Duro Canyon ranch of Charles Goodnight.

Montana range, making it necessary to turn 11,000 yearlings on the open range on the Elm and Moreau rivers. Of these we lost 40 per cent by winterkill, and that same season we shipped 2,000 locoed cows[2] from the Texas ranch to the Standing Rock pasture. Half of these died the next winter, but the total loss was on cheap yearlings and locoed cows, so the money loss was comparatively small.

The next year we bought 18,000 mixed steers, while our yearling shipment from the NUN dropped to 5,500 head. In 1904 we bought only 12,000 steers and shipped only 5,000 NUN yearlings, the two-year low in yearlings being caused by the shipment of the locoed cows in 1902, which had seriously cut the calf crop. And after that we put no more cattle on the Texas range, because that country was then settling up fast. In 1905, besides the 11,000 steers and 5,000 NUN yearlings, we also bought over 3,000 three- and four-year-old steers near Woodward, Oklahoma, for our Dakota pasture. All of these purchases were cattle I had an interest in, but did not include the many cattle bought by D. H. Clark and Company, the Sheidley Cattle Company, or other ownerships I handled from 1870 to 1891. During those years, too, we bought out a good many small ranch brands, mostly breeding stock, until we were branding 2,500 calves in Dakota every year, including calves raised from the thousand locoed cows that lived.

We sold our Texas ranch to the Elwood Glidden Wire Company of Chicago in 1905, making a little profit on the remnant of cattle there, and selling our land at $3 per acre. We had built the acreage from 54,000 to 64,000 acres, and so made over $100,000 on the land we had considered a burden to our business when we had to buy it in 1896.

In January, 1906, I sold my Lake, Tomb, and Company interest. During the years since 1891 we had shipped only matured four-year-olds. Due to this practice we usually had three crops of cattle on our range all the time, and at least 30,000 head at any one time. And once, in 1902, we had 53,000 head, after beef shipping, for a peak figure. But if you consider the fact that we made up our inventory on the second Tuesday in December, the date of our annual

2. Poisoned by eating locoweed.

meeting, but unloaded our southern shipments before July 1, you get a higher figure. For we didn't start shipping beef until August 1, so during the month of July we had 14,000 head of beef cattle on hand, making a full 67,000 head on our range at one time. (These figures are all given from memory and, if anything, the numbers are too small.)

In 1916, after trying realty and banking for nine years, I bought four hundred head of Minnesota cattle, grew them out, and made a profit at wartime prices. In 1918, I bought over 300 head of Texas cattle, had a bad winter loss, but still sold the remainder at a fair profit in 1919. But that same year I bought 4,000 head of mixed Arizona cattle that lost me one hundred per cent, my first loss on an investment in cattle.

In all my experience I found that the range from the Big Dry to the Musselshell, south of the Big Missouri, is one of the best, since it is a tangle of canyons and gulches that afford fine grass and water. On this range, which we occupied from 1896 to 1903, running a stock of about 15,000 cattle there, our losses averaged only 1⅓ per cent, the best I ever heard of for a period of seven straight years. The country under the protection of the Black Hills was fine winter range, too. From Rapid City around to Cascade Creek and out to the southeast about eighty miles, including all of the badlands along the White River and around Scenic, we never experienced a heavy winter loss on cattle. From 1891 until my windup in 1923 I occupied ranges covering practically all of Perkins County and the north half of Meade County, the big pasture on the Standing Rock reservation, the Big Dry range, including Crooked Hell and Snowy creeks in Montana, and the 360,000-acre pasture in Texas.

In 1903, after quite a severe winter, we took off 14,000 head for losses over the entire range. But we survived the loss without a whimper, and the following December at our annual meeting in Chicago we declared a legitimate 12 per cent dividend. This may sound strange, but the losses were all on inferior cattle, which we replaced with good stuff the next season; and besides, we carried a surplus of $150,000, set aside for just such emergencies.

I quit the cattle business in 1923, but not before we had one last exciting throwback to the old days. In 1922 I was running 1,500 head of southern cattle on Spring Creek, near McLaughlin, when I began to come up short quite a few beeves. A neighbor, running nearly as many cattle some fourteen miles to the northwest, was short even more than I was. So he and his grown son came over to stay all night with me and talk about it. He said he had lost 26 head of his choicest beeves on two different occasions about a month apart, and he was positive he knew who had taken them, and mine, too. But he was afraid he didn't have the kind of evidence needed to convict in court, so he proposed that we hold a lynching bee. I was worked up about as much as he was over the rustling, but I argued that we'd get enough evidence to convict if we'd just hold off a while longer and keep our eyes open. I told him the day of lynchings was past, and besides, we all had families to think about and the penalty for lynchings, if proven against a man, was about as bad as for the crime that caused the hanging. By the time he left I was pretty sure I had changed my neighbor's mind.

Soon after that an Indian was convicted for butchering beef owned by the St. Paul Cattle Loan Company. John Anderson, a former sheriff of Perkins County got the evidence that sent the Indian to the pen. John had hung, for murder, the last man ever hung in South Dakota. Well, after sending the Indian up, cattle rustling in our region just about stopped for a while and I forgot all about the lynching proposition. But my neighbor hadn't forgotten, and one night I was called to meet with a strong delegation of men at a certain schoolhouse in our neighborhood. When I got there I found the blinds all pulled down and pinned, so that not a sliver of light showed. A well-armed guard at the door spoke to me. He recognized my voice when I answered, and told me to go on in.

There were a dozen cowmen inside, and they were a worried-looking bunch. Only four were old mossbacks. The rest had only been ranching for five or ten years, and they were plenty nervous. For my neighbor had finally nailed his rustler red-handed, and the bunch was holding him there under heavy guard. Actually, they had two prisoners, and they seemed to be the only cheerful men in the room. The cowmen told me how they'd caught the rustlers butchering a beef that didn't belong to them. But one of the prisoners claimed he was only a hired man, and had supposed his boss was butchering one of his own critters. The boss had backed him up, so they were holding the second man only as a witness.

As I had the most cattle in that country, as well as more frontier experience than the rest, they asked me to take charge of the meeting. I did, and listened to all their evidence. I then told them it looked to me like they wouldn't have any trouble getting a conviction in court, but they wanted to finish it up right away with a rope. So no matter how hard I tried to persuade them to take the case to court, they still held out for a hanging.

We were still arguing when a woman suddenly dashed by the guard and tore into the schoolhouse, hollering for her husband. Of course I thought she was going to beg him not to have a hand in a hanging bee—and how she fooled me! She pointed her finger at the rustler and told how he had stolen her milk cow's calf off its picket rope, just at dusk and only a few rods from her house. So, she declared, she had come to help with the lynching and intended to help pull the thief up in the hanging tree. I jumped up then and said that if wives and sweethearts were in the know on this deal they could just count me out. The rest of the country would soon know about it, I said, and we'd all be arrested, for I well knew that our governor wouldn't take kindly to us bypassing the state laws and I sure didn't intend to be living in dread of being arrested for my part in the crime.

When I first took the chair at that meeting the rustler's gun had been handed to me. I had slipped it into my waistband, where I already had another just like it. But after I had my say the woman turned on me and told me she was sure disappointed, because she had heard I would stand up for what was right, but now she was convinced I had no confidence in women and that I'd likely do my best to see that the rustler was turned loose. When I could get a word in, I asked her if she hadn't said it was dusk when the milk cow's calf was stolen off its picket rope. She said she had, and I asked her how she could be sure that the thief was the man we had here. She came right back and said she'd know him anyplace by the graceful way he rode a horse—that he rode like a centaur, or something like that.

Then I named two other men of the same build and good horsemanship, and asked if the man she saw might have been either of them. She said yes, she could be mistaken as to which one of the three she'd seen, but she couldn't see that it made any difference, as they all deserved hanging. I admitted she had a point but told her it wasn't for us to be the judge and jury, and that I'd made up my mind that if they tried to lynch the prisoner I would toss him his gun, and then use my own in his defense. At this, the other four old mossbacks came to stand beside me. They didn't say a word, but it was easy to see they agreed with me.

Then one of the younger fellows said, "Mr. Lemmon, you've had experience in other cases like this, so can't you suggest a good way to settle this one?" I told him I could, that, as we knew the names of the rest of the rustler outfit, too, I would write a letter to each of them, and the man we were holding could name a courier from among his friends to deliver the letters. I would just write that if any of them was hereafter suspected of cattle theft, I would personally head a delegation to deal with them.

I had been doing business on that reservation since 1881, over forty years, and sort of knew my way around, I told those cowmen, but if we were going to put down cattle stealing we would have to go about it with more secrecy than they had used in this try at taking the law into their own hands. To do this, I said, we'd have to cut our active committee to less than half the number at this meeting. So I proposed that we put a slip of paper for each man in a hat. Part of the slips would be marked with a black dot, the rest would be blank. Each man there would draw out a slip and put it in his pocket without looking at it, then leave the schoolhouse, each going in a different direction. When they were out of sight and hearing of each other they were to look at their papers. Those with the dotted slips were to ride back to the schoolhouse, where I would be waiting for them. The rest would go on home. That way, only a few would know who made up the committee. While all this was going on, the prisoner was to be tied hand and foot and left with me.

When the little committee picked by the black dots got back, we talked things over and decided on just what we'd do if any more rustling happened in our neighborhood. Then I wrote the letters, and our rustler named a man to carry them to the rest of his thieving friends. After that we turned our man over to the sheriff. He was tried in court, convicted, and sentenced to two and a half years in the pen.

Up to the time I left that region, ten years later, not a man that got a letter ever again gave us any reason to suspect him of even looking twice at another man's stock. Our committee met a few times after that night, but seldom was that first meeting in the schoolhouse ever mentioned. And after that near lynching bee all the younger cowmen looked on me as their superior, which bothered me, as I never felt I was above any of them, or the lady either. For it turned out she was right as to the man we held prisoner in the schoolhouse being the fellow who swiped her milk cow's calf. I met her a good many times after that night, and although she was always friendly, she never really took me to her bosom.

By 1923 the old days of the big cattle outfits were finished. So I closed out my cattle interests. In all, I had worked with cattle for a little over fifty-three years, and during all that time I was never a desk manager. I was in the saddle most of the time in cattle-handling seasons, and I never stopped taking my regular turn at night guard until I was made general manager in 1891. As wagon boss I had always stood my two hours on second guard from twelve to two, and then got up with the cook. After breakfast I'd go with the wrangler to hunt the horses, and by the time I crawled into my bedroll again I'd have been eighteen hours in the saddle. It didn't hurt me. Actually, I throve on it.

As general manager in the heyday of our operation, I have had my men and reps covering all the territory from the lower White River, near Gregory, a Nebraska town that has since disappeared, west to Crawford, then north, taking in all the Black Hills region, then angling northwest, covering the Little Powder and Tongue rivers to the Missouri and the Yellowstone, then north by Billings to the Musselshell and Missouri, and down that river to the White River again, since at that time we had ranges on the Big Dry in Montana, the Grand River, the Moreau, and the Belle Fourche. There wasn't a time during that period that I couldn't reach any one of my wagons or reps within two days' time at the outside. In fact, I always boasted that I could ride up to any one of my crews at any noon or night camp and find everything as I expected. During my twenty years on that range I never failed to do so but once, and that was due to a wagon boss not following orders—a thing that never happened again.

One reads a lot, these days, about trail herds, stampedes, blizzards, and the like, plenty of it written by men who never ate trail dust or saw any but a movie stampede. When the real thing happened there were different ways of handling the situation, usually depending on the boss of the outfit. I had all my wagon crews carry a dozen lanterns apiece, and I always kept a lighted lantern hung inside the wagon cover on a wagon bow. This made a good beacon for directing herders to camp on dark nights. In case of a stampede every man grabbed a lighted lantern and dashed for the lead of the running cattle. It may seem strange, but the cattle soon learned to look on the lanterns as a sign of home, and instead of shying from them would quiet down so we could lead them back on the bed ground.

When a stampede started and the boys went out with the lanterns, men took the point and each flank, and the drags if needed, and soon the whole herd could be lined up from flank to lead by sighting along the lanterns. Because of our way of handling a night stampede, our Flying V and WG crews were known as the "lantern outfits," for we were the only ones in the north to carry lanterns. The Adair outfit of Texas always kept a red light burning at night, and the Goodnight a green one. A gun fired around wild steers scared them worst of all, so after passing Indian country I'd make the boys leave their guns in camp during the day. As for throwing a herd into a mill, that was the last thing we tried. In some cases there was no other way to stop a stampede, but if my men threw a beef herd into a mill before trying every other way to stop it—well, I'd soon have other men in their places. So my orders were never to put a beef herd into a mill, because you could take more pounds off the herd in a twenty-minute mill than in a mile and a half of running. The jamming together in a mill always caused a lot of damage, too.

I once took a herd of nearly a thousand longhorns from the Gulf of Mexico to Valentine, Nebraska, for shipment to market. That bunch stampeded every night of the trip, but by using lanterns we lost only two steers. A green cowhand was the cause of that herd being so spooky. At the first stop for water, after moving off the home range, the steers got nervous. There was no cow smell there, as no cow brutes had watered at that place in a long time; and the herd being homesick, as cattle usually are when leaving their home range, they didn't like it.

The watering place was small and boggy, so I cautioned the lead men to pay no attention if a few head did bog down. But I forgot to caution the tenderfoot we had in the crew, as he was supposed to be back with the drags anyway. Well, he caught sight of a few beeves bogging, and slipped up through the brush for a better look. I didn't dare yell at him to come back, as that would have stampeded those uneasy steers for sure. So I trusted to luck—and my luck didn't hold. A steer caught a glimpse of the tenderfoot moving in the brush, and away went the whole herd. At every watering place on the trip after that where the banks were high and timber close up a stampede was in order. I doubt if a gaunter, shabbier, worse-looking herd of beef steers than that one ever went on the Chicago market.

Henry Duncan, the rancher on Thunder Butte Creek in South Dakota, had a big spotted dog. The dog was resting in the shallow water at the edge of the creek under some bushes when I came along with a herd one time. We had the beeves strung out along the creek, drinking, when the dog suddenly came out of the bushes and barked. That whole herd just left the country in nothing flat. We later estimated that the bark of that dog cost the owner of the herd $1,200 in lost poundage, even after we threw the whole bunch back on the range for another six weeks.

Another time, in 1894, we planned to ship three thousand beeves from Forest City, South Dakota. The ferry on the Missouri crossing wasn't much good, so we decided to swim the herd across. We had the beeves well under way, with a boat in the lead and a halter-broke steer swimming behind it, leading the herd. We had boats on each side, too, and good cowmen in the swing and pushing up the drags. Everything was going fine until a looking glass began flashing in the faces of the leading cattle. They swung back, of course, and the whole herd followed. In the big swing back to the other side we lost seventeen beeves, smothered in the sand and water. We heard later that the ferryman, mad because we didn't hire his ramshackle outfit, caused the stampede back to the other bank.

Once I even had a herd of seven hundred beef steers stampede out of the stockyards at Valentine at eleven o'clock at night. They took out the whole side of the yards, went across fences, and tore out up a new-built railroad grade. They really flattened about twenty-five miles of that grade, which I was told hadn't yet been accepted by the railroad company. But I think the company must have paid for it, since the contractors never put in a claim against us, even though the damage must have been all of $5,000. (Valentine was the end of the track then, but the road was building on west.) The power and weight of a stampeding herd of beeves is enormous and uncontrollable. I've known of stampeding steers smashing down stockyards built of railroad ties set on end in the ground, with eight-inch planks spiked on top of the posts.

In bedding a herd of wild cattle I never bedded on the windward side of camp, that is, never where the wind blowing from camp could reach the herd. For any unusual smell or sound, even the bucking or snorting of a horse or the sound made by a man striking a match at night, could stampede the herd. And I always put the cattle at least two hundred yards from camp. After a herd had been on the trail for a month the cattle usually became broken in and traveled along in good shape, and then the cowboys had little to do but ride along and think of the good grub their mothers used to feed them. But I'll never forget one of my cowhands, James Chadoin, and the stampede he told me about. Jim hadn't had any schooling, but he sure liked to use big words. In telling about his wild stampede, he put it this way: "I was in the lead and trying to turn the leaders when all at once I and my horse and the cattle all went right over a cut bank in the dark. And it was a forty-foot *proclamation*, too, by gosh!"

There can't be many people today who don't know what a trail herd or roundup mess wagon looked like—just a covered wagon with a mess box in the rear, and the bed rolls, a sourdough keg, and a crazy cook loaded inside. The keg usually had a nail in the lid, with the sharp point turned up. This piece of furniture was sometimes used as a camp stool, but those who knew the location of the nail used it very little. It was kept for company.

I'd also like to mention the "cooney" here. This was made from a green cowhide and was hung under the wagon, below the coupling pole, with its edges lashed to the sides of the wagon. It was filled with heavy kitchen pots and pans until it was stretched and dried in the shape of a good-sized bag. We carried dry wood or cow chips in it, so as to have dry fuel for a fire when we got caught out in wet weather or when we camped where there was no fuel. The cooney also made a dry, comfortable bed ground for a small man. I often slept in one during my years of cowpunching. We always carried a ten-gallon keg of water, too, lashed to the outside of the wagon box, for dry camps. And woe to the puncher who tried to wash his hands at night at a camp off water.

Today there is quite a fad for "baby" beef, but I want to state right here that real beef comes from a fully matured steer, a four- or five-year-old. In the old days it was the matured steer that was the best eating, not a cow; but in the days when we kept cows on the range to pacify the maturing steers, it was the cows we mostly had to butcher, because the steers were raised to sell and there was no profit in dry cows—except to feed the hands. But on occasions when the manager was not around, or when, by accident, a big steer got a leg broken, we hurried up and butchered him, and then we had a feast fit for a king. Today it is seldom that I get a beefsteak that is fitting to my palate, but it is hard to make the younger generation believe this. They have the idea that grained beef is better than the grass-fattened kind, and very few of them have ever tasted a fully matured, grass-fattened beefsteak.

I just wish some of you folks who back baby beef could taste the meat of one of our old four-year-old, thirteen-hundred-pound, grass-fattened beeves. But it has been so long since I have tasted real beef myself that I have just about lost my craving for it. All I can do now is remember some of the times on the range when we put a big roast of beef ribs at long range from the evening visiting fire, and then whittled it off as it roasted and ate it with hard bread or hardtack. There was a feast you couldn't beat!

As for blizzards and hard winters, well, I knew plenty of those, too. My first hard winter was the one of '78 and '79. I was working near Julesburg that winter, and cattle drifted from west of Cheyenne down both the North and South Platte rivers and wedged into the forks, just east of North Platte City, by the thousands. During the big snowstorm that set the herds drifting southeast, a lot of cattle filled the streets of North Platte and pushed against the buildings. Some even pushed the door of the new courthouse open and filled the lower floor, crowding in to get out of the terrible storm.

When the storm was over we formed a pool outfit and went down to the forks. There we sanded the ice over the South Platte, just east of the city, and crossed some twenty-five thousand open-range cattle over the ice and let them drift down to the Medicine, where there was good feed and little snow. These cattle belonged to hundreds of different owners, so in the spring four big crews went down to gather the drift. My outfit, under Charley Ensley, brought back three thousand head; the others brought back even larger herds, and many cattle had already drifted back home before that. On our first trip down, right after the storm, we probably saw a thousand dead cattle in and around North Platte, and of course there was some loss along the drift line. Even so, the losses totaled only about seven per cent of all the drift cattle.

I remember another bad storm in the winter of 1903. I was in Chicago for our annual company meeting, and by the time I'd been there about a month I began to get anxious about our stock, for I'd learned they were having a bad winter back on the range. I got back to South Dakota on Christmas Eve and got an early start for Leaf on the Hill, our first camp in that direction. The camp was thirty miles out, and it was snowing hard. I had brought a lot of Christmas doodads for Tom McCoy and his family, who lived at the camp. I made it there in time for a late Christmas dinner, and then stayed all night.

The next day the McCoys talked me into staying for an early dinner before I started for our next camp, twenty-seven miles away on Dirt Lodge Creek. I had never been to this camp, as my building boss, George Sheets, had built it while I was gone to Chicago. I had picked the location before I left, but I didn't know that George had decided on another location, two and a half miles on down the creek,

where there was winter water. When I reached the division fence
between my two pastures, up on Hump Butte Ridge, the snow
seemed to be a lot deeper on the other side. From there on, the snow,
twelve to sixteen inches deep and crusted, slowed my team considerably. It was dark by the time I reached the place where I'd told
George to build the camp, and a blizzard was rising. When I discovered there was no camp there I figured it must be lower down,
and I knew if I traveled west I'd at least strike the hay road they'd be
using to haul hay down from the stacks to the north.

The storm got worse as I went along, and it was a dark, dark night.
Besides that, the country was a tangle of badland washouts and
gulches. When I'd come to such cuts and holes the horses would
stop, and I'd have to get out and lead them around to leveler footing.
And those poor horses, even though they were range-raised, were
trembling like leaves every time I took them by the bits. I came near
stopping several times, and twice I stopped to unhitch. But I had
only two light robes in the buggy with me, and there was nothing but
buffalo berry bushes around for fuel, so each time I changed my
mind and decided to go on. After a while the team stopped again. I
got out of the buggy and went to their heads, and that time I found
their noses hanging over a barbed wire fence. I sighted along the
fence to the right, and there I saw a dim light—a lantern shining
from a dugout window not a hundred feet away. I gave a big yell,
and out came cowboy Dick with the lantern.

Cold winters weren't only hard on cattle, they were bad for the
men, too, especially if they weren't used to them. On my first trip to
Montana I was worried over what I'd heard about winters in the
North. On the way up we went through a military post in Colorado,
and I fixed myself up by trading for a blue soldier overcoat with a
cape and brass buttons. Those coats came down to one's knees and
in warm climates were considered quite the thing for winter. When
a fellow was standing still, the cape would cover his hands and turn
water pretty well. But I want to say that when a man was on a horse
and trying hard to turn a Montana yearling, that government blue
coat was about as warm as a postage stamp stuck to the back of his
neck. I wore it, though, my first winter up there, and was even proud
of owning a coat made and paid for by Uncle Sam.

But I never actually suffered so much from the cold anywhere as I did on a trip by stage from Plainview to Lubbock, down in Texas. And that was in early March, 1900, and it wasn't even down to zero. That same night six hundred of our cows, heavy with calf, died on the bed ground down there. In the North we just don't have those body-piercing winds they have once in a while in the South.

XXII

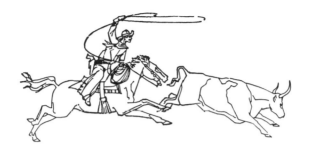

SOME CHARACTERS

A MAN IS APT to meet some strange people in the course of a
lifetime, and some great ones, too. These are a few of the ones
I ran across.

I first met Ranger Jones in 1868, when he lived a few miles out of
Cheyenne and owned a few cows. He was a Missourian, not a Texan,
but he used a five-point star as his brand. He called it the Lone Star
and was mighty proud of it. Before he came to Wyoming he had a
small freight outfit and four half-dressed daughters. Ranger got rich
and the girls grew into great riders and cowgirls, the pride of the
West.

Ranger and old Pinneo, the father of Minnie Pinneo, the world's
champion lady rider, were a lot alike, and for quite a few years the
two families of girls were much the same, too. But Pinneo was not a
money maker like Jones, who was in the first Pikes Peak gold rush,
packing in with burros. When I last saw Ranger, along in the
thirties, he was worth at least two hundred thousand dollars and had
about six thousand cattle of fine quality. As he grew rich he took to
sporting white linen shirts, which he wore with about as much grace
as a trained ape does a plug hat. Furthermore, as he was always

chewing Climax, his front was always bespattered with tobacco juice. He carried a big supply of the shirts and collars on roundups and changed to a clean shirt every morning, but by noon one end of his collar was always blowing in the breeze and his shirt front was splotched with brown.

He was probably the best-known man in Wyoming and Colorado, a rough and ready sort with many notches on his gun handle—whites, Mexicans, and Indians. He was also an entertainer of the first magnitude, and was somewhat feared, but respected, by all.

My first acquaintance with Nick and Antoine Janis was in about 1863, when they were running road ranches on the South Platte River near the American Ranch, forty or fifty miles west of Julesburg. They had been sent out several years earlier from New Orleans by the Hudson's Bay Fur Company to trade with the Indians, at which they were very successful. Even while running the road ranches they were, I think, still trading for furs for the company. About that time, too, they took unto themselves mixed-blood Sioux wives.

Soon after I met them they moved onto the North Platte River, near Fort Fetterman. A little later Nick built a trading post at what is now known as Jenney's Stockade in the southwest Black Hills, where he did a thriving business. When Professor Jenney was sent into the Black Hills by the government in '74 and '75 to investigate gold reports, he stayed at Nick's stockade, which was ever afterward called Jenney's Stockade.[1] After the fur business slowed down and Texas cattle were trailed north for stocking the range, Nick stocked a small range on the head of the Cheyenne River. When the Red Cloud reservation was set up in southwest South Dakota, he gathered his cattle, which by that time had grown to a herd of several thousand, and moved onto the White River just east of the mouth of Bordeaux Creek. His brother Antoine, who also had quite a stock of cattle, moved to the same range.

1. In 1875, while government officials were conferring in Washington with Sioux leaders on acquiring rights to the Black Hills, which had been ceded to the Indians, Walter P. Jenney, a geologist, lead an expedition into the Hills to investigate reports of gold deposits there. See Herbert S. Schell, *History of South Dakota* (Lincoln: University of Nebraska Press, 1961), pp. 130–131.

The brothers both raised large families. Their sons and daughters were educated at the Carlisle Indian school, but, though they were fine-looking people, few of them made much use of their schooling. Some came home and taught in the Indian schools in their own neighborhood. The boys, of which there were at least eight in each family, all worked on nearby ranches and turned out to be great broncobusters. R. S. Van Tassell's foreman, Johnny Bailey, hired many of them, and they were able and trusty cowhands. Both of the old Janises were good businessmen. Their families developed aristocratic ways, and the girls, of which there were many, took to dressing in silks and satins. The boys, too, wore broadcloth for dances and the like. As the older members passed away, the stocks of cattle dwindled until, the last I knew of them, there was but a sorry handful left, but their owners still wore their aristocratic airs.

About 1871 one John Richaud (pronounced Reeshaw) killed a soldier at Fort Fetterman and then went to the wild. He was of about the same rank as the Janises, had a good education, and knew well the ways and customs of the whites. Because of these accomplishments he soon became almost the head war chief in Red Cloud's band.[2] This displeased some of the older hereditary chiefs of battle victories. Richaud married Emily Janis, Nick's daughter, and the two were the envy of the whole Sioux nation, for they were a kingly and queenly pair. Richaud went on to lead so many raids and do so much damage to the whites that the government, to get him to quit his plundering and killing and come in, sent him a reprieve.

He came in then, with quite a strong following, and camped near the Spotted Tail camp on the North Platte River. Not long afterward a small gathering of chiefs got into an argument as to who among them had led the most daring raids, and one of the jealous chiefs stabbed Richaud and killed him. When his wife, Emily, was told of it, she rushed in and actually cut the Indian's heart out and slapped him in the face with it. I knew Emily as the wife of three different men—Richaud, Bob Pew, and Ben Tibbits. She was one of the best dispensers of herbs I ever knew. When we were shipping out of Valentine and Chadron she often cared for any of my cowboys

---

2. See note 2, page 145.

that got sick while in her territory. On Porcupine Creek in 1883, Lew Peck, after only one night of treatment with her herbs, was able to go back to work.

In 1880, Dr. McGillycuddy came out to the Running Water to pass on some beef steers for issue to the Indians. The steers for this issue had been dim-branded with the ID (Indian Department) brand and supposedly turned loose on the range the fall before by Captain Millett. The Captain had then turned thousands more steers on the same range. This made it necessary to clip most of the steers to get a good look at the brands. All of this was quite a ways out of the Doctor's line, so they finally settled by "giving and taking." Since Millett was an admirer of Dr. McGillycuddy's, he met him halfway and no outside arbitration was needed.

Later that same season I moved our herds north to the Cheyenne River, where we bordered on the Pine Ridge reservation, which was under Dr. McGillycuddy's supervision. The next season I began rounding up the reservation and cutting the beef issue at the agency. In this work I became fast friends with the Doctor, so much so that he and Chief Red Cloud told me I could come and go on the reservation as I pleased. The one proviso from Old Red, as we called him, was that I treat him and his sub-chiefs hospitably while rounding up on their land. This I did by saving all the lumpjaws for them and by feeding them in fine style whenever they came to our camp or mess wagon, which was often. Sometimes Old Red and a half dozen of his sub-chiefs would stay with the roundup for a week or ten days, eating well all the time. But I didn't mind, as we were grazing as many as ten thousand cattle on their reservation grass, and as I was the only cowman who could go and come there as I pleased.

It was McGillycuddy who set up the Indian police system that turned out such a big success. I don't believe the Indians ever butchered a beef animal of ours until after the police were dismissed in 1912. To my way of thinking, the Doctor was the best Indian agent of them all, except maybe Colonel James McLaughlin of Standing Rock.[3]

3. Dr. Valentine T. McGillycuddy served as Pine Ridge agent from 1879 until 1886. Although he established the first Indian police system on the Pine

After leaving the Indian Service the Doctor was a banker in Rapid City, where I lived, and we used to have many a good visit about the old days. He lost his first wife in Rapid in 1896, and after that I didn't see him for several years. Then I was invited to Deadwood for a big celebration. On the way up on the train I was sitting in the smoker, visiting with Calamity Jane, when Dr. McGillycuddy came in from the sleeping car. All three of us had been invited to the celebration, so we visited a while. Then the Doctor asked me to come back to the sleeper to meet his second wife, as he believed I knew her.

As soon as I saw her I remembered where I had seen her before. It had been years ago, and she was riding in a buggy with her father, G. E. Blanchard. With them was the girl (Harriet Abbott) that Jim Dahlman later married. They were on their way to Valentine, where Blanchard's daughter was taking the train east to college. I was on my way to Valentine, too, with a shipment of beef, so they took dinner with my outfit. Afterward I rode beside them to our night camp, six miles on east, before bidding them good-by.

I first met M. J. (Maurice) Reilly when he came out from Chicago as a kid in 1894. His first job on the range was night hawking for my outfit, the Lake, Tomb, and Lemmon Cattle Company. He stayed with us until I sold to Bird Rose in 1906, and was a wagon boss by then. Two years later he switched to the Nels Morris outfit under manager Charles Hardy, and then to the Matador [4] on the Cheyenne reservation. When the Matador's lease on that land ran out they

~~~~~~~~~~~~~~~~~~~~~~~~~~

Ridge reservation, James McLaughlin had earlier set up such a system at the Devils Lake agency. McGillycuddy's term was marked by strong dissension between the agent and Chief Red Cloud, and by disagreement, among both Indians and whites, about the Doctor's effectiveness as an agent. See James C. Olson, *Red Cloud and the Sioux Problem* (Lincoln: University of Nebraska Press, 1965), pp. 264–305.

4. The Matador Land and Cattle Company, organized in 1882 with Scottish financing, was one of the most long-lived cattle companies in America, remaining in business for sixty-nine years, until 1951. A great deal of its success was attributable to Murdo Mackenzie, who served as manager from 1890 until 1937, with the exception of a ten-year interval (1911–1921). The Matador's home range was in the Texas panhandle, its headquarters in Trinidad, Colorado. For a full account of the Matador, see W. M. Pearce, *The Matador Land and Cattle Company* (Norman: University of Oklahoma Press, 1964).

moved to the Belknap reservation in Montana, with Reilly in temporary charge.

The understanding was that a man would be sent up from the Texas Matador to be head man in Montana, but the Texas man was so long in coming that Reilly had everything on the new range organized and in good running order before he came. Reilly told me he had set things up in the style I had taught him, and when the Texas man came and changed everything around to true warm-climate style he just stepped out altogether and got a job with a big sheep outfit. From there he drifted to Canada, where he got into one of the biggest cattle deals in that country. He was buyer and beef shipping-point man for a while there. Then he came back to the Belknap for the Matador for a couple of seasons, and about that time, 1922, there was an opening for him on the old Matador in Texas, where he stayed for the next fifteen years.

In 1937 Maurice wrote me an interesting letter from Texas. Here it is:

Dear George:

This being Thanksgiving morning I thought I would stay in and write to you. I am glad you are keeping in such good health and able to travel around and see the country. I can't imagine you just sitting around resting.

I was sorry to learn of Bird Rose's death. And to think he was down here in Texas when he died, where I could have gone to see him. I had always figured on getting to see you two pals again sometime, but alas, not Bird now, who ranked only second to you in my rank of instructors, taking me from boyhood to the management of the second largest cattle deal in Texas.

We are having lots of surface tanks built under the government conservation program. Prospects for the future look brighter than for some time. Of course taxes are quite an item, having such a large acreage of a trifle over 900,000 acres in Texas alone, and several thousand in Montana near the Belknap reservation, where we mostly run sheep of late years.

Mr. Murdo Mackenzie resigned as manager of the company last fall and his [son] John was substituted in his stead. John is a fine fellow and just like his father to work for. There has been no changes made in the way of handling, and there is not likely to be as John got his education from his father, both in Texas and Montana, as well as South America. Murdo was 87 years old last April. He was down here on a visit, driving down in a car with his daughter last week. He looked fine and was as full of fun as ever. He is still a director of the company, and a good one, too.

I cannot imagine you being 80 years old. You know I have been picturing you all in my mind as being as young as when I last saw you about 25 years ago. But what stands out more than anything else is May, 1895, when I met the two Flying V trail wagons run by Oliver Rose and Jim Hudgins at Buffalo Gap. They were on the way to Orin Junction to meet shipments of Texas cattle.

I had just come out from Chicago the fall before, direct from school. They first put me on as night hawk with the horses. They had to stay overnight in the Gap to receive a new Peter Schutler wagon shipped down from Piedmont by the Hagen Co., for Jim Hudgins. The boys (some of them) got lit up and shot up the town. Fred Ahlson, who was driving through town, got to smoking his team up and shot the finest of them, a roan leader, through the foot. That ruined him, so Oliver told him to finish him and he would have to settle for him. So Fred shot him through the head, and later gave the company a satisfactory one in his stead.

With an extra team, Fred drove the new wagon out to camp that night, where we were camped on the flat south of town. We were just catching night horses when Fred, the wagon and four-horse team showed up over the hill on a lope. When the wagon went down into a dip (they had forgotten to put the coupling pin through the rear hounds and coupling pole) the front wheels jerked loose from the rest of the wagon and we could see the four work horses, the tongue, front wheels and reach, come out of the dip on a dead run and head for the camp.

After a few seconds Fred showed up, and pulling his six-shooter sent a few shots after them to insure a good job. The boys got the remuda out of the rope corral before the stampede swept it clean. I was not quite fifteen at the time, and I thought, "Gee, this is the life for me."

I remember most of the boys' names, and a new adjunct they called "Hikeout," who was finally left in his bed on the bed ground on the trail, as he was so hard to awake. His check was left under his pillow.

Well, Ed, those were the good old days and we were all young. I am hoping you continue in the best of health, as you deserve all the good things of life if anyone does. Give my regards to all the rest of my old friends.

Yours truly,

M. J. Reilly

Although I didn't get acquainted with Murdo Mackenzie until some years later, he and I were both in that Clayton, New Mexico, saloon the night the fellow had to plug the holes in the whiskey barrel with his thumbs while the other fellow whittled plugs to fit the holes. Mackenzie was born in County Ross, Scotland, in 1850, where he in a manner inherited his knowledge of livestock from his highland ancestors. His first association with the range cattle industry in this country was with the Prairie Cattle Company near Tascosa, Texas, in 1885. His next job of importance was the management of the great Matador Land and Cattle Company, which he took in 1891, succeeding Paint Campbell.

Before managing the Matador, Campbell had been a captain of the Texas Rangers. He was considered to be a very dangerous man to oust from such a good-paying and important job as the one with the Matador, and quite a few of Murdo's friends advised him not to try it. But he took it and moved right onto the ranch, where he kept a couple of expert and trusty hired gunmen with him, and so had no trouble with the Paint Campbell bunch.[5]

Soon after Murdo took over, the Matador began maturing steers in Colorado, Montana, and the Dakotas. From these ranges they reaped their greatest harvest. As Murdo himself gave it to me, he only marketed enough mature beeves to, outside of general expenses, declare an eight percent dividend each year. Many times he carried beeves over to fives so as to hold down the annual dividend and ensure marketing enough cattle to do the same thing the next year, and the next and the next. That way he was able, at all times, to

---

5. W. M. Pearce, in *The Matador Land and Cattle Company*, p. 7, identifies Campbell as Henry Harrison Campbell, who had served with the Twentieth Texas Regiment during the Civil War. He does not mention Campbell's opposition to Mackenzie's appointment as manager.

satisfy the Scottish stockholders, for that eight per cent was more than double what they usually got from their investments.

Mackenzie was sixty-one years old when he went to Brazil in 1911 to head up a land, cattle, and packing company. After eight years there he came back to Denver and took back his old job as head of the Matador. He died in 1939 at the age of eighty-nine. In my estimation Murdo Mackenzie had the greatest world-wide cattle knowledge of any man, while John Clay had the greatest in the United States. Neither of them was tops as cowboys, for they did little work in the saddle, but for running big cattle ranches they couldn't be beat.

But I'd like to say, too, that not all the top riders of those days were men. I remember Lillian Tysdal, the wife of Ole Tysdal of Newell, South Dakota. When she was a girl of seventeen she one day rode from her brothers' ranch on Beaver Dam Creek to visit a friend on the Milberg ranch on Horse Creek, seventy miles away. I pulled in at the Milberg place about five that afternoon, on my way from the Moreau to Whitewood, and found that Lillian was out with the Milberg girl after the milk cows. A few more miles on the end of that seventy-mile horseback ride meant nothing to her.

But the real riders were Edna and Inez Moses, daughters of Sam Moses, our old stock detective. In the 1880's Sam had a ranch about fourteen miles south of my L7 headquarters, and I always stopped there on my way to town. One afternoon I drove in in my buggy and Sam asked me if I'd seen anything of his girls. They were only seven and nine years old at the time, but they did most of the riding needed in looking after several hundred range cattle and a big herd of range horses. A lot of those horses were half wild, as they were only rounded up for the branding of spring colts, or for roundups or when Sam had a buyer for some of them.

I told Sam I hadn't seen the girls and he said he was getting a little uneasy about them, because they'd been gone for five hours. They had brought in a bunch of the wildest horses that morning, he said, as he wanted to brand the spring colts that day, but a dog had scared them just as they were going in the corral, and the last he'd seen of the whole outfit the girls were disappearing in the dust of the running horses. They were riding the only two horses they had kept up, so their dad had no way of going to look for them. But while we were talking about it here they came, fogging the band of wild horses right into the corral. And those little girls didn't seem to think chasing that bunch of horses thirty-five miles to the Coyote Holes and back again was anything unusual. The only thing that bothered them was that it was hours past dinner time and they were about starved to death. So as soon as they had filled up on hot biscuits and L7 beef they were right back at the branding pens to help with the work.

Back in 1872 a portable sawmill was moved in on the Little Blue, near where our family lived, about forty miles southeast of Hastings. The mill was moved in from Red Oak, Iowa, by the Slover family, and with them came Sam Seymour, a lad about fifteen years old. The first lumber sawed was used to build the first schoolhouse in that section. It was built close to the mill, and the five Slover kids and Sam Seymour went to school there, and so did us Lemmons.

Sam was not a good mixer and didn't seem to have as much nerve as the rest of us frontiersmen. Finally we discovered he was a petty thief, and because of his pilfering I mixed with him several times. He was older than I was but I always won our fights, as this was before I started having my leg broken so many times. Because most any of the boys could whip him, we looked on him as something of a coward. But, as I've said before, you can't tell by its looks how far a frog can jump, for we found out later that Sam was far from being a coward.

While he was living at the mill he finally stole something valuable and a warrant was issued for him. He beat its service, though, and I didn't see him again for about four years. Tom McCumpsey and I were passing through North Platte on our way to Ogallala when I saw him, where he was working as a slusher[6] in a saloon there. He said he was going straight and doing fairly well, and he begged us not to report him to the authorities back home in Thayer County. We told him we wouldn't tell on him. Not long after that he absconded

6. The slusher had the lowest job in the saloon, as he was the person who "swamped," or scrubbed, it out.

with some of the saloon funds. Of course the Lincoln County authorities were after him then, but he kept out of their reach. I next ran onto him on the North Platte River above the Camp Clarke bridge. Again he begged me not to tell on him, and as I considered the saloon money ill-gotten anyway, I kept still. But soon after that he skipped those parts with a string of cow horses.

In 1880 I was riding along White River near Fort Robinson when I caught up with a roundup crew to pick up a couple of outlaw steers we had lost that morning in a canyon near the stage road. In that crew the second man I laid eyes on was Sam Seymour. He came up and asked me if I was going to turn him in. I told him I didn't know of any law around there except army law, and that for the time being my hands were full with the outlaw steers. A few days later I heard that Sam and another cowboy had left the country with sixty or seventy head of saddle horses. Well, I didn't see him again until 1896, when we were branding out a herd in Billings. I was walking down the street when I saw him going into a saloon. It looked to me like he had turned in there on purpose to keep from meeting me. The marshal wasn't far away, so I called him over and told him who Sam was. He went right in the saloon after him, but he had already skipped by the back door.

Then in 1908 I had to go to Los Angeles to get my wife's signature to the deed to the Lemmon townsite. On the way home my train made a thirty-minute stop in Spokane, and I got off and was walking up and down the platform to stretch my legs. Two of my old cowboys spotted me and came over to visit a while, or so I thought at the time. They were dressed like lords and both had big diamonds in their shirt fronts. In the old days they sure hadn't dressed like that. While we were talking I happened to look across the street— and there was Seymour, heading straight for us. It looked to me like he had his eyes on my two old cowboys, but all at once he turned and went the other way, keeping his head turned away from us. I said to the boys, "What do you suppose got into Sam Seymour all of a sudden?"

They looked at me in surprise and said, "What do you mean?"

I pointed to Sam, who was going around the corner, and said, "Him."

They said, "Why, you sure don't know him," and I told them I sure did, that I'd know his hide in a tan yard.

Then they told me that if Sam knew I'd recognized him he would as lease kill me as shoot a coyote, because he was the notorious Coeur d'Alene Bob, the worst holdup man in Montana, and that he had so many disguises that only his friends and stool pigeons really knew him when he was not disguised. He specialized in big mine cleanups, they said, and would put me out of the way quick if he thought I'd give him away.

But with all their talk they couldn't make me feel uneasy, for he was still just Sam Seymour to me, the kid I'd whipped so many times on the Little Blue. I likewise figured the two dressed-up cowboys were in some way his helpers, and that they were to meet him at the depot that morning when he saw me and went the other way. But a few months later when I read that Coeur d'Alene Bob had been killed resisting arrest, it may be that I breathed a bit easier. But this shows how a timid orphan roustabout, who wasn't too bright in school and couldn't hold up his head among ordinary boys his age, could develop into a man feared by a whole territory.

One of the Slover boys who came in with the mill was named Lew. He was about two years older than myself, or sixteen, at the time. Fresh from the city of Red Oak, he dressed very citified and lorded it over us roughneck westerners. We were playing ball the first day he came to school. He stood and watched a bit, then asked if there was a vacancy for him. I spoke up and told him a little Irish boy wasn't catching on very fast and maybe he'd be willing to give up his place. The dude then stepped over to a pile of ball clubs, unbuckled a brand-new Remington revolver, belt and all, and laid it on a bench. During an inning when I wasn't at bat I went over to the bench, took the gun out of the scabbard, and was admiring it. The dude came right over and took the gun, saying it was not a nice plaything for little boys. I, of course, couldn't say anything, but I sure gave him a cool stare, for I was thinking, "Why you big stiff! I'll bet that is your first gun, and right now I could almost make one like it, as well as I know guns and how they work."

A few years later my brother Hervey married Lew's sister Lizzie, and later Lew and I had many a laugh over that little deal. For it really was his first gun and right then he couldn't hit a flock of barns with it, while I had been carrying and using one since I was nine. He finally did get to be a good shot, though, and likewise the toughest young man in the neighborhood—which meant he guzzled redeye and played cards for small stakes.

During the latter part of the season that Lawhorn and Hardigan brought in cattle and peddled them out to feeders, Lew got a job with them. He put on leather chaps and long-shanked spurs, and then he was really tough. One evening we had a dance at the school-house. We had to take the seats out to make room to dance, and in so doing a screw pulled through a seat leg and stayed in the floor. Of course Lew came down the floor with his spur rowels dragging, tough as he could be, and caught his toe on the screw head. He spilled forward on his hands, and a pint bottle of redeye, a deck of cards, and a seven-shooter pocket pistol fell out of his pockets. Father, who was floor manager, stepped up and suggested to Lew that he take off his spurs. Without stopping to pick up his stuff, he hustled over to a bench, sat down, and took them off. Then he coolly caught a girl, Ida Heberle, out of the crowd and began to dance with much grace, as they were both splendid dancers.

Father gathered up the spill and returned the pistol to Lew after the dance was over, along with some good advice, which was wasted. Father also told him his room would be preferred to his company thereafter unless he could at least get along without the bottle. Lew's father, the sawmill operator, was at one time county judge at Superior, Nebraska, and the last I heard of Lew he was a respected married man out on the West Coast.

When Pickles (Frank) Keshirak died in South Dakota in 1930, his death reminded me that his life had been a strange, and not a very happy, span. Born in Bohemia, he came to Sweet Home, Texas, in 1885 to live with an uncle, Stever Sweety. This uncle had treated him in a scandalous manner. When the boy had a spell of fever and ague, the uncle neglected him so unmercifully that filth collected in his hair in such an awful way that screw worms, the frightful warm-weather pest of Texas, took over and ate a four- or five-inch gash in his head. The gouge, half the depth of a man's finger, made a brand he carried to his dying day. While he was in this condition some neighbors named Curington stepped in and rescued him from Sweety's filth and abuse. It was probably that early ill treatment that made Pickles seem somewhat stupid and of a sour disposition, from whence he got his name. But he was never known to tell a lie or to betray a trust.

In 1888 the Curington family moved to the Black Hills and brought Pickles with them. Soon afterward I hired him as night hawk during roundup. He proved to be an able man and was never known to go to sleep on the job or to fail to bring his remuda in at the sound of the cook's gong—an iron spoon banged on the dishpan. Pickles kept his night hawk job with me on the Flying V and L7 for over twenty years, and never once asked for a different job.

Near the crossing on Rabbit Creek another little creek comes in. This little stream was long ago named Pickles Creek because, while our outfit was once camped there with a beef herd, it came time for Pickles to take his yearly bath. This was considered of great enough importance to christen the creek for him, and it has ever since been known by that name.

One time, up on the North Moreau, I drove into camp with my team and buggy and found an excited bunch of men hovering around Earl Knepper, one of the crew. Earl was bleeding like a stuck pig from a penknife cut in the fleshy part of his thigh. The boys had tried everything they knew of, even the dry puff balls on the prairie, to stop the bleeding, but nothing worked. So they borrowed my buggy and hustled him to Sturgis to a doctor. The story, as they told it to me at the time, was that Earl and Pickles were playing mumblety-peg, and the knife glanced and struck Earl in the thigh. I believed what they said, and didn't learn any different for a good many years. Then, while I was visiting Al Curington in Boise, Idaho, in 1936, he told me it was no accident but a stab in the heat of an argument over a throw of the knife by Pickles.

That wasn't the only affair of that kind that had been kept from me. There was the time that Ed Hodgkinson of Cedar River shot the neck of a broken beer bottle off Tom Vernon's head at a Fourth of July celebration in 1905. I didn't hear of that until several years after the beginning of the city of Lemmon. The concussion, they said, floored Tom for at least an hour, but Hodgkinson just holstered his gun and walked away, saying he knew Tom wasn't hurt much. He was that confident in his ability to hit what he shot at—but Tom ever after wore a white finger wave on the top of his head.

To get back to Pickles. In later years he made a trip to Canada, night hawking a band of sale horses. While he was there he bought a Buick for less money then he'd have paid in the States, and also bought some "wet goods," which he brought back in the Buick. He sold both at a nice profit in Faith, South Dakota. After that he made quite a few trips to Canada by train to buy new Buicks. As the Canadian line riders cared not how much Canadian wet goods crossed the border, they were glad to tip him off as to the best way to dodge the line riders on the American side. Pickles told me he didn't consider his trade as bootlegging, but just delivering wet goods on order.

"I never delivered a single bottle to anyone," he said, "I just delivered on order to given spots, or houses." When I last talked to him, about four years before he died, he told me he had something like four thousand dollars in the bank. He was well dressed, but as usual his clothes were a misfit, like he'd picked them out in the dark.

During the more than forty years I knew Pickles I never heard of him having anything to do with the fair sex but once, and that time it was nipped in the bud by the girl's father, Henry Duncan of Thunder Butte. Allie Duncan had worked for the Sam Sheffield family in Sturgis about 1895, and Pickles had taken her to a few shows. Then he wrote her a letter from out on the range. This caused the boys in his outfit to compose a verse of song that went like this:

> Pickles wrote a letter to Duncan's girl,
> Calling her his sweetheart and his pearl.
> Duncan got the letter and read it through,
> Now what the hell's Pickles goin' to do?

Not long after that Duncan and Pickles met—but not with a friendly handshake—and there were no more letters or theatergoings. Pickles just didn't suit old Henry Duncan. Good old Pickles. He was never known to say a disrespectful word about anyone, and my best wishes follow him to the Happy Hunting Ground.

It was this same Al Curington who told me the straight of how Pickles stabbed Knepper, who also put me in touch with Joe Elliott, our long-ago stock detective, again. Al moved out to Boise about 1930 and not long afterward wrote me that Joe was living out there. I wrote back that he must be mistaken, since Joe had certainly been killed in Wyoming, somewhere around the Devil's Tower, over thirty years before. But Al wrote again, stating that he knew Joe Elliott as well as I did, and that he was right then alive and in Boise.

In January, 1936, I went out to Nampa to visit my sister, Alpharetta Comstock. Boise was only twenty-two miles from Nampa, so first thing after getting there I called Joe by telephone and asked him if he was the Joe Elliott who was once a South Dakota stock detective. He said he was, and I then asked him if he had any idea how I got his name and address. He said he supposed out of the *Police Gazette*. I told him "No, the Rogue's Gallery," and he hollered back, "Who the hell are you?"

So I said, "I'm no detective or peace officer, I'm just old Ed Lemmon, over here at Nampa." At that, I could hear him rise up on his toes and flop back on his heels. Then he yelled, "You're sure coming to see me?" and I yelled back, "You bet I am. Tomorrow morning."

I visited with him all the next day and we had a great old time. Before I left he told me the story of his disappearance from South Dakota. He had gone back to Wyoming, he said, to go on with his investigation for our association, and not long after he got back he one day anchored his horse to the ground and began stalking a likely looking place for deer. All at once, he said, he was looking down the barrel of a Winchester and hearing orders to drop his own gun and put up his hands. The man with the gun then fired a shot in the air, and right quick five more men came out of the brush. The men told him they were going to hang him for his part in the siege and killing of Ray and Champion. He managed to convince them he couldn't have had any part in that affair, so they let him go but kept his horse and gun. They also made him promise to get out of Wyoming and to stay out for the next twenty years.

He had headed for Laramie on foot then, traveling by night and laying up by day. He didn't even try to get a ride until he was near

Douglas. He had about seventy-five dollars in his pocket, and with that he bought a ticket for Laramie and headed for the Klondike. He lived there under his mother's maiden name while he was accumulating somewhere around ten thousand dollars. With that he came back to the states and settled in Boise, took back his real name, married, and raised a nice family. But he never again set foot on Wyoming soil, nor got in touch with our association, though we still owed him about a month's wages.[7] Like myself, Joe was then about seventy-eight years old.

It was that same year that Siverene Tysdal, one of my old cowboys, and I visited Mrs. Mary Melvin McClellan, a sister of Bill Melvin, an old Hudson's Bay character. Mary had buried three husbands and was a very old lady. McClellan, her last husband, had been quite well-to-do and had left her well fixed, but at the time of my visit she was batching on the Cedar in a sod house which was, in a way, a mansion, as it had five rooms. When she went out, which was seldom of late years, she still dressed in costly old garments. It was known that she had two well-filled trunks of valuables stored in McIntosh, fifteen miles from her sod house and about thirty miles east of Lemmon.

We visited for a couple of hours, and Siverene took some snapshots of Mary and me in front of her mansion. Then he went out to crank up the car to leave, and she called me back into the house and took me to the kitchen. She opened the warming oven of her range and showed me several good-looking pies. Then she showed me her pantry, stocked with supplies galore. And then she invited me to stay and share all these things with her.

"When these are gone," she told me, "I have plenty of money to buy more. And you are the only person I've met in years who speaks my language. I know we could eke out the balance of our days here in peace, plenty, and comfort." I let her down as light as I

7. The South Dakota Stock Growers Association's financial statement for June 1, 1936–June 1, 1937, shows $125 paid to Joe Elliott for services. Mr. Lemmon probably brought the matter of Elliott's outstanding wages before the association after his visit with Elliott. (Bob Lee and Dick Williams, *Last Grass Frontier: The South Dakota Stock Growers Heritage* [Sturgis, S.D.: Black Hills Publishing Co., 1964], p. 198.)

could by explaining that my time, at least for the present, was all contracted for.

Shortly after that she was found dead in her sod house. One of her brothers came to look after things, and while ransacking the house he found two one-thousand-dollar bills. A few days later he found an oilskin bag in a mattress with three more thousand-dollar bills in it. So it looked like the old lady had meant it when she invited me to share her household in peace and plenty.

XXIII

A LOT OF INDIANS

I CAME TO KNOW a lot of Indians—Pawnee, Sioux, Cheyenne, and others—from the time I went to live on the Little Blue at the age of two and a half until now, and knew some of them very well. Many of them were my good friends, and I learned much of their tribal history and legends from them.

There was a good deal of difference between the tribes I knew, both in looks and in the things they did. The Pawnees, for instance, were, and are, inferior-looking Indians when compared to the Sioux, for they are small and shabby, while the full-blood Sioux warrior is a tall, handsome fellow. But how those Sioux feared the little Pawnees.

The Pawnee country was up where the Loup River joined the Platte, and the trail they followed to reach Sioux country, over on the Republican, crossed the Little Blue less than a mile below Liberty Farm. We often saw the Pawnees coming north with stolen Sioux ponies. The Sioux usually chased them part way, but only once that I knew of did they get any of their horses back, and that was in plain sight of our place. The only weapons they used were tomahawks and war clubs, hand to hand, and the only Indian killed in that fight was an old Pawnee squaw who happened to be along. The Sioux got their ponies back and then came on to our place, all as jolly as could be because they had whipped the Pawnees, even though they (the Sioux) outnumbered them four to one. That was in 1863, before the Sioux went on the warpath the next year.

Later on, up in western Nebraska near the Camp Clarke bridge, I saw about four hundred Cheyennes under Bill Rowland. We had a trail herd, and our boss, Bill Campbell, gave the Indians a yearling beef, just to see them kill it, buffalo-killing style, from on horseback with a Sharps carbine held in one hand and aimed at the lights [lungs]. This kills as quick as through the heart, and the target is easier to hit.

This band, headed by Dull Knife and Little Wolf, had had a part in the Custer massacre. Instead of following Sitting Bull to Canada, they had surrendered to the U.S. troops and were being taken to Indian Territory, down on the Canadian. What was left of them later broke away and came north again. The band separated, and Little Wolf and his followers spent the winter on the Dismal River in the Nebraska sandhills, where they almost stripped the country of horses. It was some of these Indians that stole the Tusler horses the night Tusler and his crew camped with me at Green's ranch on Rush Creek. The Indians were captured in the spring of '79 near Fort Keogh in Montana and about a third of the horses recovered.

Dull Knife and his followers were taken prisoner near Fort Robinson and locked up there. They broke out one cold night in January, 1879, and most of them were killed trying to get away. My brother Moroni was freighting supplies to the fort at the time, and he said several government mule teams were kept busy for hours, hauling in the frozen bodies of the men, women, and children shot down in the draws and canyons as they tried to escape into the hills. He said the soldiers just grabbed them by the legs and arms and dragged them out of the ends of the wagons to bounce on the ground on top of one another.

The battles of the Arickaree, the Washita, and the Wichita took place in 1869.[1] I have often been on the Arickaree and the Wichita

1. By the battle of the Arickaree, Lemmon is probably referring to what is more commonly known as the battle of Summit Springs, a decisive victory of

where, later, a lot of Indian bones were gathered up with the buffalo bones and shipped east by the trainload for fertilizer. I don't remember ever being on the Washita, but it was on that battlefield that an infant Indian boy was picked up by whites and kept and educated by them. He was very light for an Indian, I've been told, and was given a fine education, making it hard to tell him from a white man. He was not told that he was an Indian until he was about to marry a white girl. She wouldn't marry him then, and he went to the wild, took the name of Lost Wolf, and carried out many a raid on the whites in return for his heartbreak.

Another Indian I knew was Crow Dog, a minor chief under Spotted Tail on the Rosebud reservation. But Old Spot, as we called the chief, took a fancy to Crow Dog's wife and won her affections. Crow Dog took exception to this and shot Old Spot.[2] Crow Dog was then tried in the courts of his tribe and judged not guilty, but the Indian Department heads didn't agree with freeing the killer of the chief who was looked on by them as a good friend of Uncle Sam.

At that time George Bartlett was deputy U.S. marshal for the Rosebud and Pine Ridge reservations. He was sent to the Rosebud to bring Crow Dog in for a new trial by the Department. Since Bartlett always made our WG ranch his stopping place when traveling between the agencies, we saw most of his prisoners, including Crow

---

General Eugene A. Carr's Republican River Expedition of 1869 in which Carr's Fifth Cavalry, supported by the Pawnee Scouts under Frank North, almost annihilated Tall Bull's band of Cheyennes in a surprise attack on July 11 north of the Arickaree Fork of the Republican River. See James T. King, *War Eagle: A Life of General Eugene A. Carr* (Lincoln: University of Nebraska Press, 1963), pp. 110–113; and Luther North, *Man of the Plains: Recollections of Luther North, 1856–1882* (Lincoln: University of Nebraska Press, 1961), pp. 113–118.

In late November, 1868, a command under General George A. Custer struck a Cheyenne camp on the Washita River in Indian Territory, killing about a hundred warriors, including Chief Black Kettle, taking about fifty women and children prisoner, and scattering the band. (King, *War Eagle*, p. 90.)

2. Dr. Charles A. Eastman, a well-known, educated Sioux, wrote of Crow Dog's murder of Chief Spotted Tail in August, 1881: "Crow Dog was under a vow to slay the chief, in case he ever betrayed or disgraced the name of the Brulé Sioux. There is no doubt that he had committed crimes both public and private, having been guilty of misuse of office as well as of gross offenses against morality...." (Quoted from Eastman, *The Soul of the Indian* [New York and Boston: Houghton Mifflin, 1911], pp. 111–112, in Helen H. Blish, *A Pictographic History of the Oglala Sioux* [Lincoln: University of Nebraska Press, 1967], p. 408.)

Dog. The trial lasted through two terms of court in Deadwood, but Crow Dog was finally convicted and sentenced to be hung. Through a strong petition from his agency, which stated that he had been acquitted by his own people for killing a man who had alienated the affections of his wife after the birth of a child from their union, he won a reprieve. But by then Crow Dog had been in the Deadwood jail so long that he was looked on as a trusty and was a sort of chore boy around the place.

One evening he told some of his friends he was going home to visit his wife and family, who had been moved to the Pine Ridge reservation seventeen miles north of the agency. He asked his friends to tell the sheriff and Bartlett not to worry, that he'd come back pretty soon and everything would be all right. Then he took off on foot. But when Bartlett found it out he said it wouldn't do, and took right out on Crow Dog's trail. He found him in the Indian camp on the head of Grass Creek, enjoying his family's company. When Crow Dog saw the Marshal he reared up and told him he'd left word that he'd come back of his own accord, and he'd rather do it just that way. But Bartlett said he'd have to take him back.

It was dark by then, so Crow Dog said they'd better not start until morning. If Bartlett would go to the agency for the night, he said, and come back in the morning, he would go back with him. But when Bartlett got back the next morning he was told that Crow Dog had headed north the night before on one of his best road horses, taking another Indian along to bring the horse back. Bartlett headed straight for Deadwood, too, and when he got there he found Crow Dog back in jail, grinning at him through the bars. He had said he'd come back by himself, and that's what he did. I always thought old Crow Dog had a face like the picture of Henry Clay, with good nature and intelligence spread all over it.

Well, the day of the execution finally came, and Crow Dog dressed in his tribal death suit and walked forth without a tremor—to be hanged by the neck until dead. According to the Indian code, hanging would keep his spirit from going to the Happy Hunting Ground, but his step was steady and there was no expression whatever on his face. And right then came word that the Great Father had decided his deed was justified, and that he was free to go home or anywhere else he wanted to. And even then, I was told, his expression didn't change.[3]

After we moved to the Cheyenne River country in 1880, a lot of our cattle ranged on the Pine Ridge reservation and I often had to go to the government herd camp on White River to throw them back on our own range. I didn't always take the same route, and I sometimes took a lunch along. One day in 1881 I rode farther east than usual, working my way up a mountain-sheep path to the east end of the high table that, in 1890, was the campground of a big body of hostile Indians.

From the top of the table I rode southeast and worked down a side gulch that led to a bigger canyon that opened onto White River, just about opposite the mouth of Grass Creek. There I watered and staked my horse and ate my lunch. When I rode on again I had only gone a few rods when I came onto a cave, eight or ten feet high and wide, that opened into the side of the gulch. The sun was shining into it for about fifty feet, and the cave bottom was packed hard and smooth, as if it had been packed by a lot of use, but there weren't any animal tracks or streaks such as a snake would make. This made me curious and I thought I'd better investigate.

I picked up some sticks and made myself a torch. Then, with it in my left hand and my six-shooter in my right, I went into the dark part of the cave. It was a big one, and there didn't seem to be any places for animals to hide and jump out at me. So I went on for about another hundred feet—and then I came onto the most beautiful sight I have ever seen. The walls were covered with hangings and with other relics of all kinds (like those described by Bill Ike in *The Big Horn Sacrificial Tree*). I didn't see any white robes there, but there were a lot of others. I just stood there and gazed as far as I could see in the light of my torch. It was about all the same for forty or fifty feet, to where the cave widened to about twenty-five

---

3. Although Crow Dog had been convicted and sentenced to hang by a Deadwood district court in 1882, the decision was overturned by the United States Supreme Court, which ruled that the Dakota courts lacked jurisdiction and that Crow Dog had made sufficient retribution in the form of ponies presented to the victim's family. See Herbert S. Schell, *History of South Dakota* (Lincoln: University of Nebraska Press, 1961), p. 319. Crow Dog's miraculous gallows reprieve is not mentioned in Schell's or other accounts.

feet across by fifteen or twenty feet high, and all of it covered with relics. I didn't touch anything, so I don't know how well preserved the things were.

At first I thought I'd stumbled onto a bandit hide-out, and that this was their treasure room, and that maybe there was another way in, for I hadn't seen a single track in this passage. And if it was a bandit cave I sure didn't want to be caught there, so I made tracks for my horse and for the herd camp, eighteen miles away. The boss of the herd camp was the first man I saw when I rode in, and he said, "Ed, what's the matter, are you sick?" I said no, but he said I must be, that I was white as a sheet and trembling like a leaf.

This man had looked so familiar to me, the first time I saw him, that I asked him if we hadn't met before, maybe years ago on the Little Blue. He had said no, and that he had never before known anyone by the name of Lemmon. But he seemed to take a lot of interest in me and did me many favors, though he still insisted he hadn't known me before. Shortly after I found the cave this man quit his job and moved to Custer City onto an irrigated farm. Soon after that his health began to fail and he was told he hadn't long to live. He then asked his wife to sort his things and send certain trinkets and mementos to some of his old friends as reminders of bygone days on the frontier. During the sorting she ran onto my old penholder and the pen, the outfit I had given John Hiles in the spring of '66 when we were getting ready to leave Liberty Farm for the work on the Union Pacific railroad.

He told his wife that, since it had "Liberty Farm" written on it, a place he had often heard me speak of, he thought I must have left it on his desk and it had gotten mixed in with his things. So he asked her to mail it to me, as it must be mine. The old herd boss was dead and buried before the package and letter reached me, as I was out on roundup when it finally caught up with me. I recognized it right away, of course, and tried to figure the whole thing out. I was sure then that he was John Hiles, even though he was using another name, and I thought he must have been a bandit and might even have been the leader of a gang that had used the cave I had found for a storage place. I even thought he might have seen me go into the cave or found out I had been there, and had then destroyed the entrance to it, because I could never find it again. I thought, too, that he had sent me the penholder because he wanted me to come to him so he could tell me something, maybe a deathbed confession about the cave. But after more thought, I decided he didn't know about the cave but probably did have something important he had wanted to tell me.

Of course I did try to find the cave again, though I had decided that it was more likely an Indian sacrificial chamber rather than a bandit cave. For I remembered that Indians could come and go with their feet muffled (wrapped in cloth or fur), and moving with a glide that left no tracks. I didn't say anything to anybody, though, but made up my mind to find the cave again and then to take a witness with me and go look it over.

It was fall before I got up nerve enough to go there again, and then I carried a borrowed Winchester under my leg, but I couldn't find the cave. The next season I went again and rode every bit of that country, starting from the lower end of the gulch and tracing out every little gulch on both sides, even though I was positive the cave was in one that came in from the east side. The country there is subject to landslides, big ones sometimes, and I finally had to conclude that my Indian treasure room had been buried by one. I tried many times, too, to find out from the Indians if they knew of such a chamber, but they didn't, or else didn't want to understand what I was talking about. I told a few of my friends about it, too, telling it as if it had been told to me by someone else, but they all acted like they thought I was telling a tall tale. So this is the first time I've ever claimed the discovery.

If anyone reading this wants to look for the cave, here is the location—at least to within one mile. Take the first big gulch emptying into the White River below the badland point formed by the ridge of the Big Basin, a little above the mouth of Grass Creek. Follow up the gulch until you come to the roughs, maybe three and a half miles. As near as I can remember, it is about the fourth one on the east side of the gulch. If you find a fine, big landslide and then dig long enough, you may find my beautiful cave.

The following story was first told to me by this same Johnny Hiles when he worked for Father on the Little Blue. Before that he had been a freighter on the Santa Fe road. In the early days of staging and freighting on that road, he said, there had been a stockaded road ranch on a spring branch of living water west of Santa Fe. It was a fine camping site for all travelers on that road, but, as the whole country was then swarming with hostile Indians, a lookout had to be posted to keep watch for such dangers.

There happened to be an extra-tall cottonwood by the spring, so the ranch family put crossties high up in the tree to make a hidden platform for the lookout. Minnie, the twelve-year-old daughter of the ranchman, did most of the lookout duty. Minnie had a pet magpie that could talk, and she taught it to shout a warning if an Indian showed up. The bird got so good at the job that it could have handled it alone, except that it couldn't tell the difference between friendly and hostile Indians.

During the Civil War the government had to call in its troops from patrol duty, and the road was left open to Indian attack. So one night the hostiles came down on the ranch and massacred everybody there, including Minnie. The ranch was burned, and the bodies were later gathered up and buried on a nearby hillside. After the war, though the ranch was never rebuilt, the spring site was again used by campers. But soon it began to be told around that the place was haunted, for now and then someone would call out, "Indians, Minnie, Indians, get into the stockade quick!" But no one was ever found at the place except the campers who stopped at the spring.

Because of the stories, travelers came to fear the place so much that they took to hiring friendly Indians to go with them past the spring, where, on account of the water, nearly everyone stopped. Finally there came an emigrant train that had hired an Indian to spend the night with them there, not only because of the ghost, but so they'd have an extra hand to help night herd their stock. They had no more than started unhitching when the warning calls began. "Indians, Indians, get in the stockade quick!" The call seemed to come from the top of the big cottonwood, so the Indian climbed the tree and took a good look, but all he found was a four-inch hole in the top limb of the tree. He came back down and said the call must have been a warning from the spirits that they were to be attacked that night and that they'd better dig in the best they could. The warning calls kept up and the Indian got so scared he wouldn't go outside the camp on night guard. So they corralled the stock, and the Indian got into one of the rifle pits with his guns and wouldn't come out.

Now there was in the train a little girl about Minnie's age, and after supper she was near the spot where they ate, when a magpie flew from the tree and began picking up crumbs. Now and then it would stop eating and say, "Thank you, Minnie, thank you." The magpie came down again the next morning to clean up the breakfast crumbs and thank Minnie, but it wouldn't let the little girl lay hands on it. This cleared up the mystery, but the train had to go on, leaving the magpie to watch over the lonely graves on the hill and to shout its warning whenever it saw an Indian. Old John Slaughter, an uncle of Colonel C. C. Slaughter, the big Texas cattleman, was another who told me this story and vouched for its truth.

Red Cloud, too, was a good friend of mine. He was tall, straight, and dignified, and his people had great respect for him. I once heard him give a talk to his band while they were camped on Bordeaux Creek. He held his crowd for two hours, and it was a mighty good talk. He was quite a diplomat, too. He was called to Washington one time so the Commissioner of Indian Affairs could tell him that each Indian living with more than one wife must pick one to wed and discard the rest. The discards were to be told they must leave their husband's bed and board, and that they would then be cared for by the Department. Then the Commissioner said, "Now I presume you have more than one wife." Red Cloud said he did, and the Commissioner said, "You must go home and marry your choice and tell the others they must leave your tepee." Red Cloud thought about it a while, then said, "You go tell 'um."

There were always whites who were ready and willing to cheat the Indians and the Indian Department. Trickery of all kinds was practiced, and some of it came under my observation. Ben Arnold, who helped contractors issue beef to the agencies in the late sixties and early seventies, told me of a swindle he saw before they began to use scales. The average weight of the herd was estimated, he said, and a few head out of each herd might weigh the estimated weight, but most were far lighter. After the government put in scales in 1869, the weights fell off about thirty-six per cent. But there were still ways to steal from Uncle Sam. One outfit paid two men to go into the scale pits and take off a few nuts, letting the beams down so they'd register heavier. But these scales in some way burned, and after that they weighed a couple of average-weight cattle on the small post scale. To get this average, the beef contractor picked the heaviest animal in the issue and the agency receiver picked the lightest. Then they weighed them together and got an average.

Now comes the trickery. We had a big brindle steer with long, full horns in one issue. In the next issue the tips of his horns were gone, and in the next he had only one horn. The fourth time he was a muley [had no horns]. I never knew how we came by him for all four issues, but I was only a kid then, and not in the boss's confidence. Here is what happened. Our boss would shape up an issue of cattle all about the same size, and then he'd put in the big stag. Of course the government man couldn't find anything very much under the average weight of 850 to 1,000 pounds for his choice. So the 1,200-pound stag would bring the average weight of the whole herd up considerably.

I was told that Jack Morrow was the first fellow to pull the "counting around the hill" trick on the receiver of Indian cattle. In the early seventies Jack had a contract to furnish cattle on foot to the Indians. The receiving site was in some small, rough hills. As the lead was strung out and counted through, the steers disappeared around the hills in the roughs, and were then turned back around the hill into the tail end of the herd and counted through again, swelling the count by about eight hundred head.

Now to go back to some of my early experiences with Indians. There was Hugo Uhlig, one of our neighbors on the Little Blue, who did nothing but kill Indians. His brother, Theodore, was killed by Indians in the 1864 raid in Nebraska, only a year after the family came to America and settled near us. It was because of his brother's death that Hugo took to killing Indians, and in between his killing trips he made his home with us, resting, building up his horsepower, and laying in fresh supplies of ammunition. Hugo was not tall and he seemed kind of slow. He didn't dress in frontier style, and even wore a small, stiff hat, rather reminding me of a Jew. He didn't seem at all like a killer, and he never boasted of his kills or cut any notches on his gunstock, so no one else paid much attention to him, except my brothers and me, but he was sure a hero in our eyes, second only to Kit Carson and our father.

Hugo once told me, "Ven I first come to Hamerica the first ting I kill was a skoonk, und I shot him mit a hoe hantle. The first time I shoot I miss him, und the next time I shoot I hit him right where I missed him the first time. I poonched him und poonched him, till he fire all his hammunition away, und then I kill him." Hugo left our home in Cheyenne in the summer of 1870, headed for Elk Mountain, and we never heard of him again. The Sioux were always looking for a chance to ambush him, so I've no doubt his bones lie somewhere on that mountain in Wyoming.

Back in 1873, during the hide-hunting days in western Kansas, a party of Comanches was out on a buffalo hunt near Kiowa. I was with a trail herd that was passing that place with a herd for Great Bend'when an Indian shot a buffalo. It fell and lay as if dead, and the Indian ran up and straddled its neck, ready to cut its throat. But as he raised his knife the buffalo jumped up, with the Indian still astraddle its neck. One of its horns had slipped through his wide belt and he couldn't get loose, so it charged off with him. The Indian tried to cut his belt in two, but his hand slipped and he slit his own belly, letting his bowels out. And that buffalo actually trampled them off before anyone could do anything to help the poor Indian. One of our boys rode in and killed the buffalo, but the Indian was already dead. Even though we were not much in love with Comanches, and were used to some pretty horrible sights on the range, that one upset us all so much that we were a gloomy outfit for several days afterward.

Here is a story I heard from the old Indians I knew in South Dakota. Many years ago a band of Sioux was on the way to their homes on the Missouri, near the present Cheyenne agency, from a buffalo hunt in the west. They were traveling down Sulphur or Cherry Creek when an old squaw came down with smallpox. Being deathly afraid of the disease, the Indians left the old woman on the creek near what is now known as Squaw Buttes, close to the mouth of Frozen Man Creek, and went on. Though they didn't think the squaw could live very long, they left her a fire and a little food but not

[281]

a single weapon, either to defend herself or to kill game with. But she didn't die, and she didn't let her fire go out. Instead she set snares for rabbits and grouse, and spent the winter in a wolf den in the side of the butte. When spring came she walked home—and right in on her relatives. They had long since stopped mourning for her, so now they flew from her, thinking she was a spirit.

And once, long ago, so another story goes, the Indians along the Missouri River, below the Cheyenne River, were faced with starvation because of deep winter snows that drove out all the game. In desperation they sent couriers out in all directions to look for game, and finally located some above the Cannonball River, south of what is now Mandan, North Dakota. This was before the Indians had many horses, so their general means of transportation was the travois, strapped to big dogs. The band set out to move to where the game was, and one woman strapped her small boy babe into a travois hitched to a big female dog. When they came to what is now known as Dog Buttes, near the present town of Timber Lake, they saw a band of antelope. Using every horse that was able to run, the band took up the chase.

The dog got excited and joined in the chase, too, but burdened by the travois and her unborn pups, she soon gave out and turned into the buttes, where there were many wolf dens. There in one of the dens her litter was born. The dog then gnawed through the thongs of the travois and so released the babe, which suckled with the pups. As the years passed the boy grew a hairy coat that protected him from the weather. And in time the wolves adopted him as their leader, for they knew he was more cunning then themselves. Thereafter, with the pack at his back, he ruled the region.

He had grown to manhood before his mother came again to the buttes to mourn her lost child, but the man-wolf recognized his mother's voice and sought her out. Then she tried to lead him away, but the wolf pack barred their way. The small band of Indians that had come with her tried to help, but the wolf pack fought back in such a savage manner that they had to give up. So the mother stayed with her son and the pack for as long as she lived. Sometimes, it was claimed, the man ran on all fours with the wolves, but he could travel either way as he led the pack. The old Indians who told me the story

[282]

agree that it all happened long before their time, but they say that is why Dog Buttes were so named. And they say, too, that the Indian wolf-man was given the name Crimson Feather by his mother because, when she sat on the butte top mourning for her son, he came to her wearing a red feather in his hair. When they learned to talk to each other, he told her the feather had been dyed in human blood—probably the blood of an enemy Mandan, the Indians say.

I have talked with many old Indians who truly believe this story, and in reading the Lewis and Clark history I find they tell of a scarcity of game in the Platte region in the winter of 1804–1805, and so wintered near Mandan, where game was plentiful.

Another Indian story, which I know to be true, concerned an old Indian named Long Dog. Along with other reservation Indians, he had most of his horses taken by the government in the spring of 1878. This was done to keep them from leaving the reservation to join Sitting Bull. Long Dog had owned quite a band of ponies, so when the government paid him for them in 1881 he had several thousand dollars. With all that money in his pocket, it right away dawned on him that he should have a fine carriage for himself and his family to ride back and forth to Pierre in. He went to a carriage dealer's shop, and the first thing of beauty he saw, to his way of thinking, was a hearse with all kinds of fancy trimmings on it. The dealer tried to convince him that the fine carriage was used only for carrying the dead, but Long Dog would have no other. So the dealer finally sold it to him for eight hundred dollars.

Long Dog then went to a clothier and outfitted himself in a new suit and a stovepipe hat. With the seat cut out of the pants and the shirttail fluttering in the breeze, he loaded his family in the hearse, shut all the doors, and perched himself on the driver's seat. Whipping his ponies out of town, he headed for home, twelve miles away, where he pulled up with his family all but dead of suffocation. Never again did Long Dog hitch up to the grand carriage, but left it to rot down in the Dakota sun and wind beside his door.

I have known three cases where Indians ordered their coffins on approval and looked them over good before they died. Henry Agaard's wife was one of them. She wasn't expected to live, so they ordered the coffin—a good one, as the family was wealthy. She had it brought to her bedroom, but she didn't die at the appointed time, or for several years afterward, so they just kept it in the room until she needed it.

Another was Isadore Bone. I met a Ford car stalled on the road one day, and the Indians in it said they were going after a coffin for Isadore. I was near his home, so I drove over to offer condolences, but when I went to the door Isadore himself met me and asked me in. He understood my surprise and explained that the doctor had told him he couldn't live long and he just wanted to look his coffin over before he needed it. Old Bone was dead within forty-eight hours after they got home with it, but he had had a chance to approve it.

The third one was old Yellow Earrings, a Custer battle warrior. He didn't want to be buried in a government coffin, so he had Jack White make him a good one, and when it was delivered he got into it and tried it out. He said it was a good fit and okay, and was buried in it a few days later.

In about 1888 there appeared on the trail from the Crow reservation to the Cheyenne a Crow Indian we knew as Steps. He was so called because he had frozen his legs until they had to be taken off just below the knees. He later also lost a hand, but from a cause unknown to me. It was really surprising how fast Steps could cover the ground on his short stumps and curled-back knees, and even more surprising that he was an expert broncbuster. In fact, it seemed unbelievable that a man with such short stumps of legs could stick to a bucking horse like he could, because it sure took a tough one to throw him. Any time, any place, Steps would ride any horse a man wanted to bring out for him, and all for no more than a couple of dollars. When getting on a bad bucker, Steps would have someone hold the bronc until he was well seated, and then he seemed to ride by balancing. Only when riding the worst of them did he ever choke the horn, and often not even then.

Steps was always the spokesman for his Indian friends, and when traveling with some of them he would walk into any ranch along their way and ask for a lumpjaw beef—and he wouldn't take a thin one, either. He was quite a diplomat, too, making himself so useful that he got what he wanted. For wherever he stopped he'd have the boys at the ranch note down in a little book he carried the brands and descriptions of all their estrayed horses. This made him a traveling encyclopedia for stray horses, and that way he directed many a man to his lost stock. Sometimes, if it was on his route, he returned the horses to their rightful owners, but would never take any money for so doing; just some supplies or old clothes were all he'd accept. So Steps was always welcome at any ranch. When he rode in he would ask first thing, "Who cook?" And when the cook was pointed out he would go right up to him and say, "Go, go on," meaning "Get busy setting me out a fill."

Now Steps was an expert horse thief, but he never stole from white men, only from enemy Indians such as the Southern Utes. And he never kept the stolen horses for himself, except for a very few of the best ones. The rest he gave to his relatives and friends. He took the best of care of the ones he did keep for himself, training them to put their heads down so he could get astraddle of their necks. Then, when he gave the signal, they raised their heads, sliding him backward down their necks into the saddle.

Poor Steps met his Waterloo just above the Camp Clarke bridge on the North Platte River. He had gone alone to the Ute reservation, southwest of Denver, on a horse-stealing trip. When he came near the Ute camp he cached his horse and clumped along on his stubs and gathered up twenty-five good horses. Coming back by his own horse, he picked him up and headed north with his stolen bunch, traveling by night and keeping away from well-traveled trails. About dusk or near daylight—I forget which—he struck the river and tried to cross on the ice, which was still fairly thin, as it was early winter. About halfway across, the weight of the bunched horses was too much for the ice and they all broke through. Some fellows on the south bank saw the accident and went in to pull Steps out. They got him, all right, but the mauling he had gotten in the ice and water was too much for him. Although he lived long enough to tell the whole story of his trip, poor Steps had made his last foray after Ute horses.

And then there was Peach Springs Kate. In 1919 I went to Hackberry, Arizona, to pass on a shipment of cattle some fifteen or twenty miles out from the town. Two stations before Hackberry the train went through a station by the name of Peach Springs. It was a small village beside a strong-flowing spring. Nearby was a fine peach orchard and a nice hipped-roof house. I was told the station was named for the original owner of the land, Peach Springs Kate, who also owned the finest stock of horses in Arizona. I naturally supposed the owner was a rich Indian woman who likely wore silks and satins.

In Hackberry I asked where I could get a horse and saddle to make the trip out to look at the cattle. I was told to go to an Indian lodge on a hillside a half-mile away and see Peach Springs Kate, who looked after the livery business of the place and owned the finest stock of horses in the state. So I didn't know what to think when I went up to the shabby lodge and asked for Peach Springs Kate. But the big dirty buck who came to the door soon set me straight. He drummed on his breast and said, "Me Peach Springs Kate. Me savvy you wantum horse." I told him I did, and a saddle too. "You bet," he said.

Some fine horses were grazing near, and he was pleased when I admired them, and his good judgment in horse breeding, too. He called a twelve-year-old boy and had him drive in a small herd of the splendid horses. On orders from Kate, the boy put a saddle on the finest horse in the bunch and shortened the stirrups to fit me. I expected to use the horse the better part of two days and the price was two dollars a day. When I offered him the money, I asked if he wanted a deposit to ensure that I'd bring the outfit back.

Kate just shook his head. "Me know-um good cowman. Sure, you treat my pet horse right and pay-um when you come back. You no-um be 'fraid horse buck. Me keep-um for self and rich cowman who no ride offen or far." He had me both over- and under-estimated, for I was not rich, but I was almost always in the saddle and few men outdistanced me in long or continuous riding in those days.

When I rode up to the herd I'd gone to look at, the boss said I sure must've made a mash on old Kate, for he'd given me his own private horse and saddle to ride. I took the horse back late the next day, and Kate, after admiring his pet a few minutes and noting he was neither tired nor sweat-blemished, said, "You come some time again. I no charge you one damn cent." My meeting with Peach Springs Kate proved again that you can't tell by his looks how far a frog can jump. Fat and dirty as he was, that old Indian was plenty smart, and his lodge was packed with unbroken cases of groceries and supplies.

XXIV

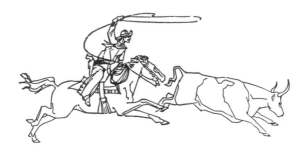

SCARLET POPPIES

I T SEEMS TO ME there should be something here about the scarlet poppies of the early West. They weren't all bad women by any means, and a lot of them had much good in their make-up.

Calamity Jane was probably the best known of any of the girls. I knew her well, as did most of the other frontiersmen. She was an ungainly person with few girlish ways, but she was a good nurse, generous with her money, and never idle. She was an expert shot, could ride, drive, manage a freight team by a jerk line or with four lines, and never complained of being tired after a hard day's work. Calamity helped a lot of folks who had neither money nor supplies. If she was out of money she never borrowed from her friends, but just stayed away from the gambling tables until someone paid back a loan. When money was plentiful she played poker and no stake was too high for her. She played to win, but if she lost she was a good sport about it.

Calamity seldom wore women's clothes. Her usual dress was a man's buckskin suit, a sombrero, six-gun, and spurs. She used to set up a little court of her own for petty offenses, pass judgment, and collect fines. She called this money her "relief fund," and spent it on the needy during the hard winter months. At such times she visited the winter camps, looking after the sick and hard up, and her presence in a sickroom was as good as a tonic. She died in 1903 and was buried in the Mount Moriah Cemetery in Deadwood.

Connie Huffman, the lady who helped Ed Comstock and the L7 boys celebrate for two weeks in Dickinson in 1905, wasn't anything like Calamity. Connie reigned in Deadwood from 1879 through 1881 or maybe a little longer, and was always a lady. And the beautiful silk dress with the brands embroidered on it became so famous that even the eastern papers printed her picture wearing it.

Nellie Bly also deserves a place in history. It was said she came west as a spy during Civil War days. I saw her a few times in Ogallala, Sidney, North Platte, Fort Robinson, and on the Red Cloud agency. She would take a town by storm with her singing, playing, and dancing. Then before the surprise of her coming had soaked in, she'd be gone again. She always hired out for a short time at the leading place in town and took a percentage of the increased earnings for her pay. It was said her harvest was always a good one. I believe she drew the line a little the finest, and commanded the most respect, of any of the girls I knew. If there was such a quality as virtue in such places, she had it. I last saw her at a resort just off the post reserve at Fort Robinson.

Brocky Moll was so named because she had a speckled face, with either freckles or smallpox pits. She was kind of pretty, small, and plump, fairly well educated, and ladylike when sober. I first saw her in Valentine in '82 or '83, about the time her husband, Dutchy, killed himself with a .45 because she flirted with one of my cowboys. After the rise of Buffalo Gap, Moll moved over there. My cowboy was still in love with her, and one time when I wanted to send him on a job he could do better than any other man in the outfit, I had to come to town and hunt him up.

He and Moll had been celebrating the night before, Charlie Degraffenried told me, then offered to help me find him. We found him, all right, sitting astraddle of a crosswalk and lamming his spurs in deep to make it move. When we came up he said, "I've got to get out to the WG. Lemmon told me last night I'd have to go to the Chocky Hall outfit today, but dammit, this horse has taken the studs [balked] on me. Charlie, old boy, I guess you'll have to get me another one, because no one can take my place with Chocky." He had been working for me for twenty years, and that was the only time I ever saw him drunk.

Billie the Kid was a young, slender girl of Cheyenne, Sidney, Ogallala, North Platte, Great Bend, and other places. I knew her during the late seventies. She carried a six-shooter and had a few notches in its stock. It was said she got them protecting her virtue, for she intended to be only a singer, dancer, and gambler. I know she was much respected by the rough element, and she could stop at any first-class hotel without question. Appointments with her had to be made in the open or in a gambling hall. As a sideline she sold gambling equipment and poolhall and fancy saloon furnishings. Some thought she was a Pinkerton agent, and she would have been a good one, as she could easily spot absconders and murderers and then tip off the higher-ups. But she never tried to make an arrest herself, nor was she ever present when anybody was arrested. Now and then she made a trip east, but no one knew where or why, for she didn't seem to have any close friends. I know she was easy to look at—and to keep one's hands off of—because besides her notched gun, her glance was not inviting. No, you just stood off and admired her from a distance.

Slippery Ann got her name from the slick way she had of getting a fellow to part with his money. She was not really a thief, just naturally oily tongued. She reigned from North Platte as far west as Laramie and Cheyenne from about 1877 to 1885, and banked a good roll because of her unusual talent. She was different from any of the other red poppies I ever saw, as she never pretended to be anything but what she was, and she didn't care where she picked her victims or who they were. She was always sympathetic to the down and out and gave a helping hand to many such, and seemed especially interested in rescuing new victims, or "tidbits," as she called them. She sent many girls home to their mothers before it was too late, paying their railroad fare herself. By doing this she made enemies of the proprietors of the joints, but when they threatened to blackball her, or tried it, she just tapped her own bank account for enough to rent and fit up a place of her own. She always attracted so much trade that it wouldn't be long until the others were ready to pay her a bonus to close up and join their ranks again.

Slippery Ann wasn't especially good-looking, and after her youth was gone she went to Omaha and bought some first-class residence properties, and then went right on visiting the slums and hunting up the downtrodden so she could offer a helping hand. I met her on one of my last trips to Omaha, and she came right up to me and said, "I used to see you in Ogallala." Then in a lower tone she added, "I am Slippery Ann." We got transfers and rode miles and miles in the late evening on a streetcar, visiting. The next day I asked Jim Dahlman, who was then mayor of Omaha, about Slippery Ann, only I used the name she was going under in Omaha, and he told me she was one of the best old ladies in the city.

Poker Alice ran a gambling house at Scooptown for more than forty years. At the last encampment at Fort Meade her hair was white but she was still a well-preserved old woman of gracious ways. The soldiers of Fort Meade were her chief customers, and from her beginning there in 1882 she kept an eagle eye on her flock of girls and met all hard knocks with a smile. Being a fine judge of character, she made a good hand in a poker game and often played, thereby building up her bank account.

In 1914 it was said that some Fort Meade soldiers, aggravated over something, planned to raid her place, which stood out by itself in the woods. Someone tipped her off, though, and she got ready for the attack. She put her girls in a back room and barred the door, then she put out all the lights and went out on the porch, where she had racked up a pile of guns. After a while she heard sounds in the brush. She called out that she knew what they were up to and was ready for them, and that they'd be better off if they left before any trouble started. Her answer was a flock of shots from the timber. When the battle was over there were two dead soldiers and a wounded one. There was an inquest and then a hearing, but Poker Alice was acquitted, and the commanding officer at the fort sent her a bouquet. In later years old Alice rode at the head of the annual Black Hills Pioneer Parade in Deadwood.

Addie Devier was a beautiful, ladylike, sweet-tempered woman with a smile for everyone. She had two of our ranch managers on

[291]

her line at the same time, and Shorty, one of my top cowpunchers, as well. Though Shorty had less worldly goods than the other two, he seemed to be a nose ahead in the race. Many a Flying V saddle horse made round trips to Custer over the rough mountain trail that season, getting Shorty home from the fifty-mile ride in time for breakfast. None of the boys gave Shorty away, so it was quite a while before I happened into the stable early one morning and saw the SL gray looking like a ganted race horse. I asked Shorty about it, and he, thinking I already knew about it, told me the whole story. All I did was tell him to ask for a day off now and then so his love affair wouldn't be so hard on our horses.

In 1893 the Queen of French Creek was a beautiful girl, slender and graceful, with a thick rope of dark hair. Her mother had plenty of money and was willing to give her everything she wanted—except let her go on the stage, the only thing she really wanted. The mother had moved to Chicago to give the girl more latitude for choosing a husband, but instead she went on the stage anyway, as a chorus girl. There she got acquainted with the end man, but he turned out to be the wrong end man. Anyway, she reigned for a while in French Creek, then went back to Chicago and into the office of a mercantile firm her mother owned. I guess she made good there, for she had persuasive ways. In French Creek she persuaded me out of one of my finest saddle horses.

About two years after the girl left our country, I was limping down Wyandotte Street in Chicago when I heard a screech behind me. It was the Queen, and she grabbed my hand and shook it like a country pump handle. "I can't help it," she said, "I haven't had a good, honest handshake since I left French Creek." She told me she always spoke to a man wearing chaps and spurs, and that she often went to the stockyards just to get a glimpse of the honest face of a cowboy coming in with a shipment of cattle from the west. She said she usually asked them if they knew Ed Lemmon, and that even if they were from Texas or Montana, they at least knew of me and would mention my crooked leg to prove it.

"Oh!" she said, "if I could just sit down on the ground with a plate of steak and baked beans and a cup of coffee that would float an iron wedge, I'd be willing to be buried on the lone prairie." The time we spent visiting flew by so fast I nearly missed my train. As I was leaving she told me to tell Frank Huss if he'd come and put his brand on her she'd follow him to h——l, but I had to tell her Frank was already hobbled by then.

The Will o' the Wisp was so called because she would be in a place for a while, then disappear. But when she came back she always seemed to know all that went on while she was gone, and the fellows speculated that she played a double part of some kind. She sure was a puzzle, until we finally learned that when she disappeared she went to North Platte—where she played the part of a loving and contented wife to a barber there. And when she was away from her husband the neighbors thought she was in a sanitarium in Omaha, taking treatments for her health. She was a small, doll-like girl and didn't look to be very healthy, but no one could outlast her on the dance floor, where she was always graceful and in perfect time to the music. In the end she was laid to rest in a pauper's grave in Cheyenne.

I first saw Brockle-faced Mary on the east outskirts of North Platte, just south of the railroad tracks. She was whaling away with a slicker, trying to put out a prairie fire that threatened her pleasure emporium. She wasn't making much headway until a bunch of us Barton and Dillon cowboys came along and helped her out. She was wearing a man's gingham shirt and a pair of hip gum boots, with the shirttail tucked into the boot tops. She had shed her skirts so they wouldn't catch fire, and every time she slapped at the fire the shirttail flopped in the breeze until the wind died down and gave her a chance to tuck it in again. But of course we were too busy to pay any attention. Then a passing handcar crew took the fluttering shirttail as a distress signal and came running with spades and shovels to throw dirt on the fire. We soon had everything under control then, and Mary's Emporium was saved.

Four years later Brockle-faced Mary, so named because of scars on her face, showed up in South Dakota with a lawfully wedded husband, Billy, who had a homestead on Battle Creek, about eight miles from our ranch. For a while Mary worked hard on the farm. Then the railroad built through and she took off for the white lights again, going to the little town of Cascade, where she ruled supreme for a year. She then came back to Billy, paid off the mortgage on their team and milk cows, and stocked the pasture. The last I knew of them in 1891 they had a well-improved homestead and were shipping a carload of grass-fat steers now and then. And Billy would point to all this and say, "Shust look at vot Mary done mit hotel in Cascade."

Frisky Phyllis reigned in Abilene, Kansas, from 1870 to '72. She was little, plump, partridge-like, light-haired, blue-eyed, and still in her teens. She was a great flirt, which was why they called her Frisky, and she always picked either the shortest or the tallest of the men in the dancehalls and saloons. She stayed with each one long enough to get a treat of some kind at the bar. According to the house rules, she got a percentage of the take, and so accumulated a fine bank account.

She was caught in the westward drift of the Texas trails, of course, and the last time I saw her she had captured a very tall "Ole" in true wedlock and was living on a small, well-stocked farm near Kiowa, Kansas. She was the apple of Ole's eye. When I happened in at their place to buy some garden truck for my wagon crew I had a nice visit with the two of them, flipped the year-old baby a quarter, and never let on that I recognized her as the old Abilene Frisky Phyllis.

Stepladder Jane, as far as I know, was born of Northwestern Construction as it neared the Black Hills back in 1885 or '86. I first saw her at Pimp Town on the south bank of the Cheyenne River, where the railroad work was held up while waiting for the bridge to be built across the river. She was one of the tallest women I have ever seen, nearly six feet, hatchet-faced, rawboned, and so limber in the middle that she twisted her body at the coupling of the waist like an owl does its neck. She was not a favorite with the boys, but the painted ladies of the town didn't dispute her leadership, because she could use a six-shooter or a beer bottle with the best, and used them freely on either sex.

She tried to be like Calamity Jane in mannishness and in skill at gambling, but never tried to handle a team or fight Indians. She got her rakeoff from all the bars and gaming tables she herded men up to, and didn't mind sleeping in boxcars or freight wagons if she had to. On the side she warned her friends if she knew of star-toters being on their trail, and was well paid for such tips. She once warned our manager, Dave Clark, that Charles Fugit was set to get him for his part in sending him to the Nebraska pen, and so probably saved his life.

In the afternoons, when the games and dancehalls were slow, Jane turned her hand to barbering. She was good at it, too, if a man kept his eyes shut while she was using the shears or razor. I hunted her up several times when the barber chairs were full and talked her into planking me down on a kitchen chair and pulling her razor out of her sock to remove my face bristles. She could be depended on, too, to have the razor in her sock or waistband to use as a weapon in a pinch. She said she'd learned to use it in St. Louis amongst the Negroes.

Jane stayed through the boom days at Pimp Town and Buffalo Gap, but couldn't keep up with Calamity Jane and the established girls at the Frontier Gem and the So Drop Inn, so she finally joined forces with an old fellow called Padden in a rough road ranch and saloon about twenty miles south of Buffalo Gap. There she was maid of all calls. Once in a while I stopped there to have my face peeled. When the railroad was finished and there was no more team freighting, Stepladder disappeared. Probably she went back to her old home in the South to eke out a respectable afterlife, for she couldn't hold patronage where there was a choice of girls. She was around thirty when I last saw her, and as she was not a heavy drinker, she was well preserved and likely had a sizable bank roll. I never knew her to have a lover, a fellow the girls of her class usually supported, since she was too homely to hold one.

Pimp Town had no post office, so all the mail came in care of the bridge contractor. But it did have a population of three hundred, a store, dancehall, and several saloons, mostly tent affairs. When the bridge was done the town disappeared overnight, hauled on wheels to the new town of Buffalo Gap. The few frame buildings there were sold to ranchers. I bought two, and in tearing down the dancehall we found the bodies of two men in the cellar. We didn't even report them. There had been enough killings in plain sight in the light of day there, without trying to solve any done in secret.

[295]

Our cow camp was only two miles from old Pimp Town, and our outfit visited there often. One day I tried to buy provisions for our roundup at the store there, but the merchant didn't have enough stock to fill my order. I loaned him our freight outfit and he brought in plenty of merchandise. After he moved on to Buffalo Gap he became a well-to-do merchant.

One night while Pimp Town was in full swing I found my night relief herders all gone. So I rode into town—and there I saw quite a sight. Out in front of the dancehall there was what looked like a corpse on a door laid across two sawhorses, and a full-fledged wake was under way. My cowboys were all standing around the corpse and now and then shooting into the air. As I rode toward them Alonzo Dow hollered at another fellow, "Hell, bunky, you've shot me." His bunky had, too, in the foot. Herb Bond, the druggist, hurried out then and dressed the wound, but the accident hardly stopped the fun at all. I asked who the dead man was. They told me no one was dead, and that the corpse was only the sleeping form of Grace, the dancehall belle of Pimp Town.

Grace wasn't a public prostitute like the other girls, but the companion of one of the leading gamblers. The cowboys had wined and dined her until she got sick, and then Herb Bond had given her some sleeping powders. She went sound asleep, all right, and didn't wake up for three hours. Sam Bell, my wagon boss, had put her on the platform, and the boys cavorted around her until their shooting woke her up. Someone brought her a robe then, as she didn't have much on; and Sam Bell passed the hat, taking in about $70. With a nice little speech of thanks for the entertainment she had furnished, he presented the money to her. This pleased her so much that she did some new dances for the boys, after which the wake broke up.

R. S. Van Tassell was the youngest businessman in Cheyenne at the time the Union Pacific tracks got there in 1867. A girl named Mae was the belle of the leading hurdy-gurdy at the same time. In nearly every boom town of the West there was a hurdy-gurdy. Such places employed pretty young girls of some refinement, girls who could make a pleasing appearance and entertain the more polished men of the frontier. Such emporiums had no bedrooms, just a well-lighted dancehall with a bar that served nothing but choice drinks. The girls got a percentage of the takings, and the management wouldn't put up with drunkenness or rough talk by either the customers or the entertainers. These places were patronized mostly by married men who had left their wives back east in the states. There men who liked to dance could while away a few hours and still not feel unfaithful to their families.

Van Tassell, unmarried at that time, liked Mae a lot, but so did a lawyer named Corlett. Corlett saw in Mae the makings of a suitable wife, so he took her from the dance emporium and sent her to Omaha, where he provided a good education for her. Then he married her, brought her back to Cheyenne, and set her up in an elegant home.

In 1895, about twenty-five years after Corlett and Mae were married, I was receiving horses from Van Tassell on his Chugwater range. While I was there he told me he had gone to an old-time hurdy-gurdy in Cheyenne a short time before. He said he was sitting at a table when Mae Corlett got up from another table and rushed over to him. There at his table she told him she just had to have one more fling on a hurdy-gurdy dance floor and that he was the only living soul there who could escort her through the turns. "You've just got to do it," she said.

Now Van knew she didn't dare do such a thing, so he went to the door and dismissed her coachman. Then he tucked her into his own coach and drove around with her for quite a while, talking her out of her wild notion. He finally took her home, woke up her husband, and delivered his wife to him, along with instructions never again to let her go to such a show unless he went, too. I knew Mae only by sight, as I was only a little over thirteen years old when I left Cheyenne in the days when she was queen of the hurdy-gurdy world.

And here I'd better tell how I met Mormon Ann again. In 1893, nearly twenty-five years after Red Pat and Mormon Ann had hustled themselves out of Cheyenne, I was delivering a herd of steers to Orin Junction in Wyoming. One night a stranger came into camp and asked for something to eat and a place to sleep. Early the next morning I saw this same tramp eating breakfast at our wagon. This happened often when we were near a railroad, so I paid no attention. Later I went over to the section house, where the section boss flagged a freight train for me. I got on, and as we picked up speed out of the station, I saw a woman catch onto the caboose and climb on. When she came in I recognized her as the tramp who had stayed at our camp. I watched her a while, and then I said, "If you're not Mormon Ann, then I don't know what I'm talking about."

"Sure," she said, "and I knew you all the time. You're one of those brats that made up the song about Pat and me and sang it in Cheyenne." I asked the conductor to let her ride the caboose to Chadron with me so I could have a long talk with her, and she sure gave me an earful. She told me how she and Pat used to tell the drunk soldiers the best way to get back to the fort, and then put on Indian clothes and lay in wait for them on the trail. Pat was armed with a blackjack, a scalping knife, and a six-shooter, she said, and if the soldier was drunk enough he blackjacked him and took his money.

Indian fashion, they'd throw the bills away and keep the silver, then dance around the unconscious man. Of course they gathered up the bills before they left. Once, after a long silence, she admitted that sometimes, when the soldiers were only partly drunk, Pat shot them down and scalped them. She declared she hadn't had any part in the killings, but said she sometimes helped hold the men while Pat hit them with the blackjack. After that talk with Ann I remembered that soldiers had every now and then been killed on the way to the fort, and that it was supposed the Indians had done it, as the country was swarming with hostiles then.

Every old Black Hills man will remember Kate the Bitch. She was a notorious road ranch keeper on the Black Hills road. Her house was just south of another one, the Dirty Woman's ranch, on the same road. They were near neighbors but bitter enemies, each being jealous of the other one. Kate was a well-educated woman, and when immigrants or stage coach passengers stopped, she visited with them and got all the news of the eastern theaters, politics, and society. Those folks would go on, wondering how such a woman could tie herself down to a place visited mostly by rough men.

They would have wondered more if they could've seen the rest of her house, or her poor, filthy, abused little four-year-old daughter, who was kept out of sight, for her looks would have spoiled a lousy buffalo hunter's appetite. But no one could top Kate in handling a beer bottle, a chair, or a six-shooter in a fight. After she quit the road ranch, though, she settled on a small cattle ranch and became a good mother. She raised her daughter well, and the girl was later wedded to a good friend of mine, a man to be proud of.

In Arizona I once happened into an establishment that was altogether different from Kate's. I had cut and passed on four thousand steers and was riding to Huachuca Station, thirty-five miles on ahead, to see that shipping cars would be there by the time the herd came in. The boys with the herd had given me directions for getting to the station, and I had ridden over some twenty-two miles of barren wasteland without seeing a drop of water or a house. Finally I saw Fort Huachuca off to my left, snuggled in a pretty little park in the Sawtooth Hills about five miles away. And then I rode suddenly onto a big adobe house of about thirty rooms, with awnings on all the windows.

It was about noon, the siesta hour, and I saw only one or two people around. I rode up and asked about the prospects for dinner for me and a feed for my horse. A woman of refinement then came to the door and courteously told me it would be all right. A Mexican took my horse, and in a few minutes I was sitting down to a fine hot dinner. When I offered to pay she said, "By no means. We seldom see a stranger here, and the pleasure is ours." So I was glad to give her the outside news, as I had just come from Kansas City. I was there for about two hours, and I never saw a thing to show that the house was anything but a well-regulated hacienda—except for some girls in the far background. But they kept their distance and not a one even tried to speak to me. Except for some Mexican stable hands, there were no men around. And one would never have surmised, from her actions and appearance, that the lady was a madam.

XXV

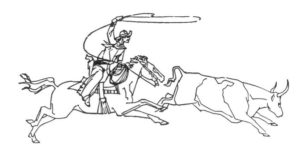

THE WEST THAT WASN'T

THESE DAYS it seems that all magazine writers like to get up blood-and-thunder stories about absconders and pursuers. They dwell on the great dangers of horses falling with their riders on dark nights, and all their gunmen shoot two guns at the same time and with deadly accuracy. There was danger of horses falling, of course, but not so much as those writers would have you believe. For all of us old mossbacks soon learned to throw our weight on the reins and then trust to the horse to keep his feet among the holes, rocks, etc. It was hard, though, to teach green hands to throw their weight on the reins to hold a horse up and steady him. But it was, and is, the best way.

I was once riding at top speed to head a big drive of cattle that was about to get in a boggy creek, when just ahead I saw a badger hole that sloped my way. There was no chance of missing it, so I threw my full weight on the reins. My horse rammed his left foreleg straight into the hole, and his shoulder cracked like a gunshot. But the hard pull on the reins kept him from falling. Tony Day of the Turkey Track heard the crack of the breaking shoulder from a quarter of a mile away. He went for another horse while I unsaddled beside the water hole, where there was good grass. Pretty quick one of my Indian friends came with his wagon and some men to help. They ditched two wheels down and rolled the horse into the wagon box and hauled him home. There the Indian made a burlap sling and a tripod to hold it up. Two months later the horse was as good as ever, and the Indian was happy with the five dollars he got for the job. Yes, many a hard fall can be saved by keeping a stiff rein.

On nights "as dark as a stack of black cats" we trusted to our horse's sight, or instinct, as the case may be. In my fifty-three years of handling cattle I was never convinced which it was. Once, back in 1869, when Father was leading a small party to the reported rich silver deposits that afterward became the famous Comstock mine, my brother Moroni was riding a stone-blind horse. This horse liked to run, and if another horse came up on him he would take the bit in his teeth and really break out. They were coming up on the rim of a canyon that was at least a thousand feet deep, when the blind horse got excited and broke straight for the canyon rim. Brother threw his whole weight on the reins, but the horse didn't even slack up until, with his front feet right on the rim, he stopped so short he shoved gravel and shale over the edge and nearly cast Brother over his head.

When coming in from night guard we always trusted to our night horses to lead us to the end of their picket ropes. A well-trained night horse never failed to stop with his head right over the dropped end of the picket rope, no matter how dark the night. So this must have been instinct, unless he had cat eyes. Lewis C. Peck rode a night horse eight years for me. That horse, named Lige because his brand was LIG, could see prairie dog and badger holes on the darkest nights, or so Peck claimed. The rest of us sometimes had falls on dark nights, but not Lewis Peck. Even so, we rather doubted his claim of such fine eyesight for his horse.

Another reason to believe horses use instinct was that when a man was confused as to directions, he could just give his horse its head and it would always go direct to the herd or to camp. There were two exceptions to this. If a horse smelled a herd of mares he would usually head for them, or if he was near his old home range he would seek it rather than the camp.

[301]

When we had stampedes during electric storms we'd see tongues of fire three or four inches long on the tips of the cattles' horns and on the tips of their ears. Horses' ears, too, would have these flames, but both cattle and horses had to be somewhat heated up from running before the blazes showed up much. On the darkest nights one could follow the herd and see its edges by these little fires.

Fiction writers always advise clapping spurs to their mounts when wanting to get the top speed out of them. This is a mistake, because the harder spurs are used the less speed one gets. Clamping spurs to a horse causes it to press away from the rowels, and that naturally slows its speed. Spurs are only for signaling a quick start, as for cutting and roping, but not for speed.

As to the fiction writer's favorite, the two-gun man—well, I never saw a two-six-shooter man who could use both at once and be accurate. Many could use first one and then the other, but not both at once. And even one gun could be dangerous in the hand of a greenhorn. Back in 1906 I was on my way to Chicago from Kansas City in a sleeping coach. A young fellow on the same coach had spent most of the day fooling with a gun. Early the next morning I got up and dressed, as I had some figuring and book work to do. A little later I heard the gunman slip out of his berth and cross over to the empty seat behind me. About a minute later the gun, a Colt's .45, went off, almost deafening me.

I thought the boy had committed suicide, so I didn't even look around when the porter yelled for help, for I had too much on my hands to spare the time to be hauled into a court of inquiry. But when the porter yelled the third time and then begged, "For God's sake, help me," I turned around and saw him lowering the young fellow to a cushion. He told me then that the gun fell out of the boy's berth and discharged when the hammer struck the seat.

"I knew that damn gun would get him into trouble. He handled it like a kid," I told the porter. It turned out that the boy had stuck the gun under his pillow the night before, the way he'd read all westerners did it, and the porter, when pulling the blankets off the berth to make it up, had knocked the gun off. At the first stop they took the young man off the train and put him in a hospital, where he died, as he was shot through the intestines.

Writers also tell that the bull teams of the early days were made up of Texas cattle. This wasn't so either. In 1863 a herd of what was called Cherokee steers passed our farm. Father bought a yoke of those steers and used them for leaders. On account of their quickness in holding the ten-yoke ox team straight they were the pride of the freight line, but they didn't have enough weight to be any good as pullers. This herd passed our ranch on what was known as the Fort Riley road, which led from Fort Riley, Kansas, to Fort Kearny, Nebraska. The steers were all peddled out as leaders, and it was possible that Russell, Majors and Waddell bought a few for that purpose. But other than those, they had very few, if any, Texas cattle in their outfit, even if some writers do insist that about half their herd of several thousand work oxen were Texas-bred. I know better, since I saw almost every work bull they owned.

Writers also make some strange statements about Slade. Some call him Henry Slade, but his name was Joe. Up until I was ten years old I saw him hundreds of times, for he was division super-intendent for Ben Holladay on the Green River division in the early sixties. They write of him as a two-gun man, but such a thing was unheard of in those days, due to the fact that nearly all guns were cap-and-ball and loaded from the muzzle. Never did I see two of those guns used at once. A man might pull them both, but he aimed and shot only one at a time.

Wild Bill Hickok, Bill Tilghman, Jack Watson, Bear River Smith, Wyatt Earp, William McDonald (of the Texas Rangers), Bat Masterson, Jim Bridger, and Kit Carson were all good, but none were two-gun men in the usual sense of the term. My brother Hervey was as good as any of them, but he never tried to aim two guns at a time, either. I've often seen him take a gun in each hand and shoot one after the other at posts while riding between them on the run, with the bridle reins in his teeth. The posts were about two rods apart, and he seldom missed either of them.

Writers today seem to believe that all old-time cowboys wore Levis. Now I never saw northern cowpunchers or cowmen wear overalls or Levis. I worked with range cattle from 1870 to 1923, and I never wore overalls until I got my first flivver, about 1907, and then I wore bib overalls. No, the only cowhands I ever saw in

overalls were a few who came up the trail from Texas. And they had
started the drive wearing six-dollar California trousers, which, on
account of being made of such firm wool goods, wore out on the
wrinkles. By the time they reached the first Kansas cow town some
of them would have to make a change, and all they could get was
overalls.

Every now and then someone wants to know if the James boys
were ever in the Black Hills. What I know about that is secondhand,
but I got it from a man I consider trustworthy beyond all doubt, Cap
Willard. Cap told me these stories twice, the second time because I
asked him to, for one tale concerned an old school chum of mine,
Johnny Slaughter. Johnny had been our neighbor on the old Ben
Holladay stage line, and had gone with us from Kearney to Cheyenne
on the Union Pacific track-building job. His father was the first
mayor of Cheyenne, and Johnny and I went to school together there
from December, 1867, to October, 1870. When the Black Hills
opened up he was one of the first stage drivers over that road.

After only a few trips he was held up near Deadwood by the Joel
Collins gang, with Sam Bass and Hefferidge as part of the outfit.
When the men jumped out of the brush and ordered "Hands up,"
the stage team got scared and Johnny couldn't hold them. So
Hefferidge shot him off the driver's seat, and he fell dead against a
stump beside the road.[1] His seat mate, the treasury guard, grabbed
the lines and drove the stage on into Deadwood. I learned later that
Collins came near killing Hefferidge for that unnecessary killing,
because it lost them the loot on the stage. It was said that Johnny's
funeral was the biggest ever held in Cheyenne, as everybody liked
and respected him.

The other story Cap told me was that Hefferidge, a spotter for the

1. Ramon F. Adams, in his preface to Charles L. Martin's *A Sketch of Sam
Bass, the Bandit* (Norman: University of Oklahoma Press, 1956), p. xxii, writes:
"Robert McKimie, better known by the name of 'Little Reddie,' killed Slaughter." McKimie had "joined the Collins gang in February, 1877, and was one
of the leading spirits of the gang, though none of the early books on Sam Bass
mention him." He also says that "Reddie admitted to Mr. Voorhees, superintendent of the Black Hills and Cheyenne Stage Co., that he fired the shot, but
claimed his gun went off accidentally. Whether it was an accident or not, the
sawed-off shotgun in McKimie's hands was filled with buckshot, and its blast
killed a man who had far more friends than enemies."

James boys, came to him in 1877 and asked if he'd like to see Jesse James. Naturally, Cap, then a deputy sheriff under Seth Bullock, said he would. Hefferidge told him he'd have to ride thirty-six miles and back for the privilege, and Cap said that would be all right. They rode to a point on Crow Creek, about due east of the site where the stockyards were later built, four or five miles from Belle Fourche. There they found a good-sized pack camp of well-out-fitted mules that Hefferidge said was on the way from the Coeur d'Alene country to Missouri. When they rode up, Jesse James stepped out some distance to meet them.

"Who's your friend?" he asked Hefferidge.

"This is Cap Willard, and he's all right. He just wants to see you and shake your hand," Hefferidge told him.

Jesse looked Cap over good, then said, "Well, he's a cool cuss, but I don't know if he's all right or not." Then he said to Cap, "I guess you'd better drag it, and quick." Cap said he didn't wait for a second invitation, but hit the breeze for Deadwood.

Now as to Frank James. Boone May was the head treasury coach guard from Deadwood to Cheyenne. His assistant was Billie Samples, a fairly new hand on the force. One day when they were off duty Boone got a tip that the coach was to be held up on Hat Creek, near the stage station. Boone proposed to Billie that they follow far enough behind the coach to keep out of sight, but close enough to be on hand at the holdup location, which would be reached after dark. This they did, and were not far behind the coach when they heard the rattle it made as it stopped. They jumped off their horses and ran to the stage, where the gang had the passengers, the driver, and the guards all lined up, ready to be relieved of their valuables.

Boone and Billie opened fire, and Boone downed the leader of the gang, a man he knew well. The other three holdup men dived into the brush and got away, but not before Boone recognized Frank James, as he knew him by sight. The dead outlaw had a two-hundred-dollar and a five-thousand-dollar reward on his head, so Boone cut off the head, tied it in his slicker, and took it to Cheyenne to claim the reward. He collected the two hundred dollars offered by the stage company, but the Express Company some way got out of paying the five thousand dollars.

From this it is plain to see that Frank James was on Hat Creek, within forty miles of the Hills and in company with Hills bandits, so he must have been in the Hills a time or two, at least. Cap said the James boys never masked when pulling a raid, but did when in camp or when hiding out or laying up in some community. As the Black Hills were full of expert gunmen, Frank and Jesse likely never showed up there except in disguise.

Now, as to trailing man or beast, I will say that I was never an expert at trailing men, but my brother Hervey was a fine man trailer. When trailing men in buzzard country, which is mostly more to the south, just watch the buzzards. They will hover above a moving man, sometimes for days. As soon as the man moves on they light to pick up the camp leavings or the offal of animals killed by campers. So if the trailer will just cast his eyes heavenward and note the direction of the buzzards' flight, he will know the course of the trailed. The same, of course, would apply to someone trailing you. The buzzard is a wise bird and seems to know whether a man, or men, are making long trips with frequent killing of game, or only a short trip. When on the trail of the long-trippers they sometimes fly so high they can barely be seen, and there they coast and circle, adjusting to the speed of the travelers. When flying low enough to keep in touch with what was going on, they soon learned to fly just out of range of the old muzzle loaders.

Another way of trailing is to cast one's gaze far ahead to see the trail made by knocking frost, dew, cobwebs, or dust from the grass. If you are where the air is dry, as in the Southwest, you can sometimes see the trail as much as a quarter of a mile ahead, but if the air is muggy the trail won't show up more than one hundred feet ahead. The farther ahead he can see, the faster the trailer can follow, of course. In this kind of trailing one never looks down to hunt for hoof or footprints, but it can only be done where there is grass of some kind for dust or moisture to lodge on.

In a sandy or rocky region where there has been no wind since the trail was made, there is always a streak made by the scuffing of heel or toe that can be seen quite a ways ahead, but not straight down. If no loose pieces of rock are dislodged in a solid rocky region, the trailer must look straight down for prints; and if the rock is too hard for that, then he must look ahead for pebbles or crusts that seem to have been turned over. These can usually be seen at a distance, but not at close range. If there is no sign on the rocky places, then the trailer should keep to the general direction of the trailed until he comes to a different surface, and then weave back and forth until he picks up the trail again.

When trailing men or beasts where there are apt to be other tracks of the same kind, you have to look for some special mark—like a crippled hoof or dragging heel or toe—that will help you trail right through other trails. Two men, unless they are drilled soldiers, hardly ever walk with the same length of stride; and if on long hikes, their stride becomes more firm, or heavy, the longer they walk. But there are also heavy-footed people in all groups, whether weary or not.

Indians are by nature better trailers than whites, though many frontiersmen such as Kit Carson, Davy Crockett, and my brother Hervey became their equal. In 1881 a full-blood Sioux by the name of Alex Adams was employed at the Pine Ridge agency camp. (He probably got his name from some government officer he served.) Of an evening when hunting the milk cow, Alex always took her trail right at the cowbarn, trailed her through hundreds of other fresh cow tracks, and found her with little trouble. And I know of one case of a tame buzzard that had been trained by Arkansas John, a freighter, to trail by scent as well as by sight. That buzzard could scent stolen goods such as log chains, whips, and gloves. All John had to do was let the buzzard smell something the loser had lately handled.

Years ago some work bulls strayed from some freighters at Spring Ranch, fifteen miles west of our Liberty Farm. Their tracks soon mixed in with those of herds of buffalo. (The only difference is that buffalo hooves are a trifle rounder than cattle or work-bull hooves.) Besides that, the trail led straight into hostile Indian country, over toward the forks of the Republican, a favorite Sioux campground. The freighters were going to try to trail the bulls, but on the advice of Ute Metcalf, the Spring Ranch proprietor, they came to our ranch to get Hervey to help them out. Hervey was only twelve years old, but Father fitted him out with a five-day supply of jerky and hardtack and a water canteen, all wrapped in a California blanket and tied on the back of his saddle. Then, riding his Blackhawk-Morgan race pony and carrying his field glasses, his Spencer carbine, and two cap-and-ball revolvers, he set out.

Father went with him until they located the trail. There he told him to break every rise on his stomach and take a good look at the country through the glasses before going on. If he sighted the cattle he was not to go near them in daylight, as Indians might be shadowing him, but was to hide himself and the pony in timber or in a gulch and wait until dark. Then he was to gather the bulls and make for Spring Ranch, guiding himself by the stars. Father didn't go with him for the good reason that there was not another pony in the country fast enough to carry him to safety beside Hervey on the race horse.

Hervey sighted the cattle late on the second or third day, gathered them, and headed for Spring Ranch. As he could take a direct course, instead of the roundabout one over which he had trailed the wandering bulls, he landed within a few miles of the ranch about daylight. Still taking no chances with straying Indians, he cached the herd in some timber on the head of Liberty Creek and rode fast for Spring Ranch, where he stopped the eastbound stage and sent word to Father to come and help him finish the delivery. The cattle had never been in much danger from the Indians, as they were leg-weary and thin, not near as good eating as buffalo or elk, and the Indians wouldn't bother wasting ammunition on them. And Brother didn't seem to think he had done anything unusual in trailing them into Indian country and bringing them back. It was just something that needed to be done.

EPILOGUE

And now as I slowly mount the last dim, distant mesa that marks the end of life's road, I have many of its rewards to enjoy. I have three sons, James, George, and Roy. James and George are ranchers like myself, enjoying comfortable homes in the Sunshine State. Roy is making good in Hollywood under the able leadership of Tom Mix.

I have a fine little town on the Milwaukee Railroad, named after me. I have lived a sober life, and some say an industrious one, for I usually put in eighteen hours a day, at least with my eyes open; and a hungry man has never left my door. I am still doing business in the same old western way, though we have no more cattle drives, see no more Longhorns or mossbacks, and I boss no more roundups, as I am now a sheepman. But life goes on in a quieter way; and better, abler, and smarter men carry on the business of stock-raising, maybe profiting from our mistakes.

I look out over the broad acres of my valley ranch and watch the fleecy bands of woollies drift as they graze. And maybe sometimes I see instead the days when the great L7's cattle ranged this valley and grazed this good prairie grass. It is hard for the old-time cowboys to line up with the changes brought by progress, bigger population, reclamation, and a new western society. But, like the Indian and the buffalo, it is our turn to bow out. So we pull our trouser legs out of our boot tops and sit in on this new game—and maybe take a few trips before we break the last rise of the last hill and join in the last roundup.

[309]

A NOTE ON THE EDITING

The first attempt at organizing an account of Ed Lemmon's life was made, probably in the late 1920's and early 1930's, by Lewis F. Crawford, superintendent of the North Dakota State Historical Society. Lemmon had turned over to him his papers—notes, memoranda, and articles published in various South Dakota newspapers, including the Lemmon *Leader* and Grand Valley *Herald*, the Belle Fourche *Bee*, and the Camp Crook *Range Gazette*—for use in writing a biography of Lemmon with special reference to the range cattle industry. While Crawford was working on the papers, Lemmon continued to send him additional manuscript material and newspaper stories; and after Crawford's death, Usher L. Burdick, a North Dakota Congressman, came into possession of all the books and papers left by Mr. Crawford. "Among them," he later wrote, "was this mass of material which Lemmon had forwarded, including cattle history, history of wild men of the west, wild women of the west, cattle trails from Texas, the cow days in the Black Hills, and data of Lemmon's experiences on the range . . . ."

In 1936, Mr. Burdick agreed to write Lemmon's story, based on the papers. In the preface to his unpublished "History of the Range Cattle Trade of the Dakotas, as told to Usher L. Burdick," he describes how he prepared the manuscript: "I assembled the material and classified it preparatory to writing the final draft, but I was confronted by the same problem that delayed Mr. Crawford. Mr. Lemmon kept up a brisk submission of articles, some of which I received in manuscript form. A great amount of this data was in slightly different form from what I already had, but there was little difference in the facts. The work of comparing these articles and hunting for new facts has been a long and arduous undertaking. Then again it was necessary to strike out some of the material which was irrelevant to the history of the cattle trade."

A copy of Mr. Burdick's typescript, along with clippings of more than one hundred of Lemmon's newspaper columns, the majority of which had appeared in the Belle Fourche *Bee* under the heading "Developing the West," was later acquired by the University of Wyoming's Western History Research Center, whose director, Dr. Gene M. Gressley, brought it to the attention of the University of Nebraska Press in 1962. By that time both Ed Lemmon and Mr. Burdick had died, and since it was not always possible to determine which portions of the manuscript were Lemmon himself speaking and which expressed Burdick's view, the Press decided to return to the primary material—Lemmon's recollections as he wrote them for local papers.

Lemmon had written his story after the fashion of most elderly people when reminiscing, recounting the events as he recalled them, with no continuity whatever. He often began a story and then was reminded of another, whereupon he promptly took off on a new tack, and perhaps even on the third, before that chapter of his life was ready for newsprint. In later episodes he would go back to the unfinished stories. Consequently, it took endless digging and sorting to put the tales together at all, and then into a meaningful sequence. The anecdotes have been arranged more or less chronologically in this book, rather than as they originally appeared in the newspapers. Although the clippings are largely undated, it is evident that most of the stories were written between 1933 and 1940 (the Epilogue appeared in 1936, although Lemmon continued to write after that). Only the chapter on "Scarlet Poppies" was taken from Burdick's manuscript, where it was apparently incorporated unedited, as Lemmon wrote it.

Another interesting feature of Ed Lemmon's stories was his use of big words. An old cattleman with little formal education, he undoubtedly spoke the simple, colorful language of the range, but not so when he "took pen in hand." Then he said, for instance, not "I knew about this," but "I was cognizant of this." His choice of impressive words sometimes threw me off the trail, making it difficult to figure out what he really meant. To him all fights were "fiascoes," whether they ended in victory or in defeat. As a result, much of the work that went into the editing of this book was that of translating the story back into everyday English. However, the experience gained from listening to two other old cowmen tell their stories (my father for *Pinnacle Jake* and John Leakey for *The West That Was*) made it much easier to write Lemmon's story as he probably would have told it in person. Whenever I was unsure about the language, I stopped and asked myself, "How would Dad have said that?"

There was also the matter of proper names, both of people and of places. In Mr. Lemmon's articles they were often spelled as they sounded, making it necessary to do a great deal of searching through maps and histories to determine proper spellings. In some cases it was impossible to verify the spellings, and I had to rely on Lemmon. I am indebted to the staff of the Nebraska State Historical Society, and especially Paul Riley, research associate, for their help in checking spellings of names and in identifying persons and events.

INDEX

[313]

Mulhall, Zach, 164–166
Mullaly, Pat, 47, 47 n.
Murphy, Paul C., 234, 235
Murray, Jim, 141

Narcelle, Narcisse, 185, 218
National Livestock Association, 203
Nebo, Charlie, 128–131, 132, 133 n.
Nelson, O. H. (Bull), 169, 239
Newman brothers, 113, 113 n., 132, 132 n.
Nichols, Mary Docia, *see* Walrath, Docia
Nixon, Tom, 91 n.
North, Frank, 273 n.
No Water Indian band, 154

Oelrichs brothers, 85
Oliver, Sam, 92
Olney, James N., 1, 1 n., 2–5, 5 n.
Ostrander brothers, 30
Owens, Jess, 21, 23
Owens, Johnny, 212

Padden (road ranch and saloon owner), 295
Panhandle Pete, 200, 201
Parker, Tom, 99
Paxton, William (Bill), 104, 104 n.
Peach Springs Kate, 285, 286, 287
Peck, L. C. (Lew), 152, 158, 218, 256, 301
Pcck, Levi, 235
Peeler, Scrub, 112, 113, 114
Petersen, B. J., 149 n.
Pew, Bob, 156, 157, 255
Philip, James (Scotty), 186, 186 n., 187, 203, 204, 205
Phillips, Charlie, 93, 94, 95
Phillips, W. F., 210
Phoebus, Oscar, 109
Pierce (cattle buyer), 205
Pierce, Johnny, 140
Pilger, Henry, 213
Pinneo (father of Minnie Pinneo), 253
Pinneo, Minnie, 253
Pitts, Miranda, 37, 66, 67
Plaster, Ben, 171
Plaster, Uncle Billie, 171
Poker Alice, 291
Powell, Al, 212
Powell, Dan, 217
Powers, Senator, 147, 148

Powers, Bruce, 231
Prairie Cattle Company, 166, 166 n., 260
Pratt, Colonel James Harvey, 82 n.
Pratt and Ferris, 82, 82 n.
Purdy (foster father of Mary Docia Nichols), 93 n.

Quantrill, William C., 171, 171 n.
Queen of French Creek, 292
Quigley, Bill, 147
Quinn, Mike, 211

Radcliffe, Mack, 94, 95
Rail, Alex, 214
Randall, Mrs. A. W. (Helen), 104–105, 104 n.–105 n.
Rankin, Dave, 107
Rankin Colony, 69 n.
Ray, Nick, 182, 268
Red Cloud, 27, 28, 32, 33, 255, 256, 257 n., 279
Red Cloud Tom, 33, 34, 35
Red Pat, 51, 52, 297, 298
Reder, A. D., 213
Reed Charles, 113, 114
Reilly, M. J. (Maurice), 257, 258, 260
Rich, Kid, 184, 185, 187
Richard, John, *see* Richaud, John
Richardson, Billy, 19 n.
Richaud, John, 145, 145 n., 255
Rideout (Mormon), 60
Riggs, Johnny, 131, 132–133, 133 n.
Riordan, Archie, 141
Riverside Cattle Company, 181
Roberts, Ed, 170, 173, 174
Robinson (early Dakota cattleman), 213
Rockefeller, John D., 172
Rogers, H. H., 172
Roosevelt, Theodore, 208, 218
Roper, Clara, 41
Roper, Joe, 30
Roper, Laura, 31, 31 n., 36, 37, 37 n., 41
Rose, Bird, 174, 175, 176, 177, 224, 257, 258
Rose, Oliver, 259
Ross, Charley, 219
Rowland (interpreter), 158
Rowland, Bill, 21, 34, 35, 272
Royce, Ben, 67, 68, 68 n.
Russell, Majors and Waddell, 12 n., 16 n., 22 n., 303